What They're Saying About Unscarred

I met Robert in 1970, 54 years later he gave an excellent toast at my 50th wedding anniversary. This book demonstrates how character can overcome adversity. If you suffer any addiction (drugs, alcohol, nicotine, etc), you WANT to read this book. Uncompromisingly honest it sets out a life no one would envy. It concludes with a great marriage, creation of successful businesses and a bio of someone you will be proud of. — Bob Posch

Robert tells an inspirational story of courage, strength, and resilience. While the autobiography discloses personal insight into the demons of addiction that exploit past traumas and prey on one's insecurities, it also provides hope to escape the darkness. From that courageous little boy wandering the streets of NYC alone to the adventurous man traveling the world with his Lady Di, Robert's journey has left him grateful and unscarred. — Mary Taylor, M.Ed.

UNSCARRED is a riveting and powerful biography that chronicles Robert Carney's struggle with addiction and his journey to recovery. The book offers a gritty, intense and compelling portrayal of the dark world of addiction and the distorted thinking of an addict. Robby's description of craving, withdrawal and shame is poignant and illustrates the weight of his battle and the effect on not only himself but all the lives he touched. His story begins by detailing his childhood, then reveals how his life completely unraveled as he progressed into full blown addiction. The second half of his book focuses on his recovery through self help groups and spirituality. He emphasizes fellowship, determination and courage as the guiding force to freedom and a new life. UNSCARRED held my attention from the first to the last page and is a must read! It offers identification and hope in this world of addiction. — Laura Kelley, Delray Beach, Fl.

The journey Robert has been through discloses a beautiful story of strength, courage and continued inspiration even in the darkest of times when he thought he lost it all. The strong foundation of recovery he has developed and continues to develop is inspirational! — Stacy Kordis, MS, LMHC, NCC, CCMHC

Robby writes an extraordinary journey that demonstrates his will to survive, despite the enormous odds against success. He brings the reader on the roller-coaster of his life, eventually finding answers to life's most important questions. — David Jahr, Book Reviewer

The material goes deep, emotionally and intellectually. The book is full of heart, mind, joy and sadness. Robert Carney has achieved something unusually vivid, blending his observations of prison life, the steps that occurred to bring him to his bottom, and then the new steps he took to start a new way of life. As a substance abuse professional, and trainer in the world of drugs and alcohol, I was privileged to read this book. I appreciated the raw, honest journey. I highly recommend this book to those suffering with addiction to see that there is always hope no matter where your addiction has taken you. I also believe family members & friends can benefit from this read to better understand what is happening for those who are under attack from addiction. — Linda Honey, LADC, NCAC

Unscarred is an excellent example of how alcohol and drugs can monopolize your life. The author, Robert Carney, draws the reader a vivid picture of his life growing up in New York, and how the drug culture caught him and eventually carried him to jail. Thankfully, and you'll have to read his journey, Robert finds hope and help for his addiction and has become an incredible recovery success story I'm sure anyone would enjoy reading. Two thumbs up on this amazing story! — Dr. Warrick Stewart, author of *Daring Love: Cultivating Compassion For Those Fighting Addiction*

It is an often raw and disturbing story. But it is also a story of hope, determination and redemption. If it helps one person overcome addiction, I am sure the author will be satisfied. — Stephen O'Beirne, attorney

If you are someone who has never personally suffered it yourself, this story provides the deep and raw understanding this world needs of what a loved one endures when in the throes of addiction. A heart-wrenching beginning, Robert recounts life events that lead him down an intensely dark path towards rock bottom and the impact it had on his mindset, actions and those around him. Just as the reader feels there is no hope left, his story provides the faith, courage and resilience of a life not only turned around but fulfilled. This is a must-read story for anyone who feels or has ever felt recovery is unreachable for themselves or a loved one. — Maggie White, @maggiecwhite

The book *Unscarred* had me captivated, angry, sad, happy. Though I know Robert's life story, having witnessed miracles of change for myself, the making of a man within a journey is awe inspiring. In Robert, God has given me my hero. By healing, our higher power has given us both the life of our dreams. I will forever cherish the blessings of understanding and faith found in Robert Carney's *Unscarred*. — Diane Carney

Unscarred

An Epic Fight to Heal
My Wounds from Addiction

Robert Carney

I dedicate this to you the reader.
We all carry many scars. Some run deep and are ugly. In the following pages, I will show you some of my scars: childhood abuse, drug addiction, prison and how I learned to live and overcome them.
I will tell you, otherwise you would not know, because I sit before you *Unscarred*.

Contents

Foreword   XII

Introduction   XV

Part One: The Boy

  1. The Monster   3

  2. Townsend Avenue   9

  3. Nobody Home   17

  4. First Grade, 1962   22

  5. Little Hustler   35

  6. In Name Only   43

  7. Junkies   48

  8. Checkers and Pistachios   52

  9. Shine, Mister?   57

 10. Big Brother   63

 11. Singapore Slings   75

 12. Playing Baseball with the Janitor   84

Part Two: The Twenty-Year Run

 13. I Can Breathe Now   90

 14. Sinister Boots   94

15.	Nickel Bags	100
16.	Big Richie	106
17.	A Long, Hard Road	117
18.	The Change Jar	126
19.	Got My Wings	129
20.	Where Did Everyone Go?	136
21.	Another Morning Shot	143
22.	A Moment of Clarity	152
23.	Zapped	163

Part Three: Corrections

24.	6 Block	176
25.	4 to 12	186
26.	The Brooklyn Court	197
27.	Penn State to State Pen	203
28.	High Inside	213

Part Four: The Insanity of It

29.	Back to Earth	222
30.	I'm Different Like That	225
31.	Recovery in Hell's Kitchen	231
32.	Forgive Me, Father, For I Have Sinned	236
33.	The Insanity of It	240
34.	Marijuana Maintenance	248
35.	The Man in the Cage	256

36. Pittsfield, Mass   261

37. Gram   266

38. Back in the Hood   282

Part Five: My Second Life

39. Day One   288

40. Freedom   304

41. Lady Di   308

42. Who's This Guy?   314

43. You da Man!   319

44. San Diego   326

45. Homer   330

46. Mikey Bats   341

47. Crash and Burn in San Diego   345

48. The Hearing   351

49. Reno   359

50. My Second Moving Company   363

51. The Gifts of Sobriety   370

Acknowledgements   374

About the Author   376

Foreword

By the time I was born in 1991, Robert Carney had already lived a thousand lives. I am the niece of Robert Carney, the author who you will read about and who you will learn to appreciate for the candor and heart that makes him the person he is today. In *Unscarred*, my uncle recounts his journey that has led him to hold all of the abundance and joy life awaiting him – when his unbridled ambition could be channeled as a force for good. I was born around the time he began to take hold of his recovery, and since then he has been a mentor, protector, and my biggest fan. He has been all of those things and more for countless others, more than any single book could truly capture.

Robert's retrospective features vignettes of characters, some vile and some angelic, and everything in between. The goal is not to sway you one or another. Instead readers will follow the narrator through moral ambiguity and weave between right and wrong. We are given an unfiltered window into the realities of addiction and the people who suffer and recover. Over my lifetime, I've met many of the characters mentioned throughout the book and over the years I have heard firsthand accounts of the stories. Robert offers memorial to the larger than life people who only live within memories or photographs. As I read this book, I can hear the voices thick with Bronx accents. I envision the hard, concrete places where life changing decisions were made.

Though much of the book is set during the roughest parts of New York City's history and the characters are all unique, sadly for many, I imagine the stories will feel very familiar. Shame, pain, loneliness, and guilt are ever-present and impartial to one's age, strength, or wealth. They prey on the vulnerable and thrive on those who have experienced trauma. These powerful emotions can rattle one's values and beliefs, or worse, let loose from their cages seductive saboteurs.

Humanity's beauty and dangers are on full display as time hardens then heals. Robert lays bare the painful experiences inflicted on an innocent child, leaving unseen wounds susceptible to infection in adulthood. Monsters take many forms in the book, depicting the lifelong fight to keep monsters caged.

What this story truly implores us readers to do is ask ourselves: what are we willing to do to heal ourselves and how far are we willing to go to help others? The relationships depicted throughout the book are a salve to wounds — tender, direct, and unflinching. Robert's story is a mirror for us all to reflect on our connections to one another, to examine what it means to love a friend and in turn help that friend love themselves. In today's world, our society is in distress, plagued by so many ills: we are more connected and yet further apart, our population is its largest yet people are lonelier, and addiction is pervasive spanning beyond substances to include technology, gambling spending, and more.

Publishing these wisdoms is a gift of hope for people and families affected by addiction in its many forms.
— Steph Halpin, author's niece

Introduction

Today is April 4, 2022. I celebrate thirty years clean and sober today, by the grace of God. I have a great life these days. I'm sixty-four, retired, and living in Florida with my beautiful wife of twenty-six years and our two Ridgeback pups, Leo and Abby. It has not always been this way. From the age of fifteen to thirty-five, I had been on my own; a criminal; an addict and alcoholic; and in and out of many institutions, detoxes, rehabs, mental wards, jails, and prisons. I've even experienced homelessness and a sense of loneliness that no living soul should ever bear.

I have found a way out of that hell. I am a decent and giving human being today. I'm not obsessed and craving a fix, or waking up hungover and wondering what happened to my face and money, or counting years, months, and days until the parole-board hearing. I will take you on a journey from being a traumatized young boy to becoming a violent criminal, hopeless addict and convict to the chair I sit in today, writing this book from my home.

Today my life is full of choices, freedom, friends, fellowship, peace of mind, and a higher power, whom I call God, that I can do business with. I was offered a way out, a second chance at a good and decent life if I was willing to put the work in and have a little faith. This second life has offered and given me so many good things that I could write a whole chapter on it. I became a son, a husband, an uncle, a brother, a friend you can depend on. I've gone from living on people's couches to furnished rooms to an apartment to owning my fifth home in the fourth state I've lived in these past thirty years. I met a beautiful woman who took a chance on me thirty years ago. We've traveled this journey together, and we can't wait to see what the next chapter holds. Her name is Diane, and she's a large part of the reason I'm writing this book.

When I first got sober in the early 1990s, I worked for a few different moving companies in New York. I got good at it and gained enough confidence along the way to start my own. I've been able to start, build up, and then sell two successful moving companies in California and Nevada. Diane deserves much of the credit for our financial success. She is my biggest fan and supporter, putting many hours into organizing our office records and payroll, plus so much more, along with working her own full-time job. Whenever I stumbled back to my corner between rounds in the business world, she would wipe me down, tend to my physical, mental, and emotional wounds, and encourage me to get through the next round—she's the best corner woman ever.

Have you ever felt less than, not good enough, or that you just didn't seem to fit in? Or maybe there was some secret recipe to make it in this life that you weren't being let in on? I've felt that way most of my life. My hope is that in the following stories, you find some hope and a recipe to make a decent and useful life for yourself, as I have.

Instead of feeling guilty or ashamed of my past misdeeds, behavior, and experiences, I've learned to use them to benefit my present life. My hope is you will see how some of your worst defects can turn into your best assets in helping yourself and others to attain goals you may not even have strived for in the past. It has become very apparent in my journey, and the one I will take you on, that everything in God's world is exactly the way it's supposed to be.

Part One: The Boy

A Day At a Time Publishing

1

The Monster

I t was getting dark as I pulled my mom's empty shopping cart home that Saturday night, with some well-earned money from helping people home with their packages from Food City on Burnside Avenue. It had been a good afternoon. I'd stopped at the candy store and had a chocolate egg cream, had picked up some jell bars for my sister Donna and me, and had bought an *Archie* comic book. I would split the remaining $2.40 with my mom and put my half in the change jar stashed away in my T-shirt drawer. I was eight years old.

I dragged the shopping cart, which was as tall as I was, up the four flights of steps to our apartment. I could hear country music playing as I rounded the third-floor landing and walked into the apartment. A man was sitting at the kitchen table, drinking beer with my mother. I had seen this guy before but couldn't place him. Maybe he was one of my father's old friends. He was middle aged, was balding, had a beer belly, and wore dark-rimmed glasses.

I put the shopping cart away in the hall closet and went to my mother's bedroom to check on my little sister, Donna, who was only three years old. When I entered the room with both hands behind my back, I asked, "Donna guess what I got for you?"

"What?" she screamed excitedly and sat up from watching television on the bed.

I pulled both arms forward and opened my palms to the two jell bars in each hand. She squealed with delight as she snatched two from my right hand. I sat on the bed next to her and watched the rest of *Bonanza* as we slowly ate our chocolate-raspberry bars.

My mom and the guy were still drinking and listening to country music when I went to my room. I thought of doing my homework so my third-grade teacher, Mrs. Baum, wouldn't publicly harass me in front of the class on Monday if it wasn't done. But I was exhausted and still had all day tomorrow to do it, so I went to bed. I fell fast asleep, but that wouldn't last long.

"Robert, wake up. My friend is going to stay over. I'll sleep in here with Donna. You go sleep in my room with him." Mom whispered the words while shaking me gently.

Half-asleep, I stumbled into her room. It was dark, and the man was already asleep on the far side of the bed. I climbed in the bed and fell back asleep. I awoke with the man on top of me and his hand covering my mouth. He stank of beer and cigarettes. His stench would stay with me for days. He pulled my pajama bottoms off and held me down. I struggled but could not get out from under the weight of his fat, smelly, hairy body. He forced his way into me, and I screamed in pain, but the sounds were muffled by his hand and the pillow he buried my face in. When the monster was done with me, he loosened his grip over my mouth, and I slid out of the bed.

I sat at the table in the dark kitchen, not knowing what to do. If I told my mother, then everyone would know, and I would be even more different. Should I just grab a kitchen knife and stab him in his sleep? No. *No one can ever know*, I thought. I spent the rest of the night mostly awake, lying on the living room couch. The next morning my mother told me to stay for breakfast. She, my sister, and the monster sat at the kitchen table eating toast and eggs. I sat at the table with my spirit broken and deeply ashamed of what had happened to me. I couldn't even look up at them.

"How did you sleep?" my mother asked.

"I had a very, very bad nightmare," I responded loudly, looking up at the monster, who would not look back at me. I then stood and left the apartment. I ran down a couple of flights of stairs, stopped, and sat on the cold marble steps and cried. "I'll get that bastard," I said to myself. As bad as I felt, I knew I could never, ever tell anyone what had happened.

When I returned to school that Monday, I raised my hand and asked to go to the bathroom around 10:00 a.m. I took my books and did not return to class that day. I ran down the three flights of metal stairs and out the exit door onto Morris Avenue. I walked down to Jerome Avenue and snuck on the downtown number 4 train. I got off on 161st Street and spent the rest of the day walking around the outside of Yankee Stadium and the courthouses on the Grand Concourse. I returned home later than usual for a school day.

"Where have you been? It's almost dinnertime," my mother yelled as I walked into the apartment.

"Out walking around." I looked down at the floor.

She took a step toward me and slapped me hard across the face.

My schoolbooks fell out of my hands and onto the floor.

"You look at me when I'm talking to you," she screamed.

I looked up at her with a cold stare. I didn't run, cry, wince, or change my facial expression. I just stared at her. My mother took a step back. "Pick up your books and go to your room. I'll call you when dinner's ready."

My little sister watched from the living room, clearly wishing she could do something to help me.

Later that week at dinner, my mother mentioned that her friend would be stopping by again that Saturday afternoon. *The monster is coming back*, I thought. I was not going to let him touch me again, I was also worried about my sister. I wanted so badly to scream at the top of my lungs to not let the monster back in again, but I was ashamed and wasn't even sure my mother would believe me. I came up with a plan.

Just around the time the monster was expected that Saturday afternoon, I went into the kitchen and took a small steak knife out of the utensil drawer. I held the handle in my hand with the blade pressed against the inside of my small arm so the blade couldn't be seen. I walked down two flights and waited on the stairs between landings. I was going to let the monster walk up the stairs as I walked down. Then as soon as he passed me, I would stab him in the ass and back of his legs, then run like hell down the stairs. I sat there waiting. An hour had passed when I heard the front door of the building open, and someone came in. I looked down between the banisters and saw a white hand moving up the black banister as the person ascended the first flight of stairs. I closed my eyes and tried to summon up all the courage I could.

When I opened my eyes, the monster was just reaching the second-floor landing, and when he turned to walk up the third flight of stairs, he saw me standing at the top of the stairs between landings, he looked down and said nothing. I walked down the stairs as he walked up. I was two steps behind him when I turned and began to raise my arm with the knife. I froze. I quickly caught my breath and lowered the knife. The monster climbed one more step, then stopped and looked back. I ran down the steps and out the door. I walked the streets for hours, beating myself up for not having the courage to stab and chase the monster away.

I couldn't help thinking about what I could have done differently to avoid the abuse. I should have bitten him, screamed, or stabbed him in his sleep when he was done. I was so ashamed that my head spun, and I couldn't stop the noise. I headed home at dusk. I worried for my little sister. I did not know what to expect when I walked into the apartment. I wasn't sure if the monster had seen the knife in my hand, everything happened so quickly.

I stood outside the apartment door, listening to the country music and shaking my head, then looking down to make sure the knife blade wasn't visible under my shirt. I took a long, deep breath and walked inside. I looked down the hallway and into the kitchen. My mother sat at the table drinking her beer, but the monster was not with her. I looked for my little sister. I went from room to room until I found her in my room, playing with her doll. The monster was nowhere to be found.

I would never see that man again. A year later I asked my mother about him, with bad intentions in mind. She said the man had been murdered by someone.

Probably a child's parent, I thought.

I was eight years old when I was attacked by the monster, but let me start at the beginning. Years earlier I'd lived in

Harlem, in Manhattan. My mother had me out of wedlock when she was nineteen. She'd become pregnant by some Irish gangster who was in and out of prison. My mother's sister, my aunt Anna, who was only sixteen at the time, lived with us and took care of me while my mother worked. We lived in an apartment that had only two rooms, and the tub was in the kitchen. I have some good memories with Aunt Anna. She was short, had long black hair, and loved the heck out of me. I have distant memories of her pushing me in a carriage and kids playing stickball in the street, or going down the dark basements of buildings with white bumpy walls, where her friends were drinking and playing cards. My aunt Anna and my mom would part ways over some problem with my father when he was out between jail stays. We then moved up to the Bronx when I was around three or four. My mother and I moved in with my father until he got arrested again. He went back to prison, and we moved into a one-bedroom apartment down the block between Townsend and Jerome Avenue. We were now alone.

2

Townsend Avenue

I dragged the chair across the linoleum floor under the kitchen window, stood on the cold plastic seat with my bare feet, and looked out. The window was ground level with the sidewalk, and I watched the children as they passed by laughing and talking on their way to school. They were older, high school age. It was early morning, and my mother had already left for work. She was waitressing at a Greek diner across the street and down the block on 176th Street and Jerome Avenue. My eyes were level with the children's feet. I was still in my pajamas and had not eaten yet. When I was hungry, I would find something in the fridge, where there was usually not much to choose from—carrots, bread, and maybe stale leftovers. Like most days, I would be alone until late afternoon, when my mother would return home and make dinner.

Watching the children from the window was the highlight of my day. I would imagine myself joining them, carrying my books and laughing and talking with them, but being only four years old, I was too young for school yet. Overcoming my fear because of the loneliness, I opened the window slightly one cold morning and whispered "hello" as a group of older schoolgirls walked by. At first they looked around at where the voice could be coming from, then one spotted my small face peering through the bottom of the slightly opened window next to the entrance of the walk-in apartment.

"Good morning to you," the schoolgirl replied.

Her three friends also stopped and waved hello. I smiled from ear to ear. I would wait every morning for that group of girls to walk by so I could say hello to them and get their waves and smiles. They always looked for me in the window when they passed by, and sometimes they would even stop for a minute and talk to me.

After the girls had passed and all the children had gone on to school, I jumped off the chair and slid it back under the kitchen table. Then I retreated to the living room. I turned the TV on, then built my little fort with the couch cushions. Using one side of the couch as a wall and the wall behind me, I set the two big cushions as a wall and roof. I dragged my blanket and pillow into the fort and waited for my mother to return from work.

I enjoyed and escaped into the TV shows: *Father Knows Best*, *Leave it to Beaver*, *I Dream of Jeannie*, *Gilligan's Island*, and cartoons, of course. I would imagine myself as part of those families or friends, instead of stuck in this apartment, hungry and waiting for my mother to come home. I feared her because of the beatings, but a part of me loved her and wanted to please her. One day I slid the kitchen chair over to the sink, climbed up, and washed a sink full of dishes and put them in the drainboard. When she came home from work and saw the clean dishes, she seemed pleased. I washed the dishes every day from then on.

One day, out of boredom, I played with matches I found on the kitchen table. I would strike the match, let it burn down, blow it out before it burned my fingers, then throw it in the garbage can. Well, one match did not go out, and the contents of the plastic garbage pail caught fire. I panicked. I slid the kitchen chair over to the sink and began filling up glasses of water to throw in the burning pail until the fire was out. I frantically tried to clean up the mess before she came home. I was not allowed out of the apartment until she returned, so I couldn't dump the burned garbage. I cleaned up the best I could and opened the kitchen window to let the smoke and smell out, but I knew what would happen when she got home. I hid within the walls of the couch fort and shuddered at what was coming.

She came home from work, smelled the smoke, and asked what happened. I tried to explain that I was only playing with the matches. I could see the rage building up in her eyes. Then I felt it from the smacks, punches, and screaming that followed. I tried to run out of the kitchen, but she had cornered me between the stove and the wall. I curled myself into a ball in the corner and covered my head with my arms until she stopped. It didn't matter that I cried—that seemed to only anger her more. The punishment for that incident would last well into the week. She locked me out of the apartment for the next few days when she left for work in the morning, then let me back in when she returned from work in the late afternoon. It was the middle of winter in New York. I was only four years old. I begged her not to put me out, but she did. One of those days I was still in my pajamas. I roamed from building to building in my neighborhood, hiding under the staircases to stay warm, then periodically running home to see if she had returned yet. After three days she let me stay in the apartment when she went to work, and I did not play with matches anymore.

My mother, Sophie, was in her early twenties. She had brown hair, brown eyes, and high cheekbones from her Russian and European descent. She was an attractive but cautious woman who did not smile much. The cautiousness probably came from her dealing with my father. My father's temper and violence were unpredictable. My mother and her sister, Frances, had been in and out of foster homes since they were infants. She and Frances had it rough growing up. They were moved to four or five different foster homes over those years. Some were okay, and some not. There were some stories of abuse, but they talked little of those years. At one point their foster parents were superintendents of a building in the Bronx, and part of the girls' job was to shovel coal into the furnace in the winter to keep the building warm. Certainly not a job for little girls. Maybe that was where my mother got her toughness.

I was shorter than most boys my age and on the thin side. I had wide ears for my little head, but a cute face, so I'm told. One night I came in from playing after dinner, and my mother noticed something on my face.

"Robert, come here," she yelled, as I tried to walk by her. "What happened to your eye?"

"I fell." One of my eyes was red and puffy.

The next night I returned home with a fat lip.

"What happened?" she asked again.

"I fell off the stoop playing."

On the third night I came home with a bloody nose.

My mother went crazy. "Who did that to you?" she screamed.

I started crying and said a boy around the corner named Joey Stroker had been chasing and beating me up whenever he saw me. She grabbed me by the hand while saying, "Let's go. You show me who this Joey Stroker is."

I was delighted. My mother was going to protect me from the bully. She walked around to Townsend Avenue with me in tow, until I spotted him across the street. He was with two other boys, and he was a couple of years older and bigger than me.

I pointed. "There he is. The one in the blue shirt."

"Okay, here's what's going to happen," she said. "You are going to go over there and kick his ass, or I'm going to kick yours." I looked up at her in disbelief, but I knew she meant it. I looked at her, then across the street at the bully. She gave me a little shove. I stepped off the curb and walked across the street toward him, moving faster as I approached the sidewalk where the boys were standing.

Before we said a word, I landed the first blow to Joey Stroker's face, then began swinging wildly. Joey swung back, and we hit the floor and rolled out into the street. A yellow taxi was approaching but had to stop because of us fighting in the street. The taxi honked his horn, but that didn't stop the fight. The bully's pinky ended up in my mouth, and I bit down on it hard and continued punching him in the face with my free hand. Joey let out a yowl and started crying.

My mom stood over us in the street and said, "That's good. You can let him up now."

I released his pinky from my mouth, stopped punching, and stood. He lay there holding his finger and wiping his bloody nose. There were several cars behind the taxi now, beeping their horns.

My mother put her arm on my shoulder and pulled me next to her as we walked home. "Don't you worry," she said with half a smile. "He won't bother you anymore."

I learned that day that I could fight back. I also learned that I would have to depend on myself in such situations, which would occur again. Even though I stayed to myself, I would be taunted by the other kids on the block.

As mean as my mother was, I still craved her attention and approval. Perhaps out of fear, there were many beatings, and she had left me for weeks at a time with different people, but always came back to get me. She had once dropped me off with a very kind Black family at a big house in the country, with other children there. I remember how scared and alone I felt when she drove off with a guy. I thought of chasing the car, but it was going too fast. She came back to get me a month or so later. The Black family had treated me well and even offered to keep me if my mom couldn't take care of me. My mother paid the woman, thanked her, and took me by the hand and marched me out to the awaiting car. I was glad she came back for me.

My mother fed and clothed me the best she could, but it was obvious I was not well taken care of and disheveled most of the time. My mother also had a bit of a reputation in the neighborhood. I had heard teenage boys talking about her a couple of times. Even at this young age, I knew what they were talking about because I saw the men she would bring home from the bar or who would occasionally stop by the apartment in the evenings. At least they didn't beat her like my father did. Fortunately, my father wasn't around much, which I did not understand.

I looked around at the kids and families in the neighborhood. They mostly had two parents, some siblings, and seemed happy. The same as the family TV shows I watched from my couch fort. I wondered what happened to me. How did I end up in this apartment with this woman who I was sure did not like me, was mean and beat me, but whose attention and approval I craved?

There was an older woman in the neighborhood who took a liking to me. One summer afternoon I was hanging around the other kids on Townsend Avenue, and they were listening to the newest crave, the Beatles, on their radios and laughing and talking. Townsend Avenue was full of kids of all ages that day, sitting on cars and stoops, flirting with one another. "I want to hold your hand" by the Beatles could be heard from several radios. I did not join any group of kids but was close enough to be around them. I climbed the side of the building and grabbed on to the metal ladder that hung from the fire escape. I swung back and forth on the fire escape ladder, when I heard the old gray-haired woman call out to me. While leaning on the windowsill and looking out the window from across the street on the third floor, the woman smiled and waved me over.

I climbed down off the fire escape to the sidewalk and crossed the street. I looked up at her and pointed to myself. "Me?"

"Yes," she yelled back. "What's your name?"

"Robert," I shouted over the city's background noise, looking up at her.

"Hi, Robert. My name is Judy. Would you like to join me for lunch?"

I looked around, then back up at her and nodded. I was hungry, it was getting near noon, and I was pretty sure my mom was still in bed from being out the night before.

"Apartment three b," she yelled down and waved me up.

I walked up the stoop steps then ran up the three flights taking two steps at a time. The smiling heavyset gray-haired woman in her flowered house dress stood in the doorway when I reached the third floor. She invited me in and asked me to wash up while she made me a peanut butter and jelly sandwich and a glass of milk.

During the summer in the 1960w, many older women in New York neighborhoods would lean on their windowsills and watch the kids playing and people hanging out. She must have spotted me always off on my own, disheveled and dirty, and realized my situation.

I sat at the kitchen table and gobbled down the sandwich and a piece of blueberry pie. Judy and I became good friends. If I was out on Townsend Ave, I always looked up at her window. If she was there, she would wave me up for a meal, and we would talk and laugh for a while. I liked her apartment. It was filled with furniture and pictures and rugs, almost to the point of being crowded. It felt cozy, nothing like the barren one bedroom I shared with my mother. Judy's husband had passed, and her only daughter had married, so she enjoyed my company.

When winter came, Judy told me to just come by on Saturday afternoons and we would eat lunch and visit. I looked forward to that. It would be like that in my early childhood years—there were some good people who sympathized with my situation and would reach out to help. That help would be needed sooner than later.

3

Nobody Home

My mother had become pregnant by my father in the brief time we had all lived together months earlier. My mom worked right up until the day she gave birth to my sister, Donna. The ambulance had taken her right from the restaurant to the hospital that day.

When she didn't return home from work that afternoon, I panicked. I slid the kitchen chair to the door, climbed up, unlocked it, and went over to the Greek diner looking for her. They told me she had gone to have the baby. I went back to the apartment, crawled into my couch fort, and waited.

Later that night, after dark, Pat, one of my mom's friends, came. She was a pretty woman in her early twenties, with long black hair she kept in a ponytail. She brought me to her home, where she lived with her brother, sister, and mother. They were all in their early twenties, except for the gray-haired raspy-voiced mom, who seemed to be much older, and she wasn't too happy having me there. Pat explained to her that it would only be for a few days, until Sophie came home from the hospital with the baby. Pat and her family were the supers of a building on Townsend Avenue. Their apartment was down concrete steps in the basement of the building. They set up a cot for me to sleep on.

Days and nights passed. I waited for Mom to take me home to meet my new brother or sister. After a week I panicked and sneaked out of the basement and ran the two blocks back to the walk-in apartment to see if she'd returned but had forgotten me. I knocked and knocked on the door to no avail, then I put my ear to the door. It was silent inside. I finally gave up. As I descended the concrete steps to Pat's basement apartment, I knew there would be a price to pay. I had asked a few times if I could check the apartment to see if my mom had come home from the hospital yet, and they'd said no, that they would tell me when she returned. Pat and her siblings were at work, so it was only the old lady I had to face, and she was none too happy with me for running off like that.

"Where were you?" the old lady asked as I tried to sneak back into the basement apartment.

"I went to see if my mom had come home yet."

There was no screaming and slapping. The old lady just pointed to a yellow vinyl-and-metal step chair that sat in the corner of the kitchen. "Go sit."

I sat on the chair facing the wall. I would spend many hours in that chair over the next week. I ran off two more times to check the apartment. On my last attempt, the old lady had hidden my sneakers, so when I saw my chance to run, I grabbed a pair of well-worn galoshes near the door. It was cold and wet outside, so I needed something over my socks. I scampered up the concrete steps to the sidewalk with galoshes in hand. I slipped my much smaller feet into the huge galoshes. They belonged to Pat's older brother and were three times the size of my feet, but I managed to buckle them up and shuffle off to check on the walk-in apartment again. Snow flurries were falling, and I was having a hard time walking, but I finally made it. Again I knocked and knocked and put my ear to the door, but once more, no answer. I started back to the super's apartment knowing it was going to be a long day staring at the wall in the kitchen on the yellow metal footstool.

I shuffled toward Townsend Avenue, when I spotted her walking down the hill with her long coat on and carrying a grocery bag. I stopped and stared to make sure my eyes weren't playing tricks on me. I thought I had seen her before, but it had just been my imagination, I'd concluded.

It was her all right. I ran toward her as fast as I could, with the huge galoshes on my feet. When I reached her, I wrapped my little arms around her legs and held on tight.

She bent and hugged me with her free arm. "Where did you get those boots?" She laughed.

"They took my sneakers." Tears trickled down my cheeks.

"Well, I'm home now, and I brought your little sister home with me. Let's go see her." She took me by the hand, and we walked down the hill with the snowflakes getting bigger and coming down faster now. They melted on my face and lips. I was overjoyed. She was all I knew.

I welcomed Donna, but I didn't expect the changes that came with her arrival. My mother left me with my newborn sister when she went to work in the diner. I watched over her as best I could, but I was only five and didn't know what to do when she wouldn't stop crying. I changed her diapers when they were dirty and refilled her milk bottle, but sometimes she just kept crying. I stood there looking down into the playpen, watching her cry, and felt helpless that I couldn't do anything.

There was an old woman named Helen who lived next door in the second walk-in apartment. I knocked on her door and asked her for help a couple of times when Donna wouldn't stop crying. She was a sweet old lady and would come over and rock my little sister and sing softly to her until she stopped. But after a few times, she politely told me to go across the street to the diner and tell my mom. I went across the street to the diner and told her. My mother told me not to worry, that Donna would soon cry herself to sleep. Then she told me to sit at the counter and have a bowl of soup. She had never offered to feed me there before, and I was hungry, but I felt guilty because my little sister was home alone crying in the playpen, and it was raining and thundering, with lightning. I sat at the counter and ate a bowl of vegetable soup. I didn't want my mother to be angry with me, and I was hungry, but I was worried and hurried back to my sister.

A few weeks after Donna had come home, my mother took Donna and me out one Sunday morning to visit our father. My mother said my father was sick and we were going to see him in the hospital. We dressed up, and my mother put the Donna in the carriage. We took the number 4 trains a few stops down to River Avenue in the Bronx. Then we walked a couple of blocks and ended up across the street from a big white building—it practically took up the whole block. It stood about five stories, with black horizontal windows with bars you could not see into. My mother told me that she was going to go in and visit my father, but she wanted me to walk back and forth with the baby carriage across the street and occasionally wave up at the windows, because although we could not see him, he could see us. I did as I was told. I did notice that there were no doctors or nurses coming or going from the building, but mostly men in blue uniforms that looked like cops, and the occasional regular person. It occurred to me that this was no hospital but one of the jails I had heard about, where they put bad men. I walked back and forth with my little sister in the carriage for nearly two hours, occasionally waving up at the black barred windows. My mother finally emerged from the building, and we went back home on the train. My mother said my father was getting better, and I just shook my head and kept my mouth shut and my thoughts to myself.

After a month of me watching my sister, my mother finally found a babysitter. She lived only a couple of blocks from our apartment, and Mom would drop us off in the morning and pick us up after work. I was glad my little sister was being tended to, but I didn't like going there. The woman had two other children, and one was handicapped and in a wheelchair. He needed a lot of attention. I spent most of my days there playing in the street in front of the house or on the five or six concrete steps that led up to the Concourse.

4

First Grade, 1962

I didn't make it to kindergarten and started first grade a month after the school year began. Pat had come by the babysitter's house one day and taken me over to Public School 70, because my mother was working. Pat registered me in the main office, then left me there. It was lunchtime, so the woman in the office took me to the lunchroom. She opened the lunchroom door and told a school monitor (students helping teachers) that I was in Ms. Howard's class. The school monitor told me to find a seat and he would take me to my class after lunch. There were over a hundred children sitting at lunch tables with their food, eating, laughing, talking, and children in line with their plastic food trays, getting lunch. The many kids bustling around and the loud chatter frightened me. I had not been around that many children ever. I stood there frozen, not knowing where to sit. I noticed the other children were dressed nicely in slacks, shoes, and jackets, and the girls in dresses, and I was in jeans and sneakers and a sweatshirt. I felt out of place. I spotted an exit door along the wall in the lunchroom and headed for it. I looked back and saw that the school monitor was watching me and walking in my direction across the busy, noisy lunchroom.

I pushed on the exit door, and it opened. I stepped out into the sunlight and ran as fast as I could toward home. I looked back, and the school monitor, an older boy, was running after me. He caught up to me a block away and grabbed me by the arms and told me to relax and that everything was okay, but he had to bring me back to the school.

I started to fight back. "Please let me go. You will have to drag me all the way back, and I will just run away again the first chance I get. I only live a few blocks from here, and I know my way home."

The monitor looked down at me still trying to catch my breath, then looked around and loosened his grip on my arms. He let go of me and watched me run off under the underpass for the Concourse and toward Townsend Avenue.

I was brought back to school later that week, this time by my mother. I was still nervous, but I stayed put this time. I did my best to blend in, but I was not up to par with the other children when it came to the schoolwork. I hadn't learned my ABCs or numbers, which made it difficult to do homework. After school my mother would have me sit at the kitchen table with my books until my homework was done. There was much I did not understand in those first few months when it came to my homework, and my mother became impatient with me.

I sat at the end of the table against the wall. She came in the kitchen and asked if I was done. When I said, "No. I don't understand it," she slammed my head against the wall. After a few weeks there was a slight indentation in the wall. I began to learn quickly how to read and write and lie about having my homework finished.

I also looked forward to going to school. The teacher showed me some attention, and they offered milk around 10:00 a.m. and lunch around noon. The teacher sometimes gave me extra small milk containers to take home, if there were any left over. I felt oddly out of place among the other children. I could tell by the way they were dressed and well kept, and how they interacted with each other, that I was different.

It was cold that winter, and on the weekends when my mother slept in, I would slip out of my bedroom window into the alley early in the morning to wander the streets. Each time I went out, I would walk a little farther away from home. I ventured down Jerome Avenue one morning and walked under the number 4 train El all the way to Tremont Avenue. It was a busy street with lots of stores, some of them just opening. It was cold and windy that morning, and my hands and ears were frozen. I tried covering my ears with my frozen hands but couldn't stop them from stinging.

I followed a family into John's Bargain Store to warm up for a minute. I wandered through the store and stayed close to families with kids so I wouldn't stand out. I saw other kids with their parents, and they were trying on hats, gloves, and jackets. I stopped at a table with hats for children. The hats were big and furry and had flaps you could pull down over your ears and a strap that snapped under your chin. I had seen a mother trying one on her son when I'd first walked in. The first one I tried on was much too big for a six-year-old, as it fell over my eyes. I put it back and tried another. This one fit perfectly. I pulled the flaps down over my frozen ears and snapped the strap under my chin. The furry material felt good against my ears. I looked around and followed a woman and her two daughters down the middle aisle and out the front door. I followed them a few more feet down Tremont Avenue, then ran as fast as I could toward Jerome. I couldn't believe I did it. I got away with the hat. My head, face, and ears were protected and warm from the cold and wind.

I thought about the time my mother had taken me to Alexander's on Fordham Road a month earlier. The jacket I'd worn was getting worn and much too light for me to make it through another winter. She walked me over to the coat rack in the children's department. Then took a big heavy blue peacoat off the rack and had me try it on. It was a little big on me, but it was warm. She buttoned it up, looked around, then pulled the price tag off the sleeve and put it in her pocket. She dropped my old jacket on the floor and kicked it under the coat rack. "Okay," she said. "Let's go," and down the escalator and out the front door we went. Once we were clear of the store, she looked down at me, put her index finger in front of her mouth as if to say *shhhhh*, mussed my hair, and laughed.

Walking up Jerome Avenue this cold morning with my new hat on, I buried my hands in my peacoat pockets.

When I got home, my mom had just gotten up and asked me, "Where did you get that hat?"

I was startled. "I went shopping with Billy Jones and his mom on Tremont Avenue. She bought him this hat, but when they got home, she realized it was too small for him, so she gave it to me," I replied, staring at her with wide eyes.

She looked at me and said "Okay," slightly nodding her head yes. *That was easy*, I thought.

The following Saturday, I slipped out of my bedroom window into the alley, while my mother stayed sleeping in the living room on the pull-out couch. I headed back down Jerome toward Tremont Avenue. I went back to John's Bargain Store, and this time I stole a warm pair of leather gloves. I skipped up Jerome Avenue with my furry hat on and clapped my gloved hands together. Maybe I wouldn't have to freeze again this winter.

When I arrived home, my mom was already up and cleaning the apartment. She had stayed in the night before, so she had her wits about her this morning. "Where were you, and where did you get those gloves from?"

I took a step back and nervously stuttered, "I went shopping with B-B-Billy and his mom again."

She looked at me with squinted eyes and a scowl. "Let me guess. The gloves were too small for him."

"Yes," I replied, wide eyed.

"You little bastard," she screamed. "You've been stealing this stuff. I'll show you what happens when you steal." She marched into the kitchen and turned the front two burners on top of the stove on. Then she grabbed me by the wrists and began dragging me toward the stove. I realized what she was trying to do and began screaming and trying to pull away from her and the flames. She tried her hardest to place my small hands into the flames. I could feel the heat on my palms before I finally broke loose. I escaped from her grasp and ran into my room, slamming the door shut behind me, and hid on the other side of the bed, on the floor.

I could hear her screaming, "I brought you into this world and I can take you out of it—don't you forget that."

I waited there on the floor shaking, but she didn't come in after me. I stayed there for the remainder of the day. She let me keep the hat and gloves.

Later that week, two well-dressed men came to the apartment and installed a pay phone on the hallway wall, next to the kitchen. The phone rang constantly during the day until early evening. My mother would answer the phone and write a name and numbers down on small pieces of paper. Then around 6:00 p.m. she would collect all the pieces of paper, put them in a small paper bag, and leave the house for about a half hour every night. She had stopped working in the diner once the pay phone was installed. Things had gotten better for us during those few months. The fridge was usually full, we had some new furniture and some new clothes, and my mother was home most of the time to take care of Donna.

One night when I was coming in from playing on the block, there was a police car with its light flashing and an unmarked car outside our walk-in apartment. I walked down the three steps to the apartment, and the door was open. My mother stood there all dressed up and ready to go out, with her hands cuffed behind her back. The plainclothes cops were searching for the betting slips in the kitchen cabinets and drawers, while the uniformed cops were ripping the pay-phone off the hallway wall.

I stood there looking at my mom.

"Take Donna and go next door to Helen's. I'll be home in a few hours," she yelled to me. I did as I was told, and as promised, she was home in a few hours.

Apparently she had been taking illegal numbers over that pay phone, and whomever she was working for was well connected, because she was out quickly. The gangsters seemed to be attracted to her, because one had climbed through the living room window one night and made her get dressed and took her out against her will and at gunpoint. She was able to flag down a cop at some point during the night, and they arrested him. It made the *Daily News* the next day, pictures and all. I didn't even know she was gone until the police brought her home early the next morning. That was a rough year for the three of us.

Christmas was soon approaching, and it was the weekend, so I had some free time. I was hanging around 175th Street and Jerome Avenue, where they were selling Christmas trees. They had a big metal drum filled with wood and huge flames dancing out of the top of it. It was getting dark and cold, but I did not want to go home yet. I stood close to the drum so I could get warm. I saw a woman buy a large Christmas tree and start to drag it away. She must have been on her way home from work.

I walked up to her. "Miss, do you need some help getting the tree home?"

"Yes," she replied.

I helped her drag the tree for four blocks and up one flight of stairs, and she gave me a dime. I thanked her and ran back to the Christmas tree lot. I helped four more people home with their trees that night and earned myself seventy-five cents. I went back the next few days, right up until Christmas Eve, and helped more people home with their trees.

I earned a few bucks in those couple of days. I took my earnings and went to a gift store on Jerome Ave that was still open and bought my mother a lighter and a can of lighter fluid for a Christmas gift, because she smoked. I asked the woman to gift wrap it for me and then I gave it to my mother on Christmas morning.

She thanked me, then asked, "Where did you get the money for this?"

"I helped people carry Christmas trees home from the tree lot," I replied.

She looked at me, nodded, and half smiled. That was a tough Christmas for the three of us, but my mother did manage to put a couple of things under the tree for Donna and me.

I learned some things that Christmas. I learned that there were ways to make money, even for a little guy like me. I just had to find them. It made me feel good to buy my mother a gift and to have some money in my pocket and that I could use it to make other people happy, if I wanted.

A few weeks after Christmas, I awoke early, with the sun, on a Saturday morning. My mother was sleeping in and I didn't have to watch my little sister. I threw on my clothes from the day before and out the window I went, to run the streets all day. I had found a new excitement now—sneaking on the number 4 train on Jerome Avenue that ran on the El above the street. I would wait for people to buy tokens and go through the turnstile, then I would walk right up behind them and slip under the turnstile. The man in the token booth never said anything, I sometimes thought I was invisible. Each time I snuck on the 4 train, I would take it one stop farther uptown: Burnside Ave, 183rd Street, Fordham Road. I would get off the train, check out the neighborhood, then back on the downtown side of the train and home again. I would have to count the stops each way so I wouldn't get lost, as I did not know how to read yet.

That Saturday morning I had taken the number 4 train one stop uptown and got off at Burnside Ave. There were many stores on Burnside Avenue, much like Tremont Avenue. I followed some people into Woolworth's Department Store and wandered into the toy department. I was playing with a silver metal cowboy cap gun. I looked around, then slid the cap gun into my waistband and pulled my shirt over it, then pushed a small box of caps into my pants pocket. I started for the door, but as I rounded the aisle toward the exit, a young man stepped in front of me and lightly placed his hand on my shoulder. He lifted my shirt. "What do we have here?"

I took the toy gun out from my waistband and handed it to him.

As the manager took the gun, I broke free and ran like the wind for the door. The manager did not give chase—he just stood there looking at me running and then looking at the gun in his hand and shook his head in disbelief. I ran all the way back to the train, snuck on, and rode the one stop downtown back to my neighborhood. When back on Townsend Avenue, I hung around the other kids, listening to music on the radios and waiting until it was time to go up to Judy's apartment for lunch and our Saturday afternoon get together. I enjoyed my time and lunch with Judy, but it was getting late, and I had been gone all day. So I thanked Judy for lunch and hugged her, then headed home.

As I approached the walk-in apartment around the corner on 176th Street, I could hear the country music coming out of the living room window in the alley. I knew what that meant—she would be drinking. If Mom didn't go out on a weekend night, she would drink, listen to country music, and get depressed. I hoped she had cooked dinner and was not angry enough with me to beat me. I walked down the three steps of the walk-in and up to the front door. When I got older and spoke of my childhood, I would always say, "I had a rough start in life. My mother did the best she could with what she had, but that I had seen a lot of things a child shouldn't have to see." Well, this is one of those things.

I opened and walked through the door. She stood there all dressed up to go out, crying with her arms hanging by her sides and her wrists dripping blood on the floor, a small pool of blood on each side of her.

I panicked. I ran next door and pounded on the neighbor's door and screamed, "Please call the police or ambulance. My mother is bleeding and going to die." The blond woman opened her door, looked in the apartment at my mother, and said, "Okay, I'll call the ambulance," and closed her door.

An ambulance arrived in about ten minutes. Two young medics wrapped my mother's wrists and took her to the hospital. I told them that a neighbor was going to come over and watch us. I then wiped the blood up off the wooden living room floor. I fed Donna a jar of baby food, gave her a bottle, and put her to bed. I then made myself a peanut butter and jelly sandwich. I put on my pajamas, put the TV on in the living room, built my couch fort, climbed in with my blanket and pillow, and waited. I was shaking and scared. I couldn't help thinking what would happen to us if she died. It was a long night.

My mother returned early the next morning, her wrists stitched and bandaged. From that day on things would get progressively better for the three of us. While in the hospital for her suicide attempt, my mother was put in touch with a social worker, who set her up with social services. Mom accepted the help from social services (welfare) with rent and food money. She no longer had to work, so I would not have to be left alone to care for my younger sister. She would not have to work until 11:00 p.m. in the factory or be answering the pay phone for five hours straight and taking illegal numbers for the gangsters. My mother would finally catch a break.

I noticed that there was food in the fridge on a regular basis. My mother now had money to food shop regularly, and once a month she would take her shopping cart and return with a large block of yellow cheese, a big silver metal can of peanut butter, a white box full of raisins, powdered milk (which I couldn't bring myself to drink or even use in my cereal), a big bag of lentils to make soup with, and other canned goods. Donna and I looked forward to my mother coming home with that food from her monthly trip to welfare. There seemed to be a routine in our home now. My mother began to pay a little more attention to Donna, myself, and the household now. Dinner was on the table every night at 5:30, which presented a new problem for me.

My mother would now give me a big plate of food for dinner. Donna was still eating baby food and a bottle. Mom would pick at the food as she cooked it, so I sat at the kitchen table alone with a portion that would feed a grown man or more. I was not allowed to leave the table until the plate was cleared. I ate what I could and then forced what I could into my small stomach until I couldn't eat another mouthful. I sat and stared at the food for hours, not understanding what was happening. My mother would yell things about kids starving in Biafra, and I thought of the commercials of skinny little Black babies starving in Africa. Maybe she had gone to bed hungry many nights when she was a foster child, or maybe she was trying to make up for me having gone hungry many a night when she left me alone. I did not understand. My mother would occasionally stick her head in the kitchen and look at the plate, then at me and shrug her shoulders, as if I had a choice.

After a month or so I began to figure out ways to clear my dinner plate. I began stuffing my pockets with food: potatoes, hamburger and meats, bread. I learned to eat the softer foods and stuff the solid pieces in my pockets. Once I was out of the apartment, I would run to the garbage cans in the alley and empty them. Sometimes when my pockets were already full, I would throw what I couldn't eat behind the fridge in the kitchen. That eventually attracted mice, so I could no longer do that. We had a small dog for a few months, and that dog helped me out with my dinner problem tremendously. I was becoming attached to the dog. I came home from school one day and it was gone. I asked my mother about the dog, she said it had run away. There was no more talk of the dog.

A few months after my mother started receiving welfare money, we moved a few blocks uptown to a fourth-floor two-bedroom apartment on Morris Ave, just off Burnside.

We had finally moved in and spent our first night there. I had awakened early Saturday morning. The apartment was big and bright from the sun shining in through the living room windows in the front. My mother and Donna shared the front bedroom, which was through a set of French doors in the living room. I got the back bedroom. My windows looked out over the backyard, which held lots of brick, windows, clotheslines, and fire escapes. I liked the change from the small and dark walk-in apartment.

The following school year, I began third grade in PS 79, the school right up the block from our new apartment. I had met a few of the kids on the block that summer but still kept to myself. Now that my mother wasn't working and was receiving help from social services, she paid more attention to dressing and feeding Donna and me. I still received an occasional slap, punch, or outright beating from her, but not as often as before. I did not scream or cry as much now ... I just covered up and took it.

5

Little Hustler

That first summer on Morris Avenue, I was looking out the window early one morning as the garbage truck was coming through. I watched as the garbage men picked up the metal garbage cans and banged them on the opening at the back of the truck until they were empty, then dropped the empty cans down on the sidewalk. There were ten to fifteen cans at each building. I stared at all the empty cans along the block and got an idea. I dressed and then ran down to my super's apartment in the basement and knocked on the door. It was only 7:00 a.m. I hoped I hadn't awakened him. The super's German shepherd started barking, and I got nervous and almost ran away, but the door flung open. There stood the older Black man with the gray beard, holding his barking shepherd by the collar. He looked down at me and said, "What can I do for you, young man?"

"Well, sir, I was wondering if I could bring in those empty garbage cans for you on Wednesday mornings after the garbage truck comes through. You could stay sleeping and I would line the cans up nice and neat along the backyard wall. I would only charge you a quarter."

The old man stood in the doorway, holding his dog, and looked me up and down. "I think I would like to sleep in on Wednesday mornings," he man replied with a smile. He reached in his pocket and then handed me a quarter.

"Thank you. I'll get those cans in for you right now, and I'll see you next week."

"All right then," the super replied, and closed the door.

I ran out front and carried each metal can in and placed them along the wall in the backyard, then went on to the next building.

I knocked on five more super's doors that morning, and four more agreed to my proposition. By 9:30 I had earned $1.25. Yes, I liked this new block and my new friend, money. I hadn't made any real friends yet, but I kept myself busy just the same. My mom became friends with a woman across the street, named Fay. Fay was large, around two hundred pound, and had long black hair. She was also large in life too, always laughing and talking to everybody. Fay's sister Josie was the manager of Food City on Burnside Avenue and had a son named Jeff. Fay's job was to watch and care for Jeff while Josie worked. Jeff was a little older than me and pretty much got whatever he wanted. I did not care much for Jeff. My mom and Fay became good friends. They would sit outside during the summer evenings on their folding chairs with the other ladies on the block, watching us kids run through the water from the fire hydrant or playing stickball.

I paid attention to the older kids when they were playing stickball on their block. Home plate was the sewer at the bottom of the hill. They picked a parked car on each side of the street, about six cars up the hill, to be first and third base, and the sewer at the top of the hill was second base. The batter would toss the ball up in the air, some guys would hit it on the way down, and others would let it bounce once or twice before hitting it with the long wooden stick. A real stickball bat was thick and had black tape wrapped around the bottom of it—otherwise you just used a cutoff broom or old mop stick. If you hit a fly ball past the German deli at the top of the hill, it was a home run. One setback was that the open sewers on each corner would swallow up the Spalding balls if the fielders weren't quick enough. It ended many stickball games before they were over. I remembered a guy fishing Spaldings out of a sewer with wire clothes hangers when I was walking through neighborhoods on one of my adventures.

I got up with the sunrise that Saturday morning and headed out with two wire hangers and a brown paper bag. I walked up the hill to the corner of Morris Avenue. Looking down through the open holes of the sewer, I could see five balls bobbing up and down in the sewer water about six feet below. I fashioned two of the wire hangers together with a small circle on the end of the wire to scoop the balls out of the water. I lay completely flat on the cold metal sewer and stuck my arm through the opening where the rainwater would flow down, stretching my arm as far as it would go with the wire hanger. I managed to fish all five out in about a half hour. That morning I hit two more sewers where kids played stickball and went home with around a dozen balls in pretty good shape, but, like myself, they needed a good washing after hanging around the sewers. I checked out the candy store on Burnside Avenue—they sold Spaldings for fifteen cents apiece. So I sold them back to the kids on the block for five cents each—sometimes they would buy three or four at a time. On the Saturday mornings I ventured out with my wire hanger and paper bag, I always found new sewers where the kids played stickball, to fish Spaldings out of. I was not much for sports, but I certainly liked figuring out ways to make money.

Donna, my mom, and I were all doing okay on Morris Avenue. She was giving my little sister a lot of attention, and I was grateful for that. The men would still come and go, but not as often, but she dated some for a while. I always stayed clear of them and the apartment as much as I could when she was drinking and had company.

My mother asked me to help bring groceries home one day, as she had a hard time pulling the full shopping cart up the four flights of stairs. I went with her to the supermarket and noticed something when I was on the checkout line. Some people had two or three bags to carry home, and not everyone had a shopping cart. They'd probably bought more than they intended to. When we got home and I helped her up the four flights, she emptied the cart, and I asked her if I could borrow the shopping cart.

She shrugged her shoulders. "Sure. Just bring it back in one piece."

I pulled the empty shopping cart behind me the two blocks back to Food City. Then I went in the exit door and positioned myself at the end of the last checkout register. I watched the checkout girls fill the brown paper bags with food and give the customers their change. I waited about ten minutes, but then I spotted her. An older woman by herself and carrying two heavy shopping bags. As she walked past me, I asked her, "Ma'am, do you need some help home with those bags?"

The older woman looked down at me—I was not much bigger than the shopping cart—and she said, "You know, I think I do." I quickly opened the shopping cart and helped the woman place the bags in it. I pulled the cart behind me for two and a half blocks, walking alongside and talking with the woman.

I followed her into her building and pulled the shopping cart up the one flight of stairs one step at a time. "Can I give you a hand with that?" The older woman asked, more than once, seeing me struggle.

"No thank you," I replied. "I got it." After the woman helped me lift the two bags out of the cart, she handed me twenty cents. I looked at the two dimes in my hand, then looked up at her. "Thank you, ma'am."

"No, thank you," the woman replied.

I folded up my mom's shopping cart, carried it down the flight of stairs, and headed back to Food City. I helped four more people home with their groceries that Saturday afternoon and evening. When it started getting dark, I took the shopping cart and headed home for dinner. I earned $1.20 that day and gave my mom half.

I put my earnings in a jar in my T-shirt drawer, along with some of the change I made from fishing the Spaldings out of the sewers and my garbage can gig on Wednesdays. I returned to Food City on Friday nights after school and on Saturdays, and my jar started to fill up. I would always give my mother half of the money I earned.

Donna walked now, and I played with her every chance I could. I doted over her and worried if my Mom would beat her the way she beat me. We were playing in my room one morning, and Donna opened the bottom drawer of my six-drawer dresser and stepped on it to see what was on top. The entire dresser began to topple over on her, when I ran over and was able to grab the top and get under it. I was pinned between the dresser and the bottom of my bed. Donna had let out a yell and crawled out from under it.

My mom came running into the bedroom and lifted the dresser off me and screamed, "What the hell is going on in here?" She stared at me and Donna, who was standing near the window, the morning sun bouncing off her tiny face. I knew that voice and the look on my mother's face.

Donna went to say something, and I yelled, "I stepped on the bottom drawer, and it tipped over by accident."

She shoved me into the wall and yelled, "Don't do that again," and walked out. I looked over at Donna and let out a long sigh of relief. I watched carefully—so far, Mom had not beat my sister.

The apartment on Morris Avenue had begun to take on a look I had not seen before. My mom got a minibar and a new couch for the living room, along with a used but nice bedroom set for herself. She began to wax the wooden floors, wash the windows, and clean the house on a regular basis. The apartment was spotless most of the time. I welcomed the semblance of normalcy, but above all, I welcomed not being left alone for long periods of time or left alone to care for my little sister. I seemed to be doing well in third grade in my new school. My third grade teacher, Mrs. Johnson, seemed to like me. I also got some new clothes and shoes from my mom, to start school with, so I didn't stand out as much. I tried to stay quiet and blend in as best I could. If I kept quiet and to myself, no one would know about the drinking or the beatings and the men coming and going at my home.

I had to get a bigger jar from all the money I was earning and saving, even after giving my mother a good portion of it. Having some money saved away made me feel good. But that was when things would take a drastic turn. It was when she let the monster in. I was never the same kid after the sexual assault. Carrying that secret and the guilt and shame around wore on me.

My mother began getting calls from my school. The teacher said that I was becoming disruptive and could not focus on the schoolwork and that I would ask to go to the bathroom and not return to class. My mother continued to beat me, but it did not affect me anymore. I would not give her the satisfaction of crying or covering up anymore. I just took it.

I slid one of the unfiltered cigarettes out of the red pack of Pall Malls my mother had left on the kitchen table. I grabbed a book of matches and ran down the four flights of stairs and up the block. There was a driveway next to the German deli on the corner. Down the driveway, behind the deli, were four garages that made up a small building. I tucked the cigarette on the top of my ear, climbed to the top of the fence that separated the backyards, and onto the black tarred roof. The garage roof was my secret hiding place.

I grabbed the cigarette that was tucked on the top of my ear and lit it. I took a puff and began coughing. I took a smaller drag the next time and was able to hold it in and blow it out without coughing. I'd watched my mother and other grown-ups smoking and wondered what the big deal was. Before I was halfway through smoking the cigarette, my head spun, and my heart raced from the nicotine. I liked it. It made me feel different, and I would do anything to feel different. It was a couple of days before I stole my next cigarette, but within a few weeks I was a nine-year-old boy who was a daily smoker, buying packs of Parliament filtered cigarettes for twenty-five cents a pack from the German deli on Burnside Avenue.

I would use the money from my odd jobs. Sometimes my mother would send me, with a list, to the bodega around the corner on 180th Street, where she had a tab. I would just add on a pack of Parliaments if I was short on money.

I started smoking in the bathroom of the apartment. One day as I walked out of the bathroom after smoking, my mother said, "Were you just smoking in there?"

"No." Of course, a cloud of smoke followed me out of the bathroom. My mother smacked me hard across the face. But once again I just stood there staring at her, not giving her the satisfaction of seeing me cry or cringe. She shook her head and walked away.

I was also smoking in the bathroom at school. I began to have a hard time concentrating or focusing on my schoolwork. I would raise my hand and ask to go to the bathroom a couple of times a day, where I would smoke my cigarettes if I had them. Sometimes I would return to class; sometimes I wouldn't.

6

In Name Only

My mother got no help from my father with raising me. Even when he was out of prison, the only time he showed up for me was for my Holy Communion in the Catholic church, and that was only for show. One of my father's friends (Charlie the Bird) was asked to be my godfather.

I got to see my father three times that last year on Morris Avenue. The first time, he took us all out to dinner against my mother's will, and ended up stabbing her in the face with his fork during a violent outburst. The second time, he took her all over downtown from bar to bar and dinner and gift shops, only for her to find out he was passing counterfeit twenties. The third time would be my last.

It had been a while since I had seen him. My mother told me that my father would be stopping by later that afternoon. I played in the snow outside the building alone, waiting for him. We lived on a hill, and as the snow melted, it flowed down the street. I was making a passageway in the snow for the water to flow down just off the curb, when I spotted a man walking down the block. He wore a long winter coat, nice black shoes, and a hat. I kept glancing back as the man moved closer. At last glance I could clearly see his face—it was him. My father locked eyes with me for a couple of seconds, then looked straight ahead and walked past me and up into the building. I tried to tell myself that maybe he didn't recognize me because of the big winter hat with the floppy ears, but sadly, I thought he might have.

I played in the snow for another hour, then went upstairs. It was late Saturday afternoon, and the country music was playing. My mother and father were sitting in the living room, drinking beer and talking. My little sister sat next to my mother on the couch. I nodded hello to them and headed to my room.

My mother yelled, "Robert, your father is going to the German deli. Why don't you go with him?"

I followed my father out the apartment and down the stairs. He didn't speak much to me when he was around. Although, I did notice that he would sometimes stare and seem to size me up. We were leaving the deli after my father purchased a couple of quarts of Schaefer beer. I watched as he counted change out on the countertop, and he had just enough to pay. We left the deli and were crossing the snow-covered street as the sun was going down. I noticed something lying on the frozen slush in the street and ran over and picked it up—a ten-dollar bill. My father said, "Hey, what did you get there?" I proudly lifted my hand up, clutching the wet bill tightly between my thumb and forefinger so it wouldn't blow away. "Look what I found."

My father leaned over and snatched the bill from my fingers and slid it into his pocket. He put his finger to his lips and said, "Shhh. We'll surprise your mom later."

I waited, but my father never mentioned the ten dollars. That would be the last time I would see him alive.

That summer I was called home from a camping trip I went on with Fay and some of the kids from the block. When I entered the apartment, I could see my mother was visibly shaken and had been crying. I walked into my room, followed by my mom.

She sat at the end of my bed and beckoned me to sit next to her. "I have some bad news, Robert. Your father died last night." She brought the napkin to her eyes and wiped her tears.

I sat motionless on the end of the bed next to her. *I should be crying. It was my father.* So I hugged my mother and worked up a few alligator tears for a man I did not know, but feared. I sat with her for a moment while we both cried, then I went to check on my little sister. That would be the one and only time I would force myself to cry.

The funeral was held at St. Brendan's Catholic Church in the North Bronx. It was a cool, brisk Monday morning. My mother and I dressed in our Sunday best and took a cab to the church. As we walked from the cab to the church, my mother looked down at me and said, "Robert, we may not get a warm welcome in the church from your father's family. If anyone says anything, just keep looking straight ahead and keep walking with me."

"Okay, Mom, but why would they be mean to us?"

"Well, your father had a few women in his life, and some had his children, but his family only recognizes the woman he married and their son, Raymond, but I'll be damned if we're not going to pay our respects today," she said, as she pushed the church door open.

As we entered, I looked up at the sun coming through the stained-glass window above the altar, beaming light down on the casket. I drew a deep breath and scanned the rows of brown wooden pews and the people scattered about. One large group in the front, and near the casket, turned and gave my mother and me a long, hard look. She and I stood still there for a couple of moments. Men started to get up from their wives and families and walk toward my mother and me at the back of the church. There were a total of six suited men. As they reached us, each man gave my mother a kiss and hug, then patted me on the back. Many heads turned to stare at the commotion in the back of the church, and there were whispers of who we were and how much I looked like my father.

The six men formed a horseshoe around my mother and me and escorted us up to the closed casket. She put her hand on the casket and said a prayer as her tears fell. I prayed also. I overheard one of the men whisper to her, "Sophie, you were the only one he ever loved." My father's crew stood with my mother and me until we finished praying, then dispersed back into the wooden pews. She took me by the hand and, with her head held high, walked through the stares and whispers and out of the church. We walked to 204th Street and stopped in a fountain candy store, where my mother treated herself and me to a couple of chocolate egg creams and pretzels.

As we drank our egg creams, my mother looked down at me and said, "Well, I guess it's just us again," and messed up my hair.

I continued doing my odd jobs and sharing what I made with my mother, but I stayed to myself. I also worried about my father and where he may be heading in the next world. From what I had learned in the Catholic Church, my father was not going to a good place.

When my mother was out shopping with my sister, and I had time alone at the apartment, I would pray for my father. I would kneel on the side of my bed and repeat the Our Father and Hail Mary for up to an hour or more, in hopes that my prayers would help my father not have to suffer as much for his sins.

7

Junkies

In 1967 I was ten years old and became friends with the Cola family that last year on Morris Avenue, who helped me tremendously. I started hanging around with Billy Cola, who was my age and lived across the street. We both liked to smoke cigarettes, so we had that in common. Billy had three brothers, two sisters, two very cool parents, and a Doberman pinscher named Ringo. I would spend many overnight weekends with them, and if they went to the drive-in, I would just pile in with them in their station wagon. I loved the whole family scene and how they all looked out for each other and me. I blended right in with the Colas, and they enjoyed having me around. The oldest daughter's boyfriend's name was Robby, so they nicknamed me Little Robby. The Colas' apartment was a great place for me to escape to. After a year or so, the Colas moved up to the North Bronx. I missed them.

We moved uptown a few months later. We had lived on Morris Avenue for about two years. We moved because my mother said the neighborhood was getting bad. What made the neighborhoods bad were the drugs. Once the drugs were there, it was time to go.

My mother called me over to the window one afternoon. "See that window on the ground floor at the end of the building?" She pointed across the street. "Well, the junkies come by at night and tap on the window. It opens a little, then they slide their money under it, then the dealers push the dope back out and the junkies take off up and down the block. It is definitely time for us to move."

The whole idea of the desperate junkies piqued my interest. I would quietly sneak over to the living room window at night, when my mother and Donna were sleeping, and watch the junkies cop their dope from the window below, which was illuminated by the streetlight. Once the junkies got their dope, they scampered up or down the block to go get fixed. I was mesmerized by the whole scene.

I had only met one junkie my whole short life, and his name was Monty. He was a friend of my mother who would stop by and visit her occasionally, usually when he was doing well. He was a tall, skinny, blond-headed guy in his twenties. He always had a paperback book sticking out of the back pocket of his jeans. I only knew Monty was a junkie because my mother had said so.

Monty had stopped the old apartment years ago when I was five-years-old, when we hadn't gotten on welfare yet. I had been crying in my bedroom, and Monty had asked my mother, "What's wrong with Robert? Why is he crying like that?"

My mother replied, "He's been like that for a couple of days now from a bad toothache, but I don't have the money to get the tooth pulled."

Monty peered into the bedroom, and I was holding the left side of my jaw and crying. "Get your sneakers on, Robert," Monty said. "Let's see if we can get that tooth fixed for you." Monty turned to my mom and said, "Sophie, you can't leave him like that. I'll take him up to Royal Hospital and see if we can get that tooth pulled."

"Okay," she replied.

Monty and I walked the six blocks to Royal Hospital on the Grand Concourse and Burnside Avenue that day. He talked to the hospital staff, and the next thing you knew, I was sitting in a dental chair and the dental assistant was asking me my name and address.

"My name is Robert Carney, and I live at 2005 Townsend Avenue," I answered.

"Excuse me, ma'am," Monty interrupted. "We've moved since then, and our new address is 2604 Walton Avenue." Monty just looked over at me and winked.

Moments later the dentist came in and pulled my tooth. The dental assistant gave me some gauze to put on my bleeding gums and led me into another room to recover, then left me.

I had only been sitting there a minute when Monty peeked his head into the recovery room and put his index finger to his lips for me to stay quiet. He walked over and picked up my little five-year-old body and threw me over his shoulder. He carried me down the hallway and through a metal door, and down the stairwell we went. Within two minutes we were out of the hospital and turning the corner onto Burnside Avenue.

When we were two blocks away, he took me off his shoulder, set me down, and asked, "How are you feeling?"

"Much better, thank you," I replied, and we walked the six blocks back home.

We stopped at a candy store, and Monty bought me a couple of pretzels and chocolate jelly bars to eat later when I felt better.

That was all I had known about junkies, until looking out that window and watching them cop their dope under the streetlight that night.

8

Checkers and Pistachios

A few months later, we moved uptown to 194th and Briggs Avenue, just north of Fordham Road. The new neighborhood was mostly White, Irish, Italian, and Jewish. I was half-Irish myself, from my father's side, and I fantasized that I might fit in and make some new friends here, maybe even join an Irish gang, if they had any. I was now ten, and my mom registered me in the sixth grade at Public School 46, just up the block from our new apartment. The new place was on the first floor, and it was a five-room apartment, so we each had our own bedroom.

That first year on Briggs Avenue was a hard adjustment. I did not have my little hustles to make money anymore, and I was not making any new friends, so I stayed to myself most of the time. I was also constantly being haunted by the sexual assault incident. The slightest thought of it made me feel ashamed, as if I had done something wrong. I never understood that.

I started visiting the library down the block and around the corner on Bainbridge Avenue. I would check out adventure books and read them after school in my room. It was my newest escape, and it worked. I would spend hours alone in my room reading after school and on weekends. My mother would stick her head in the room occasionally to ask me if I was okay.

I also started having problems at school. Part of my homework assignment every night consisted of writing fifty or one hundred times, "I will not talk during class" or "I will not get out of my seat," or whatever—it was an ongoing thing. I had become very withdrawn, and the demon's voice in my head was becoming louder and louder.

One Saturday afternoon after spending much of the winter in my room reading, I went to the bathroom and took the razor blade out of the razor that was in the bathroom cabinet. I went back into my room, closed the door, and sliced each wrist five or six times. I lay down on my single bed and let each arm hang off the sides and closed my eyes.

A short while later my mother walked by the room and saw the door closed, and she knocked, but no answer. She walked by a few minutes later and knocked again. This time she yelled to me, "Are you all right in there?" There was no answer, so she opened the door. She saw me lying there on my bed and my arm hanging off the side, the blood dripping from my wrist and forming a small puddle on the linoleum floor.

"Oh my God, what did you do?" she screamed. She tore a T-shirt in half and wrapped my wrists and rushed me to a doctor's office around the corner from our apartment. The doctor stitched my wrists up and asked me why I did that. I just shrugged my shoulders and said I was tired of feeling bad.

My mother became concerned about me and contacted a priest who was an old friend of my father. Monsignor Moore set me up to see a psychiatrist once a week at the Catholic

Charities on the Grand Concourse, just south of Fordham Road in the Bronx. I was scheduled to see Dr. Pelosi after school on Thursdays. On my first visit, I went directly from school to my 4:00 p.m. appointment. I walked the five blocks down the Concourse, then into the white building and up the long flight of wooden stairs. I announced myself to the receptionist and sat and waited for what seemed like hours, checking out the other people in the waiting room. I noticed I was the only child there.

Finally a big, balding head with black-rimmed glasses popped out of the door leading to the offices. "Robert Carney," the man said softly.

I raised my hand, and the man motioned me through the door. "I'm Doctor Pelosi," he said and shook my small hand with his big, sweaty paw.

I wiped my hand on my jeans and followed him down the hallway.

The doctor was a very large man, over six feet tall and around three hundred pounds. When we entered the office, I sat in the chair in front of the desk, and Dr. Pelosi made his way behind the desk and settled into the swivel chair. I watched as the doctor struggled to fit his backside between the two armrests, and I listened as all the air (hsssssssss) left the leather cushioned chair when the doc finally settled in his seat. I just smiled to myself and looked around the office and out the window at the blue sky and clouds behind the doctor and tried not to laugh.

"So, Robert, how are you doing today?"

"I'm okay, Doc. How are you?"

"I'm doing okay, Robert. Is it okay to call you Robert?"

"Sure," I said, while shrugging my shoulders.

"I understand you're having some problems at school and at home," the doctor continued.

"That's right," I replied. "I don't like sitting in the class all day, and I really don't get along with the other kids so well. I'd rather ride the trains and check out different parts of the city."

The doctor let out a laugh. "So would I. What about your home life? I understand you cut your wrists a couple of weeks ago. Would you like to talk about that?"

I got very quiet and shrugged my shoulders again.

I thought, *You mean, talk about all the beatings, being left places with people I don't know, about the drinking and men coming and going, and the sexual assault that haunts me daily with shame and guilt? No, not today, Doc. I'm not giving my mother up for her unusual cruelty, and the sexual assault is coming to my grave with me.* Then I raised my head and said verbally, "Not today, Doc."

"That's okay. We can save that for another time. Do you like playing checkers?"

"Yes," I replied, and we played checkers for the remainder of the session.

On my way to our second session, I stopped in Krums, a large candy store on the Grand Concourse near the Catholic Charities. There were all kinds of chocolates, barrels of taffy, and varieties of nuts. I filled my pockets with pistachios and headed to my appointment.

The doctor sat in his chair, hsssssssss, then pulled out the checkerboard. "Do you like pistachios, Doc?"

"Sure," he replied.

I stood and emptied my pockets of pistachios onto the desk, and we played checkers and ate pistachio nuts every week for the better part of a year—we were both worthy opponents at checkers.

At our third session, the doctor asked, "So, Robert, what's happening at home? Is that something you would like to talk about? Whatever we talk about is between us, and it may make you feel better."

"Not really, Doc," I replied. "I know my mother's doing the best she can, but sometimes she's not a very nice person, and I really don't like the people she brings to the house. We just don't get along."

"Okay," the doctor replied, and we continued to play checkers and have small talk. I would not disclose the sexual assault incident or the beatings, not to him or anyone else, ever.

Dr. Pelosi gave me an IQ test and asked me to bring my mother in the following session. I brought her with me the next week and told her about the air hissing out of the doctor's chair. When the doctor sat down, we both bit our lips to keep from cracking up. The doctor asked me if he could talk to my mother alone for a few minutes, so I excused myself to the waiting room. My mother emerged about twenty minutes later, and the doctor said he would see me next week.

"Well, you're no dummy," my mother said as we walked out onto the Grand Concourse. "The doctor says you have an IQ of 136, which he says is higher than normal, so it's not that you can't do the schoolwork. He says he thinks you're just bored in school." I thought about that as we walked up the Concourse. "Dummy" was one of her nicknames for me, especially when I had trouble doing my homework. No, I was no dummy.

9

Shine, Mister?

I liked the new neighborhood and school; I also continued my sessions with Dr. Pelosi. I still had some problems getting along with the teachers and other kids and sitting still in school, but my thoughts of suicide had subsided. I made a couple of occasional friends on my new block, but my thoughts and energy had turned to earning money again. I was still smoking cigarettes when I could get them.

I went from store to store in my new neighborhood, asking if they needed help stocking shelves or cleaning up or whatever. Apparently I was too young and small, or "light in the ass," as one store owner remarked, but my insistence finally paid off. A Jewish butcher on 198th Street told me to come by on Fridays at five. He would then drive me to Co Op city and sit in the car while I delivered kosher meats to different customers in the buildings. I also found a cleaners on Kingsbridge Road that let me deliver cleaned and pressed clothes to customers on Saturdays.

I had found an old wooden shoeshine box sticking out of a metal garbage can in my old building. It was filled with brushes, rags, and three different colors of shoe polishes. When you flipped over half the top, a wooden foot imprint appeared, to set your foot on. I took the shoeshine box and went to Fordham and Jerome Avenue to catch the people coming off the train from work, but I got no takers. I guess people did not want to stand and get a shine after working all day.

I noticed there were many bars in my new Irish neighborhood, maybe two on every block. I took the wooden shoeshine box out of the closet once again and set out that Friday afternoon. I thought I would catch the guys coming home from work with their paychecks and they might splurge on a shine. My first stop was the Poe Park Tavern on Kingsbridge Road, just up the block from our apartment. It was six o'clock on a cool spring night, and the bar was packed with older working-class men on their way home from work. The loud talking, laughter, thick cigarette smoke, and music coming from the jukebox were a new world to me as I approached my first couple of prospects.

"Want a shoeshine, mister?" I yelled to the first man at the end of the bar.

"No thank you," replied the man.

The second man I asked swung his swivel chair around and looked down at me and my shoeshine box. "How much?" asked the gray-suited gentleman.

"I don't know," I replied, "How about a quarter?"

"Okay, shine 'em up," said my first customer.

I knelt, flipped open the shoeshine box, set the man's left foot on the foot stand, and did everything I learned from asking an old man about shining shoes. I wiped down the dull black leather shoe with my then white rag, applied some black polish, brushed it out, then shined it up with my shine rag. I did the same to the right shoe, and the gentleman looked down at his shoes and said, "Good job," then handed me a buck and said, "Keep the change." I shined three more pairs of shoes in that bar, then visited another five bars that night. I went home with close to ten bucks, of which I gave half to my mother.

I had hit the jackpot—I had found a way to make some money. Yes, I liked money. I always felt better with a few bucks in my pocket. I would shine shoes every Thursday, Friday, and Saturday nights. Within a short while I added six more bars to my route.

I felt those twelve bars were mine to shine in exclusively. If I walked into one of those bars and saw another kid shining shoes, I would wait for him outside the bar, then explain that that was my bar, and so were all the bars along my route. I also explained that this was a warning, and if I caught them shining in there again, there would be a problem. And yes, I had a couple of problems. Of the five boys I caught infringing on my territory, three heeded my warning and found other bars to shine in. One sized me up and told me to fuck off, and at it we went. We squared off in front of McDonough's Pub on 194th Street. Rolling up and down the block, punching each other, until the intruder realized that the few pounds and a couple of inches he had on me were not helping him. I was told I hit hard for my size, and there didn't seem to be any quit in me. The intruder finally backed up, grabbed his shine box, and ran down 194th Street, screaming obscenities as he fled.

I wiped the blood from my bottom lip and walked over to my shine box, which had fallen over, and some of my brushes and polish had scattered over the sidewalk. I kneeled to gather my stuff, when I looked up and saw a group of men staring out the large front window of McDonough's Pub. They were all smiling and nodding their heads at me. They waved me in, and a bunch of them took shines while praising my street-fighting abilities for such a small kid. I enjoyed the attention and floated to the next bar.

I prided myself on how shiny and fast I could shine a pair of shoes. I also learned to snap my shine rag to some of the tunes on the jukebox. I got to know some of my customers on a first-name basis, and they seemed to like me.

My second altercation came about six months after I started shining. I walked into the Raven Bar on Webster Avenue and saw a kid giving a shine. I walked back out of the bar and waited. It was a kid from the other side of Fordham Road, one I had already given a warning to. The kid emerged from the bar a few minutes later. I looked the boy in the eye and said, "I thought I asked you not to work these few bars along my route?"

"I'll shine wherever the fuck I want," the kid responded.

I put my shine box down and my hands up. "Fine, then let's get at it."

Bar patrons started to gather at the bay windows to watch the commotion. The kid put his shine box down and pulled a curved linoleum cutter out of it as he came up. I jumped back and picked up my wooden shoeshine box for protection. The kid took a swipe at me with the cutter. I stepped out of the way and slammed the corner of my shoeshine box into the side of his head. He dropped the cutter and fell to one knee, and blood trickled down over his left ear. I kicked the black-handled cutter into the street and raised my box over the kid's head again. "I'll give you to the count of three to pick up your shine box and get the fuck out of here." The kid scrambled to his feet, snatched up his box, and took off down Webster Avenue toward Fordham. I looked up at the patrons in the bar window. There were no smiles this time, only open mouths and wide eyes. I made sure my shoeshine box wasn't broken, then headed on to my next bar. I saw no more intruders on my bar route.

I worked my shoeshine business three days a week, all year long, except if the weather was too bad. I took off on holidays, except for one Christmas Eve. Donna had been talking about the Dancerina Doll for the last month—a doll that played music and twirled around. It was a big hit that year. My mother planned on getting it but ran out of money that Christmas. When I found out late that afternoon on Christmas Eve, I grabbed my shine box and hit the bars. It was cold and windy, with some snow flurries, so not many people were out that evening. I had to come up with $23.00 for the doll. I had $8.00 saved, so I only needed $15.00 more to get the doll. I finished my route and was still short, so I crossed Fordham Road and visited some new bars. I was sure I was encroaching on someone's territory. By 8:30 p.m. I had hit the $23.00 mark and ran over to Sears on Webster Avenue and Fordham Road and purchased one of the last remaining Dancerina dolls. I stumbled into our apartment around 9:30 that Christmas Eve, with my shoeshine box and a shopping bag.

My mother looked at me and said, "Did you get it?"

I handed her the shopping bag. She hugged me and said, "Good job."

I was elated.

Donna turned six that year and started first grade. I turned eleven and was in sixth grade. My little sister seemed to adjust well in school, and as far as I could see, my mother had not laid hands on her. I was grateful for that. I wondered why I had gotten beaten so badly, so often. The beatings had finally stopped, a smack here and there, but nothing like it was. I think things had begun to change when my sister came along.

10

Big Brother

Dr. Pelosi suggested I get a Catholic Big Brother through the Catholic Charities. I was twelve years old at the time, and he thought I needed a good male role model in my life. The first Big Brother did not work out. He was a young business type and had taken me to a soccer game, then a Yankee game. Neither sport interested me. I also smoked cigarettes on a daily basis then. When I went out with him, he had asked me not to smoke, but I lit up anyway and said, "Hey, didn't they tell you I was a smoker?"

When I had my next session with Dr. Pelosi and he told me the first Big Brother backed out, I was not disappointed. A few weeks later, my mother had gotten a call from Dr. Pelosi, who said they had found me a new Big Brother. The following week I was asked to bring my mother with me to meet the new guy at my next session.

Bob Posch, the college student who had volunteered for the Big Brother program, had asked for their hardest case, their most troubled young boy. He wanted a challenge. He was told that this boy was a smoker, had a history of playing hooky from school, fighting, and running away from home. Bob was expecting a big, tough, leather-jacket-wearing thug with a cigarette dangling from his lips to walk in. Instead he saw a cute-faced short and skinny kid with big ears walk in with his mom, smiling.

Bob stood about five foot nine and was in pretty good shape. He had short brown hair and wore a long winter coat, black jeans and shoes, and a collared shirt with a pullover sweater. He carried a white cloth bag over his shoulder that had the words *Manhattan College* in big green letters across it. He offered me a piece of gum, which I took. We had some small talk, shook hands, and arranged our first meeting.

On our first outing, we attended a Manhattan College versus Fordham University basketball game at Madison Square Garden. I was still reeling from the ride down on the number 1 train. It was filled with Manhattan College students who called themselves Jaspers, who were drinking and singing college songs and peeing between cars. They were having a blast, and so was the I. During the game, the Jaspers threw rolls of toilet paper that would unroll as they flew toward the court. At one point they had to stop the game to clear the court of toilet paper.

After the game Bob and I walked and ended up in front of the Empire State Building. "Have you ever been to the top?" he asked.

"No, I haven't," I replied. *Could it get any better than this?* I thought, still feeling the excitement of the game and the ride down on the train. The elevator ride to the top of the Empire State Building seemed to take forever, and I was sure I left my stomach somewhere between the twentieth and twenty-fifth floor. It was a brisk March evening as we watched, from the observation deck, the sun go down over New York. I was in awe.

Bob gave me a nudge with his elbow. "You see that guy over there with the two women and kids?"

"Yes, what about him?"

"That's Cassius Clay, the boxer. Go get a postcard and get his autograph. He changed his name, so call him Mr. Muhammad Ali."

I had heard of him, as everyone had.

Bob gave me a dollar, and I ran over to the counter and bought a postcard with King Kong wrapped around the top of the Empire State Building, swiping at a plane. I then ran over to the larger-than-life, smiling Black man and asked, "Can I have your autograph, Mr. Ali?"

Ali looked down at me holding the postcard and pen and said, "Come here." He picked me up in his arms and said, "What's your name?"

"Robby," I replied, wide eyed.

"Robby," he said, "can you believe it—nobody out there can beat me." He waved his arm from left to right over the city. "I'll have my belts back within a year." Ali had just gotten out of prison for avoiding the draft. He put me down, then turned to Bob, put his dukes up, gave a couple of feint jabs, and said, "Want to go a couple of rounds?"

Bob took a step back and laughed. "No thank you, Mr. Ali. I've seen some of your fights." Muhammad Ali then autographed the postcard and talked and joked with Bob and me. His wife finally called him, and he said it was nice meeting us and walked to his family.

I had the time of my life that night, and Bob let me smoke my cigarettes in peace. Although Bob always offered me a stick of gum when I was lighting up, saying, "Cavities are better than cancer." Bob took me camping, bowling, ice skating, the movies, the Statue of Liberty, and sometimes let me bring some of my townie friends with me. He even brought me out to Merrick, Long Island, to meet his parents and sister and hang out for the weekend. I looked forward to the time spent with him.

The Kennedy Home

Things were still not going well for me at home. The beatings and verbal abuse had stopped, but the drinking on the weekends and men continued. My mother had been seeing one man steadily during that time. He was a businessman named Fred, and he was about twenty years older than my mother. I did not get along with, or like, Fred. There had been an incident when my mother had dated Fred a few years back. She had gone out for beer, and I had walked into the apartment and saw Fred holding my little sister in his arms. Donna was only two or three years old. I became extremely uncomfortable with the way he was holding her and screamed at him to put her down and not touch her again. I took my sister into my room until my Mom returned. I took my mother to the side when she got back and told her what happened, but apparently it went in one ear and out the other. Nothing was ever said, but I kept a close eye on my sister when he was around.

One Friday night the doorbell rang, and my mother said, "Watch this." She opened the door slightly, said a few words, then snatched the bag of beer out of Fred's arms and slammed the door on him.

I thought, *What a sucker.*

More recently, my mom was trying to push Fred out the front door, and he pushed her up against the wall. I heard her yell and ran out of my room and punched Fred in the side of his temple, which caused him to lose his balance, and my mother was able to push him out the door. Nevertheless, Fred began coming to the apartment on a regular basis. I would make myself scarce when he was around, but I made my little sister promise to tell me if he ever touched her. Then I knew what I would have to do. Fred and I hardly spoke a word to each other.

I barely made it out of the sixth grade, as a result of my behavior and absences, but because of my reading and comprehension skills, they moved me on. I came home from school one day, and my mother informed me that she felt she could not control me any longer and that I would be going to live in a place called the Kennedy Home this coming weekend. "It's a home for children run by the Catholic Charities. I spoke with Dr. Pelosi, and there's nothing more I can do with you," she calmly said.

"Are you sure it's not because your new boyfriend doesn't like having me around?" I asked.

"No," she answered. "He has nothing to do with it. It's because of your school absences and your not listening to me."

"How long do I have to stay there?" I asked.

"I don't know. It depends on your behavior and how well you do in school."

That Sunday, on a cold and windy October morning, my mother was finishing packing the open suitcase on my bed. I just stood there watching her. She left the room for a minute, and I slipped a carton of Marlboros and a lighter into the suitcase and under the clothes.

I carried the suitcase out to Fred's 1963 Ford Fairlane and put it in the trunk. Fred would not even make eye contact with me as he slammed the trunk down. I sat in the backseat with my sister as we drove down Fordham Road toward Pelham Parkway. It was cloudy and cold out as the snow flurries began to fall. It was surreal. I could not believe she was sending me off. We made a left on Stillwell Avenue and pulled up in front of the Kennedy Home. It was a large, fenced area with grass and trees, dotted with a dozen or small red brick buildings. I hugged my little sister and said I would be home soon. She held me tight and did not want to let go. Fred opened the trunk, handed me my suitcase, then got back in the car. My mother and I walked up the white stone steps to the entrance.

A Catholic nun met us at the door, and we followed her to the room I would be sharing with four other boys. We passed a television room filled with boys my age glued to the screen and hanging out. The nun left us to unpack the suitcase into the locker next to the single bed. My mother was unpacking the suitcase, when she spotted the red carton of Marlboro cigarettes. She looked at them, then up at me, then quickly shoved them into the locker under my clothes. She emptied the suitcase, hugged me and said, "Be good. I will talk with you soon," and left with the empty suitcase in hand. I stared out the window next to my gray steel locker at the barren trees and cloudy sky, as my mother walked down the white stone steps with my empty suitcase. She placed it in the backseat next to my sister, got in the car, and they drove off. I swallowed hard and did my best not to cry.

The nun who met us at the door came into the room and explained all the rules to me, then took me to the television room and introduced me to a few of the boys.

The Kennedy Home was not a lockdown facility for juvenile delinquents, but you did need permission to leave the grounds, and it was considered a privilege. It was a children's home run by the Catholic Charities and Catholic nuns, for neglected boys and girls who had lost their parents or whose parents could not take care of them for financial or other reasons.

I lay in my single bed that night, staring out the window at the streetlight and listening to the other boys settle in, 9:00 p.m. and lights out. When all was settled and silent, I slipped out of my bed and quietly dressed. I grabbed the couple of bucks I had and a pack of cigarettes and peeked out into the hallway. There was a nun sitting at a dimly lit desk, reading, at the end of the hallway of the five rooms on that floor. I made a right and tiptoed to the end of the hallway and down the flight of stairs. I pushed open the heavy metal door as quietly as I could and slipped out into the night. I climbed over the six-foot chain-link fence and jogged down Stillwell Avenue to Pelham Parkway. Two buses and two hours later, I was knocking on the door of my Big Brother's dorm room in Jasper Hall at Manhattan College.

Bob had let me in and asked what happened. "I'm not staying at that place. I'll live on the streets if I have to." He explained that because I was only twelve, I had to do what my mother and Dr. Pelosi said, but that he would be there for me the whole time and when I got out and that he was always going to be my Big Brother.

"Well, spend the night with me tonight, and we'll see what happens tomorrow," Bob said.

He got a call the next morning from Dr. Pelosi, who asked if he had seen me. "Yes, he's here with me," Bob said.

"Please return him to the Kennedy Home. He is legally in their care now," replied the doctor. So Bob gave me another pep talk and took me back to the Kennedy Home.

I had been there about a week when the strangest thing happened. Each child was given a net bag to put their dirty clothes in and leave hanging in a room with shelves down the hallway. Each child's name was written on a piece of white tape and taped to a section of the shelf where the nuns would put their folded clean clothes every week. Each piece of clothing had the child's first initial and last name written on the tag inside the clothing. I found a shirt in my pile with the initial R. and the last name *Carney* written in it. I took it to the nun on duty and said I found it in my pile, but it wasn't mine. The nun said it probably belonged to Ray Carney, who lived in Hayes Cottage with the older boys, and it got mixed up.

I asked where Hayes Cottage was and ran the shirt over. I asked for Ray at the door, and my half brother Ray emerged from the cottage. We had not seen each other since I was three and he was seven, while living on 176th Street, a lifetime ago. Two weeks later Ray was hit by a car on Pelham Parkway on his way back from high school. He was in a coma for a couple of months, then awoke. I went to visit him in Jacobi hospital a few times, then he was sent to rehab, and we didn't meet again for many years.

I attended school within the Kennedy Home for the first few months, then I was allowed to attend outside public school for the remainder of the school year. I met with a social worker every couple of weeks at the Kennedy Home. His name was Mr. Quigley. He was younger, thinner, and dressed more casually than Dr. Pelosi. He wore jeans, penny loafers, and corduroy jackets, but he had the same black-rimmed glasses and asked the same questions.

"So how are you feeling today, Robby?"

"I'm doing okay, Mr. Pelosi, but I don't like not being able to come and go as I like."

"Well, you'll have to earn that privilege," Mr. Pelosi replied. He would always bring up the home situation. "So when you think about having to come here, and your whole home situation and your mother's boyfriend, how do you feel?"

"Not so good, sort of kicked aside," I answered.

"Does it make you feel angry?" Mr. Pelosi would ask.

"Well, I'm not happy that I had to come here partly because of that asshole."

"You know that you can express that anger in this office," Mr. Pelosi replied. "You can yell, scream, bang on the desk, or even throw a chair against the wall if you like."

I just looked up at him and said, "I'm okay, thanks," and he would end the session.

When that first happened, I told my Big Brother about our sessions on my weekly phone call. Bob told me, "Never, ever act out or get violent in any way while you are there. They will only use it to diagnose and label you, and you'll end up there until you're eighteen or sent to a worse place."

So I held my head and did not act out for the remainder of my time at the Kennedy Home. I got along well with the other kids, perhaps because they were all throwaways like me. Because the place was run by Catholic nuns, I tried to always be on my best behavior, and I wanted to get out of there. After a few months, I was allowed to leave the facility and go to regular public school with the other kids. I finished seventh grade at JHS 127 in the Parkchester section of the Bronx. I did well at JHS 127, both in grades and attendance.

I was released from the Kennedy Home ten months later at the end of that school year. I returned to my mother and sister on Briggs Avenue, with the promise that I would attend school regularly and live under my mother's rules. Fred still came and went, but he totally ignored me when he was there, and that was just fine with me.

I would spend weekends at Manhattan College with my Big Brother. Bob was involved with the student government, so I was always helping with their events, serving beer at the dances, running the projector for movie night, which was advertised to be *Laurel and Hardy* but was actually soft porn, to my delight. There were also pie-throwing events to recruit Big Brothers. I spent as much time as I could at the college. They let me slide through the cafeteria line without a punch card many times, saying only "It's Posch's little brother." The highlight of my childhood would be the time we spent on our adventures and my time hanging with Bob at Manhattan College. He tried to give me all the time and guidance he could spare, but my unstable home life and the streets were hard to compete with.

I had started the eighth grade at Paul Hoffman Junior High School 45 off Fordham Road. I was now thirteen and tried my best to attend school regularly. I still stayed to myself for the most part and showed up at school regularly, but did the minimum amount of schoolwork.

I began to branch out and make some friends. I started to hang around the Public School 46 schoolyard, just up the block from our apartment and where I had gone to grammar school. Public School 46 and Our Lady of Refuge Church were across the street from each, and both had after-school programs where the kids could play basketball, Ping-Pong, bumper pool, or just hang out.

I had my first altercation at the PS 46 gym playing basketball on a Saturday afternoon. I had some words with one of the older guys, named Frankie. He called me a little punk, and I told him to fuck off. Frankie took off his garrison belt and waved it at me, then chased me out onto 196th Street, where there was construction going on. I stopped running and picked up a good-sized rock and turned around. A group of kids had followed us out onto the street. I hardly knew any of them, but the older boy seemed to know them all. "Go ahead, you little punk. You don't have the balls to throw that rock," yelled Frankie, who had about a foot and fifty pounds on me.

I glanced around at the crowd of kids, then at Frankie. I cocked my arm back and threw that rock as hard as I could. He lifted his arm to block it, and that's where the rock hit him, on the forearm. Everyone gasped. Frankie cursed and yelled at me, then chased me for three blocks until he tired and gave up.

I had avoided the schoolyard for about a week, hoping I wouldn't run into him and things would calm down. I was back there a week later playing basketball, when he walked in the schoolyard with a cast on his arm. I stopped dribbling and passed the ball, ready to run. Frankie caught my eye, raised his other arm, and said, "It's okay. I'm not gonna chase you. We're good, you crazy little bastard," and started laughing.

I walked over, shook his hand, and said, "Sorry about the arm." Frankie and I were okay from then on. The older crew even took me camping with them after that.

I had made some friends in the schoolyard that summer: Tommy, Ken, Tom, and Wally, who had just moved up from the projects in the South Bronx. Wally had gotten teased a lot at first because he dressed, talked, and walked like some of the Blacks he grew up with in the projects. One good summer in the schoolyard and he fit right in with the Irish boys.

I cut school one day and was hanging out in the PS 46 schoolyard with a few of my new friends. We were playing basketball and smoking cigarettes, when my mother walked into the schoolyard. She was there to see my little sister perform in a school play in the auditorium that morning with her third-grade class. It was only 10:00 a.m. She made eye contact with me and started screaming, "You get home. I'll deal with you later." I knew the sound of that voice and that look.

"Oh shit," I said, and nodded goodbye to my friends, picked up my school books, and headed down Briggs Avenue.

11

Singapore Slings

I wasn't going home to wait on that altercation, but I had to get out of the schoolyard so she wouldn't cause a scene and embarrass me in front of my new friends. Instead, I went to visit a kid that I was friends with from my old neighborhood on Morris Avenue, who had moved in with his grandmother on the Grand Concourse: Joe, a.k.a Shmoey. He was two years older than me and tall for his age, but we had much in common. We both had mothers who drank a lot and had boyfriends we didn't get along with. Shmoey and I would steal fruit from the fruit stand on Morris Avenue and Burnside. I would cause a distraction while he grabbed whatever fruit he could and ran down the alley next to the fruit stand. We would share cigarettes and jump on the back of trucks as they slowly turned up the hill onto Morris Avenue from Burnside. Sometimes we rode them all the way to Fordham Road.

I climbed the four flights of stairs up to Shmoey's grandmother's apartment. I rang the bell, and Shmoey opened the door. "What's up, no school today?" Shmoey asked. I told him what happened and that I wasn't looking forward to going home later. I said hello to Shmoey's grandmother, who looked quite old and frail but had her purse and looked ready to go out.

Shmoey walked out of the bedroom with a small suitcase in hand.

"Where are you going?" I asked.

"I'm not sure, either Florida or Canada. I haven't decided yet. Do you want to come?"

"Are you serious?"

"Yes," Shmoey replied. "I talked my grandmother into giving me a thousand bucks. I caught her in a good mood this morning."

"Yes, I'll go," I answered, still not sure if he was serious. The three of us walked out of the building and down the Concourse toward Dollar Savings Bank.

When we arrived outside the bank, Shmoey turned to me and handed me his suitcase and said, "Wait out here with my bag, and when you see me coming out, wave down a cab."

"What about your grandmother?" I asked.

"She'll be fine. She's going to do some shopping and take a cab home."

I said goodbye to his grandmother and in the bank they went. I stood outside, peering in every few minutes to see them waiting in line for a teller.

Finally they made it up to the bank teller and were taken care of. Shmoey gave his grandmother a hug and headed for the door. I waved a cab down as Shmoey exited the bank. We jumped in the backseat, and Shmoey said, "Kennedy Airport please."

I looked over at Shmoey and said, "Did you get the money?"

He reached back and pulled a white envelope out of his back pocket and opened it. It was full of cash, mostly twenties and some fifties. "Okay," I said, and leaned back with my spiral notebook on my lap.

When the cab arrived at JFK, Shmoey said there was a plane leaving for Montreal, Canada, in two hours and to let him do the talking at the ticket counter. "Two tickets for the 1:10 to Montreal please," Shmoey said to the young female ticket agent.

"How old are you guys?" she asked.

"I'm eighteen, and my brother is sixteen. Our parents will be waiting for us at the airport in Montreal when we land," Shmoey answered.

She nodded. "Okay." She printed out the two tickets with the names he had given her and handed them to him. We were only thirteen and fifteen, but Shmoey was five foot eight and could pass for eighteen years old.

Two hours later I was looking out the window of the Boeing 727 as it began to roll down the runway. I was wearing jeans, sneakers, and a T-shirt, with my spiral schoolbook still resting on my lap. I watched the short-skirted stewardess walk by with drinks on her tray, then looked at Shmoey in the next seat, and broke out laughing. "Holy shit, we did it."

When we landed in Montreal, Shmoey exchanged some American money for Canadian currency at the airport. He handed me a handful of colorful bills. "Here, put this in your pocket so you have some dough on you."

I stood there looking at the colorful bills in my hand and wondered if this was a dream and I'd be waking up any minute.

"Thanks, Shmoey," I said as I stuffed the bills into my pocket.

"Next we gotta get some threads," Shmoey said.

We walked outside the airport and got into one of the waiting cabs. "Take us to a motel close to the Expo," Shmoey said. It was early September of 1970, and the Man and His World summer fair was still going on where the 1967 Expo had taken place.

"I know the perfect place," replied the mustached cabbie with his French accent. "My name is Marcel, and I am at your beck and call. You can call me anytime, and I will pick you up and take you anywhere." He handed us each his business card. "I know Montreal and Quebec like the back of my hand." He laughed.

We checked into the motel and called Marcel later that afternoon to take us to a men's clothing store in downtown Montreal. Marcel dropped us off at Boutique Men's and said to call him when we were done shopping. We walked into the store wearing jeans, T-shirts, and dirty sneakers. An hour later we walked out dressed in slacks, black leather shoes, and button-down shirts, each carrying a shopping bag of newly purchased clothes.

Back at the motel, we walked a couple of blocks to a Chinese restaurant for dinner. The waiter took our meal orders, then asked Shmoey what he would like to drink. "A Singapore Sling please." Then the waiter looked over at me.

"Make it two," I mumbled. The waiter nodded and wrote it down. I couldn't believe it. The Chinese waiter returned shortly with two tall, thin-frosted glasses filled with ice, a red liquid on the bottom, and a clear liquid on top, with slices of lemon, cherries, and a small, colorful umbrella floating on top. I looked over at Shmoey and thanked him again, and we toasted to a great vacation.

This must be a dream, I thought.

The next few days Marcel drove us all over Montreal and Quebec: the Expo, the Notre Dame Basilica, the Public

Square in Old Montreal, to name a few. We visited the Expo twice in the evenings, for the carnival atmosphere. I won a couple of dolls to bring home to my little sister, a huge white-stuffed rabbit, and a wooden Pinocchio puppet doll with strings.

Four days had passed, and I had not contacted my mother and sister to let them know I was okay. I knew they would be worried about me, and it started to bother me. I had run away before, but only for a night or two, then I would call home to let them know I was okay, and they would talk me into coming home again.

That night back at the motel, I said to Shmoey, "Did you see a pay phone in the front office? I'm going to give my mom and sister a call, just to let them know I'm all right."

"What, are you homesick?" Shmoey teased.

"No, I just don't want them worrying."

"She's not worried about you," Shmoey replied. "All they care about is their drinking and boyfriends."

"You're probably right," I said. "But I'm calling them anyway, just to let them know I'm alive."

"Okay." Shmoey shrugged his shoulders.

I gathered up some change and went to the front office, hoping they had a pay phone, and they did. Even the Canadian coins were different, but I figured out what $1.25 was and deposited it in the phone at the operator's request, for the first three minutes. The phone rang once, and my mother answered. I could tell from her first words that she had not been drinking.

"Hello? Hey, Mom, It's me. I just wanted to let you know I'm all right and I'll be home in a few days."

"Where are you?" she asked.

"I'm okay and will be home soon." I answered.

"Please deposit $1.25 for the next three minutes," the operator chimed in.

"Where is this call coming from?" my mother asked.

"Montreal, Canada," answered the operator.

I deposited the $1.25, but the phone went quiet for a minute. "Mom, are you still there?"

The line seemed to go silent, then Donna's voice came through the phone. "Are you okay, Robert? Where are you?"

"I'm fine, kiddo, and I have some presents for you. What happened to Mom?"

"She slid down the wall and is sitting on the kitchen floor under the phone," Donna replied.

"Put her back on the phone, and I will see you in a couple of days."

"Okay," and she handed the phone back to my mother.

"Did the operator say you were in Canada?"

"Yes, Mom, but I'm okay and will be home soon. I'll call and let you know when I'm flying back."

"But you're only thirteen years old," yelled my mother.

I hung up and went back to the motel room. I felt much better—at least they knew I was alive and well.

Shmoey had looked up a priest he knew from the Bronx who was a friend of his family, and we visited him at his church the next day. He was young for a priest but seemed concerned enough about Shmoey and his family situation.

Father Ryan had taken us to a nearby restaurant for lunch. "So how are your mom and sisters, Joseph?" Father Ryan asked as we ate our burgers.

"Katie turned eighteen and moved in with her boyfriend. Maureen just started high school, and Mom is still drinking and has a new boyfriend, so I moved in with my grandmother on the Concourse."

"What does your mom think of that?" Father Ryan asked.

"She doesn't want me there, but it's been over a month now, and I'm not going back and dealing with her new boyfriend." Shmoey then took another bite of his burger.

Father Ryan shook his head from side to side and laughed. "I'll give your mom a call, Joe, and let her know you're okay."

He then looked over at me. "How about you, Robby? Does your family know where you are?"

"Yes, Father. I have a similar family situation as Joe, but I did call home yesterday and let them know I was all right."

"Good," Father Ryan responded. "I understand your boys' family situation, but pray and ask God for help, and remember, your mothers are only human and doing the best they can."

We looked at each other, rolled our eyes, and laughed. "Okay, Father, we will," we said, almost in unison.

Father Ryan asked me for my home phone number in case of an emergency.

Three days later I was on a flight back to New York. Shmoey wanted to stay another week, but I'd had my fill. I stared out the window in wonder the whole flight home. Watching the sun go down over New York from the air was a sight I wouldn't soon forget. My flight home landed in JFK around 6:00 p.m.

I exited the plane and walked down the boarding bridge in my new silver silk sharkskin pants, black suede playboy shoes, and a black turtleneck pullover shirt, carrying the huge stuffed rabbit and wooden Pinocchio doll for my little sister. I planned on taking the subway home and surprising my mother and Donna. As I walked down the boarding bridge, I spotted my mother, sister, and Mr. Quigley, from the Kennedy Home, among the people waiting for their family and friends to deplane.

Shmoey had gotten me a ride to the airport from Father Ryan in Canada, so he must have called ahead to my mom to let her know I was on my way home. I panicked for a second at the thought of going back to the Kennedy Home. I lowered my head and tried to block my face with the big stuffed rabbit, but my mom and sister had already spotted me.

Donna ran straight to me and wrapped her arms around me. I kneeled, hugged her, and said, "I got these for you at the fair," and gave her the dolls.

My mother just stood there shaking her head. "Where did you get those clothes? You look like a little man."

Mr. Quigley put his hands up. "Don't worry. I'm not here to take you back. Your mom just called and asked if I would give her a ride to the airport to pick you up. I'm very curious—tell me all about your trip on the ride home."

The whole ride home I excitedly told them about the Expo, the plane ride, the different language, the colorful money, and some of the sights I had seen. Mr. Quigley dropped us off at our apartment, and that would be the last time I would see him. There would be no repercussions for my adventure, only amazement that it had happened. I saved some of the Canadian money and airline tickets as souvenirs.

A couple of months had gone by since the Montreal adventure, and things were going smoothly at home and at school. I kept my distance from Fred, who would stay over and drink with my mother on the weekends. I took Donna to the movies and even horseback riding on Pelham Parkway some Sundays with the money I earned shining shoes.

12

Playing Baseball with the Janitor

It was Saturday afternoon, and I was playing basketball with my friend Bert in the Public School 46 gym. They had an after-school and Saturday program where they opened the gym up to the neighborhood kids. A young, stocky janitor in his blue uniform picked the ball up and took a shot, then another and another. I looked over at the janitor and said, "Yo, man, we're playing a game over here."

"Take it easy, Shorty. I'm just taking a few shots," replied the janitor.

"Fuck you. We're in the middle of a game," I yelled back.

The young janitor stepped up to me and smacked me across the face.

I was startled and took a step back. I looked up at the janitor, who was twice my size, and said, "All right, mother-fucker, you're gonna pay for that." and I ran out of the school building.

"Little wiseass," I heard the janitor say as he took another shot with the basketball.

Bert just stood there looking at the janitor and shaking his head. "You probably shouldn't have done that—that kid is crazy."

Another kid from across the gym yelled, "He'll probably be back with a bat or something. He's a little nuts that one."

The janitor began to get nervous and looked around the gym.

I ran out of the school building and jogged down Briggs Avenue to 194th Street and our apartment. I nodded to my sister as I passed her room, then went into my room and into the closet to get the Louisville Slugger I kept there.

My mother yelled from the kitchen, "Dinner will be ready in less than an hour."

"Okay, I'll be right back," I yelled as I left the apartment with the bat. I walked quickly up Briggs Avenue with the bat swinging back and forth by my side as I passed the private houses on each side of the street.

A couple of the Luigi brothers were sitting out on their porch across the street. "Where are you going with that bat, Robby? You don't play baseball?" Mikey Luigi said as he laughed.

"I'll be playing baseball with that fucking janitor up at the school in about five minutes," I said as I passed their house.

"Oh shit," Mikey yelled. "There he goes again." Then Mikey, Marty, and Butchy Luigi followed me up to the school.

I walked into the side entrance of Public School 46 with the bat in hand. Bert was still taking shots with the basketball. I looked over at Bert and questioningly shrugged my shoulders. He nodded over at the sink closet, where the janitor was hiding. I quietly walked over to the sink closet with the bat in my right hand and swung the door open with my left. My first swing came quickly as the janitor tried to block it. The bat cracked him right in the elbow as he tried to run out of the sink closet. My second swing caught the janitor in the back as he ran from the closet. He almost went down but kept his footing. He ran through the school and out of the heavy metal doors onto Bainbridge Avenue.

I chased him out onto the street, followed by the Luigi's and ten or twelve kids from the school program who saw the whole scene in the gym. The man stumbled and fell between two parked cars, as a cop car, sirens blaring, turned the corner onto Bainbridge Avenue. Luckily for him, the janitor had called the cops after the other kids had warned him.

I looked back over my shoulder and saw the cop car. I took a step back and tossed the bat under one of the cars. The cops pulled up right behind me and jumped out of the car. One cop yelled at me, "Don't move. You stay right there." The other cop ran over to the man in the street, who was lying between two parked cars. "Are you all right?" the cop asked the janitor.

"What happened here?" the cop asked, while standing be- hind me and looking down at the man and group of kids who now stood quietly on the sidewalk.

The janitor pointed at me and said, "That crazy little bas- tard hit me in the back and elbow with the bat he threw under the car."

"He smacked me first," I shouted back. A couple of the kids on the sidewalk backed me up.

"That's right, Officer. A few of us saw what happened, and he did hit Robby first."

An ambulance pulled up and took the janitor away. The cops grabbed me and my bat and put me in the backseat of the cop car. "Where do you live, kid?" the cop asked.

I gave them my address, and off we went. One cop knocked on the apartment door while the other cop held my arm in one hand and the baseball bat with the other.

My mother answered the door. "What's going on, Officer?"

"Are you this boy's mother?"

"Yes I am," she answered. "What did he do?"

"Your son cracked the janitor twice with this bat up at the public school."

I looked down at the floor and shrugged my shoulders.

"What happened?" my mother asked me.

"We were playing basketball, and he took the ball. I asked for it back a couple of times, and we got into words, and he smacked me."

"The janitor smacked you?" she asked.

"Yes."

"Well, there you have it, Officers. I guess he won't be smacking him anymore," my mom said, matter of fact.

The two officers looked at each other, shook their heads from side to side, and walked out of the building, leaving me and my bat with my mother.

"Well, come on," she said. "Dinner is almost ready."

Part Two: The Twenty-Year Run

A Day At a Time Publishing

13

I Can Breathe Now

It was a cool fall night as the college kids from Fordham University in the Bronx started filling up the bars along Webster Avenue.

"Yo, bro. I heard they only charge a dollar a pitcher on Friday nights," Rick said to me daringly. We were both fifteen years old.

"I got a few bucks on me. We don't even have fake IDs, but I'll give it a shot. After all, they can only say no," I shot back.

"Well, there's a first time for everything," he answered, as we walked into the bar.

The place was lined with students and pitchers of beer on the bar. "Rocket Man" by Elton John blared out of the jukebox. We made our way into the back room, which was empty except for eight small square tables with red-and-white checkered tablecloths on them. We sat at one of the tables and nervously waited to be served. A big, round, red-faced, gray-haired man, with a white shirt and black bow tie and white apron, walked into the back room.

"What can I get you boys?"

"We'll take a pitcher of beer," I replied.

The old man turned and headed to the bar. He returned shortly with our first pitcher and two beer glasses. We slapped each other five and drank the first of a few pitchers that night. We couldn't believe we'd finally been served in a real bar and hadn't even been carded.

We stayed in the back room, knowing we would stand out as "townies" and probably get carded if we went up front. Townies are what the college students called us local teens and young people who were from, and lived in, the area surrounding the college. The college preppies wore their Fordham U sweatshirts or jackets, along with button-down collared shirts and jeans with penny loafers. We sat in the back room and drank our beer in our dirty T-shirts, jeans, and sneakers, trying not to draw any attention to ourselves. We had a few more pitchers and stumbled out of that fine establishment as proud as peacocks that we had finally been served in a bar.

Rick was a good friend. We came from similar homes. We were the broken kids who found each other. He and I were the same height and weight, which was handy when you had a limited amount of clothes and wanted to wear something different. We also had mothers who drank too much and had boyfriends named Fred. Yes, we had much in common.

This night would not be the first time I got drunk—that was two years earlier. It was just what we did on the weekends in my neighborhood. Every weekend and in the summer, the back wall of the schoolyard would be lined up with the older teenagers drinking, listening to music, and passing an occasional joint around.

At thirteen, Tommy, Ken, and myself got this older guy, Billy, to buy us two pints of cheap wine, but only if we bought him one. We were curious about what the big deal was with drinking. We drank that wine on the grounds of Mt. Saint Ursula, a girls high school in our neighborhood, on a hot summer night. The grounds were fenced in and had plenty of grass and some trees. I clearly remember the awful taste of the wine as it went down, but then the warmth that went through my body and the ease of tension that made its way to my head. We sat in the grass, passing the wine bottles back and forth and laughing, smoking cigarettes, and sharing stories about our fucked-up homes, about girls we had crushes on, and about things we would never normally talk about. We knew we would keep one another's secrets and be friends for life. A couple of hours later we wobbled out of Mt. Saint Ursula, and each of us made our way home.

I stumbled into my room and fell on the bed. The room began to spin. I held on to the bed tight but leaned my head off the side and began throwing up. The bedroom door swung open, and my mother stood in the doorway.

"What's wrong with you? Are you okay?"

"I'm sick," I answered as I spewed more purple fluid onto the linoleum floor.

"Jesus Christ," she screamed. "Are you drunk?" She began cleaning up the wine and my dinner off the floor and gave me a cold rag for my face.

I passed out on the bed and awoke the next day, still dressed and woozy, with some purple stains on my white T-shirt. I showered, dressed, and came out for breakfast. My sister started laughing at me, and my mother just shook her head. She was familiar with the drinking game.

By midafternoon my head had cleared, and I thought about the night before. Not so much about the room spinning or getting sick and being yelled at, but more about the warm feeling and lightheadedness the wine had given me. I recalled the laughing and camaraderie with my friends, and more importantly, about not worrying about anything for a couple of hours. Worrying had stolen my childhood. I worried about everything all the time and could not turn my mind off, until now. By age fourteen I had already developed ulcers. After that night of drinking in Mt. Saint Ursula, I knew I had found the oxygen I needed to breathe on this planet.

That Friday afternoon at school, as we were heading back to our classes after lunch, I listened to the other kids talking.

"Who are the Yankees playing this weekend?" one kid yelled.

"Joey, are you coming camping with us this weekend?" another boy yelled to his friend.

Some girl was asking her friends what was playing at the Loew's Paradise Theater on Saturday.

None of that mattered to me. My only thoughts were, *How much money did I have saved to drink with? Who was getting it for us?* and *Where were we gonna drink it?* It was Friday afternoon, and I was staring at the clock, counting the hours and minutes until 3:00 p.m. and school let out, so I could rush home, do my homework, eat dinner, then meet the boys, get some booze, and start drinking and turn off the worry machine so I could breathe freely for a while.

Between drinking with the schoolyard kids, and now having graduated to smoking pot and my growing reputation as a crazy kid, I was starting to fit right in.

14

Sinister Boots

Jimmy B. was the president of about a dozen young guys who called themselves the Sinisters. One of their trademarks was that they wore motorcycle boots, which we schoolyard guys called Sinister boots. If they got you down, you were sure to get stomped with them. The guys were around my age, sixteen to nineteen. They hung out on the Grand Concourse in the Bronx. We were aware of each other because the schoolyard was only four blocks away.

Jimmy's younger brother Mack had come through our schoolyard a week ago, talking smack about his brother and the Sinisters and how they'd come down and kick everyone's ass. I offered him a one-on-one right there. We squared off, and I landed three quick shots to his face. He went down and waved me off.

"All right, all right, you win," he said as he scrambled to his feet. They made their way out of the yard, Mack mumbling under his breath, "You're fucking dead. We'll be back," as he and his friend sped up the block.

I just shook my head as the six or seven schoolyard boys patted me on the back and said, "Good one, Rob." The praise and pats on the back felt good.

I went up to the Concourse a week later, looking for my friend Ken, who I knew was dealing weed. There were about ten Sinisters scattered up and down the block as I crossed the street and made my way toward Ken. "Hey, Ken, you got anything?" I asked.

Within a minute the Sinisters realized who I was and circled me. Ken and I finished our transaction, and one big dude in a tight sweatshirt, jeans, and Sinister boots said, "Are you Robby Carney?"

"That's me," I answered with a smirk.

"You're the one who kicked my brother's ass in the schoolyard a few nights ago?"

"I am." I looked down. I was surrounded by seven pairs of black leather Sinister boots, and the circle around me grew smaller. I knew it wouldn't be long before they beat me down and stomped me out.

I heard Ken's voice from beyond the circle yell, "I wouldn't do that, Jimmy. There's a lot of guys in that schoolyard who would show up for him." There was a long silence as Jimmy stood there staring at me, his guys just waiting for the word to attack.

I looked over at him. "I'll tell you what—you come down to the schoolyard any day or night of the week, and I'll give you a fair one right there."

He looked at me for a second and nodded to his boys. "Let him go. I'll be seeing you real soon."

A couple of guys took a step back and opened the circle of boots that had been slowly closing in on me. Ken looked at me with eyes wide, which said, *Get the fuck out of here now before he changes his mind.* I slipped through the opening in the circle, stepped off the curb, and disappeared around the corner in disbelief that I made it out of there.

A week passed, and Jimmy was true to his word. He wanted his fair one to redeem his brother. Wally, Mack, Dave, and I were standing in front of the deli across from Our Lady of Refuge Church. We had just left the church's rec center after playing some basketball. It was a cold night—we could see our breath escape our mouths as we passed a quart of beer around. I noticed Ken walking toward us from the schoolyard.

He had his hands in the side pockets of his pea coat, and his chin and mouth buried in the top of the coat. He lifted his blond head up and wiped his runny nose. "Hey, Robby, Jimmy is waiting for you up at the yard."

"Really, how many guys does he have with him?" I asked.

"Two, Zef and Stitch." He shrugged and looked a little worried for me. "All right, tell him I'm on my way."

The four of us started walking toward the schoolyard. Dave reached into the metal garbage can on the corner and pulled out a pipe, then stashed it under his jacket.

Dave was my age, seventeen. He came from a big Irish family of six kids—four boys and two girls. We would have keggers in his basement. His mom had recently died of cancer. I had been at Dave's house a month before she passed. His mom had been preparing dinner, and I'd asked "Hi, Mrs. Walls. How are you feeling?"

"Besides dying, I'm feeling okay," she'd answered.

"Oh," I'd replied, dumbfounded, and followed Dave upstairs.

The four of us entered the schoolyard. It was dark, cold, and empty except for the three Sinisters, who stood near the back wall on the blacktop, covered in light from the streetlamp. Ken stood off to the side, leaning against the back wall. Jimmy B. took off his leather jacket and dropped it to the floor when he saw me walk in. He stood there in his jeans, Sinister boots, and black tight sweatshirt. He had me by about three inches in height and thirty pounds in weight. I looked at him standing there at the back of the yard, under the streetlight, and thought, *Shit, he looks a lot bigger now.* I laughed.

Mack, who played league football and was about Jimmy's size, said, "I'll fight him for you, Robby. He's a big fucker."

"Thanks, Mack, but I'll have to deal with him sooner or later. If he gets me down and stars stomping me with those fucking boots, you know what to do." I took my dungaree jacket off and handed it to Wally. I whispered to all three of them, "Watch my back. I know that Zef the Albanian carries a switchblade with him, and he's used it before."

We walked thirty yards to the back of the schoolyard. A cold wind was blowing, and the yard was empty except for us. As I got closer, I thought, *I might get my ass kicked here tonight, but he's gonna remember he was in a fight.* When we got within ten yards of them, I broke into a run and charged him. He looked startled when I landed the first punch to the side of his head. He grabbed me, leaned his weight on me, and pushed me down, pulling my long-sleeve shirt over my head. Everything went dark for a second. I reached back over my shoulder and pulled the shirt completely off me and wrapped it around his neck, slid out from under his weight, and pulled him backward by the neck. I landed two good shots to his face with my free hand, and backward he fell.

He hit the blacktop with a thud. I scrambled on top of him, pinning both his arms down with my right knee and left hand, placing all my weight on his chest. *Crack, crack, crack.* I smashed his face with my free right hand.

"Okay, Okay," he yelled. "That's it."

I stopped punching and slid off him. I walked toward my guys.

Then his voice came from behind me. "Where are you going? We're not done yet." He pushed off the ground and put his hands back up.

Shit. Can I get lucky again? I rushed him. He was still dazed from the shots he had already taken. I stuck my leg behind his and pushed hard. He went back down easily. I resumed my position on top of him and started smashing his face again.

He yelled "okay" again.

"You're not getting back up this time, asshole." I kept landing shots to his face and head with my free hand.

I heard a click behind me. I turned my head. It was Zef snapping open his switchblade. Dave jumped in front of him and pulled the long metal pipe out from under his jacket.

"I wouldn't do that, motherfucker. It's a fair one," Dave said as he raised the pipe.

Zef backed up with both hands raised.

I landed three more shots and could see Jimmy was losing consciousness. I stopped punching and shoved off.

Wally handed me my jacket, and I heard Jimmy call my name again.

"Robby."

I turned. Zef and Stitch had helped him to his feet.

"You gave me a fair one, and you beat me," he said. "As far as I'm concerned, we're good." I walked over to him and shook his hand. His left eye was black and puffed, his nose was bleeding, and the cold air escaped his bloodied lips.

Dan, Mack, Wally, and I walked back to the church rec center. I asked Mack to watch the door of the bathroom for me. I needed a minute. I walked over to the sink and turned the hot water on, dropped to my knees, and placed both swollen hands under the hot water. I had broken a couple of knuckles, and my hands were frozen. I stood and walked to the bathroom door, thinking, *Nobody will be beating, starving, or hurting this boy today, no, not today.*

15

Nickel Bags

It was a cool spring night as I walked the three long blocks home from my job at Sultan's on Fordham Road. I entered the apartment, and my mother was standing outside my bedroom, with her arms crossed and that cold stare she had.

Donna stuck her head out of her room and said, "Ooooooh, you're in trouble," with a smirk on her face. I just shook my head and walked toward my bedroom.

I turned into my room and saw the problem. My single bed looked like the cover of a *High Times* magazine. On top of the black-and-green checkered bedspread lay my half pound of weed in a plastic ziplock baggie, my triple beam scale, a box of small brown manilla envelopes, a shoebox, with the top off, filled with cash, and my 32-caliber handgun with an extra clip lying next to it. All nicely displayed on my bed. My mother had found my stash up in the closet behind my camping equipment.

"So this is what you do now—you're a drug dealer? I wondered where the extra money you gave me was coming from," she said, her voice filled with disappointment.

"Mom," I replied, "it's just pot. Everybody smokes pot."

"Well, I don't smoke pot," she shot back. "And what's the gun for? If they don't pay, you shoot them?"

"No, it's just for protection when I have a lot of money on me."

"Well, I want this stuff out of my house. I'll help you with anything, but I won't help you with this." By the calm, stern sound of her voice, I knew she meant it.

"I'll have it out of here by tomorrow," I replied quietly.

The next day I found a furnished room in a private house on a nice, quiet, tree-lined street around the corner from the schoolyard. It was a small room on the top floor at the back of the house. The ceiling on one side of the room was slanted because of the pitch in the roof. I covered that part of the ceiling with black-light posters and black lights. I added a small fridge, two big speakers, and my eight-track cassette/radio player to the room.

I didn't sleep there at first. I only used the room to get high and to store and bag up my weed. I had the boys over to help me bag up that first time, Wally, Pete, and Rick. I found this one-half-inch slab of fiberglass about six feet long and two feet wide. I laid the fiberglass across the two large speakers. We sat there for a couple of hours, smoking, drinking, listening to Led Zeppelin, the Stones, Hendrix, and bagging up all those nickels.

Pete, a short Italian kid with long frizzy black hair down to his shoulders, yelled, "Yo, Rob, do you have any Humble Pie? I fuckin love them," as he dropped another bagged nickel into the shopping bag on the floor.

"I got 'Rockin' the Fillmore' in that stack of eight tracks next to you on the table," I answered.

He twisted the cap off a cold Heineken and began to look through the tapes. Pete played neighborhood league football. He was short but fast. He played middle linebacker, and they say he hit hard for his size. Pete lived with his grandparents and older brother, Gerard. His mother had passed away when he was a youngster, and his dad was here and there, so he and his brother ended up with his grandparents.

Wally and Rick also came from broken families affected by alcohol. Rick was the youngest of four, one older brother and two older sisters. His mom was real cool. We could always party in the basement of their house or crash there if we wanted to.

Wally had been my best friend since I was twelve. He was a big Irish kid who came from a big Irish family. Wally's mom and three sisters all had red hair and freckles. His father was a big, quiet man. Wally's mom had banned his father from the house for a time because of his drinking, but he had sobered up and became part of the family again. He was a union man, the teamsters, and he took good care of his family, but it was too late for Wally. Like myself, he had already been gobbled up by the streets.

We all found each other and somehow found comfort with each other and the booze, drugs, and music. We would do anything to escape our homes. We were the fifteen- and sixteen- and seventeen-year-olds who ran the streets all night and didn't get in trouble because no one came looking for us. The battle between the streets and our parents was over, and the streets had won.

Two six packs of beer and four joints later, the pound of weed was bagged up. Everyone got some headgear to take with them, and I started filling my pockets with nickels. My jeans pockets, my socks, vest pockets, and a small paper bag full of nickels, and off to the schoolyard we went. It was near six o'clock Friday night, and the customers were already lined up.

We entered the blacktopped schoolyard that was fenced in on both avenues and sat between Public School 46 and two five-story buildings, our slice of heaven. Dave and Ken were standing under one of the two steel basketball hoops, drinking beer and smoking.

"In the little yard," Dave yelled, and nodded toward the steps behind the fence. I veered off into the little yard, where three kids were sitting there.

"What do you need?" I asked.

"You got nickels?" asked the young blond hippie chick.

"I do, and the weed's good."

"How's the count?" Her boyfriend, with a ponytail and mirrored sunglasses, chimed in.

"Check it out." I pulled one of the fat little manilla envelopes out of my vest pocket. "You'll get at least five or six nice joints out of that," I added.

"Cool," the hippy chick said. "We'll take four."

"And I'll take three," said the young jock with the buzz cut.

I pulled the rest of the nickels out of my left sock and stuffed the cash in my pocket. I exited the little yard and walked to the small wall under the buildings to join the rest of the boys, who were drinking and passing joints around.

"I see you re-upped," Dave said. "How is it?"

"It's pretty good. Picked up a pound last night, Blonde Lebanese." I pulled out a joint, lit it, and passed it around.

"Put an ounce aside for my old man. He's looking," Pete said.

"No problem," I replied.

Pete nodded toward the entrance of the schoolyard, where a few more customers had wandered in. I waved them over to the entrance of the little yard so we'd be out of sight.

I made three more trips to the stash room before I called it quits around nine o'clock that night. Then off we went to the college bars on Webster Avenue with our fake IDs.

A week later I pulled up in front of the yard on my new 350 Harley-Davidson. I was so short that both my feet could not touch the ground at the same time when I came to a stop. I had to lean over and place one foot on the ground, while the other leg hung over the bike.

"Nice. Where did you get that?" Rick asked.

"Yeah, I bought it off Kenny yesterday for a $1,000 cash. He bought it with the money he got when he was in a car accident, but he got bored with it, so I lucked out."

"Did you get your license yet, Robby?" Pete asked.

"Not yet. I just had him sign the registration over to me and drove off. I'll get one soon enough." I laughed.

Besides my previous year hanging with Gabrielle, my childhood sweetheart, that summer would be the one I would try to recreate for years to come. The money, the reputation, the Harley, the girls. Everything was so new, and I was invincible … or so I thought.

I had just walked into the apartment from working at Sultan's on Fordham Road and was getting ready to eat dinner and rush to my second job, dealing weed in the schoolyard. My mother looked at Donna and me seriously at the dinner table.

"Hey, guys, there's something I have to ask you. Fred asked me to marry him yesterday. I didn't give him an answer yet. If I do, we could move out to Brooklyn to his family's house,

and you guys could have a new start. What do you think?"
Fred had been spending many a weekend at our house the
last few months.

"Hey, Mom, that's a decision you have to make. You're the
one who would have to live with him full time. I'll be seventeen in a few months, and I already have one foot out the
door, so it would just be you and Donna. Do you love him?" I
asked her skeptically.

"I've only loved one man, and that was your father," she
responded sadly.

"It doesn't matter to me. Whatever makes you happy,
Mom," Donna chimed.

They were married by a judge in a courthouse in downtown
Brooklyn two weeks later. A week later, my mother and sister
moved out to Brooklyn. I lived in the apartment for one
month alone before they moved everything to Brooklyn. A
truck showed up at the end of the month and took all the
furniture out. I moved in with my childhood friend Rick and
his family around the corner. I continued selling pot in the
schoolyard and kept my furnished room to stash my drugs
and money.

16

Big Richie

Richie walked into the schoolyard with his little gray shih tzu on a long, thin leash. They looked odd together. He stood a bit over six feet and was well rounded at 250 pounds. He wore a white button-down shirt, black dress pants, plain black leather shoes, and a black sport jacket. Not the kind of jacket and shoes you would wear to look sharp, but maybe to pass a dress code at an accounting firm. He topped it off with short, perfectly cut black hair. I would have taken him for a disheveled teacher or accountant whose wife forced him to walk that tiny, cute little dog.

I had spotted him a number of times walking by the schoolyard with his little dog and peering in while we sat on the concrete steps in the little yard and played cards for money and drank beer. The little yard was off to the side of the schoolyard, so I could sell my nickel bags mostly out of sight. There was a small, square metal sewer cap next to the concrete steps that I could lift up and stuff a bag of fifty or so nickels in, only taking out a few at a time when I needed them, so that if I did get busted, I wouldn't have that much on me.

This particular day Big Richie and his tiny dog walked right into the little yard and up to where we were playing cards. I had wondered if he was an undercover cop. There was certainly a lot more foot traffic coming through the schoolyard these past couple of months due to my weed business. He caught my eye and waved for me to come over. I folded my terrible poker hand and stood.

"Hey, man, what can I do for you?" I asked as I knelt down to pet the little gray ball of fur.

"I just wanted to cop a bag of weed," he answered.

"Weed, there's no weed around here," I said.

"I know what you're thinking," he said as he shrugged his shoulders. "But I'm not a cop. I'm Richie, and this is Tiger. I live right across the street." He pointed to a third-floor window in the building across from the yard. "I'm just a guy who likes to get high." He smiled.

I looked up at the window, then at him and the dog, and reached down in my sock and pulled out a nickel.

Big Richie and Tiger would stop by the yard once a week for a nickel or two. The third time he came to buy weed, he had a proposition for me.

"Hey, Rob, I have something you might be interested in. Can you stop by my apartment in a half hour?"

I handed him the two nickels of weed and took his money, eyeing him questioningly.

"I'm in apartment 3D," he said as he and Tiger took off without waiting for my response.

A half hour went by, and my curiosity got the best of me. *I hope this guy's not a perv or anything.* I gave Wally some nickels to sell while I went across the street to check it out.

I climbed the three flights of stairs and rang the bell to apartment 3D. I could hear Tiger yapping. Richie invited me into his apartment, which looked a bit disheveled, like himself.

"Can I get you a soda or water?"

"No thanks, Richie. So what's up?"

He waved me over to the window that overlooked the schoolyard.

"I've been watching your operation for a little while now, and you have a good business going there. You keep your main stash in the sewer by the steps, so you only have a few bags on you at a time, and now you have your big freckled friend catching the customers coming in from the Bainbridge side, so there's not too much traffic coming through the schoolyard. Smart idea."

"Besides knowing that you're spying on me, why did you ask me up here?" I asked impatiently.

Richie reached into his pocket and pulled out a clear ziplock bag filled with white powder and put it on the kitchen table. "That's why."

"What is it?"

"It's crystal methedrine, you know, speed. I have a large supply of it if you want to make some real money."

I looked at him, then Tiger, then the bag of white powder on the table. *This big, nerdy dude is actually a speed dealer. No fucking way.*

"Thanks, Richie, but I'm gonna pass on that one. This isn't that kind of neighborhood. Some weed, a few pills, maybe some acid occasionally, but nothing like that. I wouldn't want to bring it into the area."

Richie's eyes widened, and he looked surprised.

"Okay." He shrugged his shoulders. "But take this with you. It's on me," as he handed me the bag of white powder. "There's a few grams in there. When you're out partying tonight, let some of your weed customers check it out, but I wouldn't mess with it if I were you."

I stuffed the bag of white powder in my pocket and headed for the door.

"Before you leave, take my number in case you change your mind." He scribbled it on a piece of paper and handed it to me.

Later that night at the Wagon Wheel, one of the local bars that hosted live bands or DJs on the weekends, I ran into a couple of my weed customers and turned them on to a few sniffs of the white powder. Word spread quickly throughout the bar that I was dealing speed and it was good.

My friend and weed customer Nora, a tall dark-haired Irish beauty from the neighborhood, joined me at the bar.

"Hey, barkeep, give this guy whatever he's drinking on me," she yelled. Then looked down at me with a smile. "Hey, Robby, I heard you got some speed."

"I do, and they say it's pretty good."

"Can you sell me a fifty-dollar piece?"

"Sure," I said. "I'll meet you in the alley next to the bar. Do you have something I can put it in?"

"I'll just use the foil from my cigarette pack," she answered.

It went on like that for the next three hours until the speed was gone. I didn't really know what I was doing as I went from the alley to the men's room, pouring the white powder into foils, folded pieces of paper, bills, or whatever they could find to hold it in.

"Give me fifty, twenty, or thirty dollars' worth," they asked. And $740 later I was sold out, and they were still coming back for more. I called Big Richie the next day and met with him to buy an ounce of crystal meth, which he showed me how to bag up into half grams. I was used to doubling my money with the weed, but this was a different ball game altogether. I was more than tripling my money now, and the customers were nonstop. My clientele also changed.

It was about 9:30 at night when the three guys entered the schoolyard. Wally, Rick, and I were standing just inside the metal fence, and the yard was empty. I recognized one of the guys I had sold a gram to the night before. He looked a little wild eyed, as if he had been up for a couple of days. I had a bad feeling.

"Hey, man, are you holding?" he asked, as one wandered behind me.

Wally's eyes never left him. My eyes were darting in every direction.

"Yeah, I got something. What do you want?"

"I want an eight ball," he replied.

An eight ball is an eighth of an ounce.

"I need some notice for that," I replied, as my eyes darted from one to the other. "I have a few half grams on me now," I added.

"Watch it," Rick yelled.

The two guys in front of me took off running. I turned, and the guy behind me was on the floor unconscious, his head bleeding and a knife in his hand.

"He was gonna stab you," Wally said as he held the pipe in his hand. The three of us ran like the wind out of the schoolyard and down the block to my stash room. I put a Jimi Hendrix tape in the eight-track cartridge, opened a few beers, and passed a joint around as the ambulance and police sirens passed under my window overlooking Briggs Avenue.

I will have to start carrying my gun full time now. I took another swig of beer.

The third time I met Big Richie for an ounce, he had me meet him at the opening of the Kingsbridge underpass that went under the Grand Concourse on Kingsbridge Road, at one in the afternoon. It was a long, dark walk under the underpass.

"How's business?" he asked.

"Great. The money's rolling in," I said with a smile as I slipped him a wad of cash and he passed me the ounce.

"Remember what I said about using this shit. I shoot a bundle of dope a day, but this speed shit never ends. And watch your back with your new customers now. This isn't weed. it's a whole new game."

"I know. I've already had to deal with some shit, and I won't mess with it. I can see what it does to them," I replied.

"All right, I'll talk with you soon," he said as we exited the other side of the dark underpass.

I watched him cross Kingsbridge Road as I walked up toward the Concourse. *Big Richie, the big, nerdy accountant-looking dude with the little furball of a dog, dope fiend, and speed dealer ... who would have ever guessed?*

The shoeboxes were filling up. I began selling weight in speed and fronting guys some so I could spend less time on the street dealing, which meant less chance of getting busted. Then there were the trips to some upstate colleges, an ounce here, two ounces there. I envied the college life I would never see. It looked like one big party. One of the guys I was fronting speed to was able to put together my biggest sale yet to some of his friends at Syracuse University.

"Hey, Kenny, how's business?" I asked as I delivered his next half ounce to him. He was living at his girlfriend's apartment in Riverdale in the Bronx. Kenny was nineteen, two years older than me, and an original hippie. He was tall, skinny, with long brown hair, a mellow but cool hippy. His girlfriend, Amy, on the other hand, was a short, thin woman in her late twenties who was stoned on pills all the time, but Kenny was head over heels for her. It surprised me when he wanted to start dealing speed.

"Business is good, man. In fact, I have a dude up in Syracuse University that wants a quarter pound. Can you handle it?"

"No problem, Kenny," I answered.

We worked out a price and were set to leave that Saturday morning at eight for the long ride upstate. Kevin's friend, Mark, was going to drive us up there in his Cadillac. Mark was a heavyset Italian dude who always had his greased black hair combed back and wore a leather sports coat over his white T-shirt. He was also the buyer's friend in Syracuse. I didn't know much about him, but I had seen him around the neighborhood with the right people.

It was a cool, cloudy, and dreary Saturday morning when I left my furnished room with the four ounces of speed slung over my shoulder in a knapsack. This would be my biggest drug sale yet. I had already experienced a few close calls with the cops and the robbers, and came up unscathed. I felt invincible. If I was doing this good at seventeen, imagine where I would be at twenty. I rang the doorbell in the lobby of the building of Kenny's girlfriend's apartment. After what seemed like forever, she answered and buzzed me up.

"Where's Kenny?" I asked after she let me in.

She was a mess. Her hair and clothes were in disarray as she stumbled back to the living room couch and fell on it. "He's lying on the other side of the coffee table." She pointed at his sprawled body on the living room floor. I couldn't wake him up.

"He might be dead. My bottle of pills is empty." she mumbled before she passed out again. I knelt next to Kenny and shook his arm, with no response. I placed my hand on his cheek, and it was cold. I knelt there for a minute and took Kenny's cold hand into mine and asked God to look out for him. My quiet moment was interrupted by the downstairs buzzer. It was Mark. I buzzed him up and let him in. Amy just nodded back out on the couch. She disgusted me.

"Are we good to go?" Mark asked as he entered the apartment.

"Mark, Kenny is dead on the living room floor. I think he accidentally overdosed on her pills. There's an empty prescription bottle on the coffee table.."

"Do you have the speed?" Mark asked.

"Yeah, I got it."

"Well, let's get out of here. It's my connection at Syracuse anyway, and they'll be waiting for us," he said anxiously.

"Look, Mark," I said angrily. "We can go later today or tomorrow, but I'm not leaving Kenny here like this, with this stoned-out bitch. Here is what we're gonna do. Where is your caddy parked?"

"It's downstairs in front of the building."

"I want you to take this." I handed him the knapsack. "Hide it in the car. Then drive it a block or two, lock it up, and come back here on foot. I'm gonna call the cops and wait for them to come and deal with Kenny's body."

"Okay." He headed out the door with the knapsack.

"Hi, 911. How can I help you?" said the woman's calm voice through the phone.

"Yes, I just found my friend Kenny overdosed at his girlfriend's apartment.

"Are you sure he's not breathing?"

"Yes, ma'am, he's not breathing or moving, and he's ice cold. His girlfriend says he took whatever was left in pill bottle. I'd put her on with you, but she's stoned out and useless right now."

"That's fine. Just give me the exact address, and I'll dispatch a police car immediately," she said.

I buzzed Mark back up and let him in. "The cops are on the way, Mark. Let's make sure Kenny doesn't have anything on him that would draw any attention." I pulled four half grams of speed out of one of Kenny's front jeans pockets, then about two hundred dollars in bills, a small phone book, and his wallet out of the rest of his pockets. I threw the four grams behind her refrigerator in the kitchen, then put the rest back in his pockets.

Two detectives in plain clothes arrived. I recognized one of them from my neighborhood. The detective's name was Officer Fielding, a real supercop. He stood about six foot, in good shape, with black hair and trimmed beard, in his thirties. He supposedly had one of the highest arrest records in New York. He also lived directly across the street from my childhood sweetheart's parents, and he was on a hello basis with her mother, Natalie.

"What happened here?" Officer Fielding asked as he knelt next to Kenny's body and placed two fingers on the side of Kenny's neck to feel for a pulse.

"I got here about a half hour ago to meet up with Kenny and Mark. We were supposed to take a trip upstate to check out a motorcycle, and this is how I found him."

Kenny's stoner girlfriend was finally sitting up and babbling about the empty pill bottle.

"Take her statement," Officer Fielding said to his younger and eager-looking partner. He then started emptying Kenny's pockets. When he took the small phone book out of Kenny's front pocket, he opened it and began reading. Then he looked up at Mark and me a few times, then back down at the phonebook.

"Are we free to go?" I asked the detective.

"Sure, you can go, but let me have your names, phone numbers, and addresses, and don't leave town for a couple of days."

We gave him our information, and out the door and into the elevator we went.

"What was up with the phone book?" I asked Mark as the elevator went down.

"That wasn't his phone book. That book is what Kenny used to keep a tally on people he fronted speed to."

"Shit," I said. "I thought that cop was looking at us weird. I got rid of the speed Kenny had on him." As we stepped out into the courtyard, I could see Mark's black caddy still double parked right in front of the building.

"What the fuck, Mark. I told you to move the car."

"I know. But I figured it would be all right. They don't know whose car it is. Let's just get in the car and head up to Syracuse and do this deal," he replied as we walked out of the courtyard and onto the sidewalk.

"Mark, don't go near the car. Just keep walking with me. We'll come back for it later."

But he stepped into the street, walked to the driver's door, unlocked it, and opened it. I stood staring at him from the curb.

"Is that your car?" A voice came from the courtyard as Detective Fielding exited the building. Mark just stood there, all 240 pounds of him, with his mouth hung open. The detective made his way to the car and asked Mark for the keys, then told him to stay right there while he searched the front seat of the Caddy. The detective backed out of the car a minute later with the knapsack in his hand. He opened the knapsack and pulled out one of the ounces of speed.

"You're busted," he said as he held the ounce of white powder in front of Mark's face. I took a deep breath, turned, and slowly walked the twenty yards to the corner. Each step I took, I waited to hear, "Where are you going?" but it never came. *After all, it wasn't my car.* I finally turned the corner and was in the wind.

I had gotten away again, but this time with an awful taste in my mouth. Kenny was gone for good. A young, mellow, cool kid with his whole life in front of him. Snatched up by the world of drugs. The consequences of being in the drug world had only begun to raise its ugly head.

17

A Long, Hard Road

Three things were keeping me from being completely swept away into the criminal and drug world at the age of seventeen. One, I still had my job at Sultan's on Fordham Road and was now working full time. Second, I still looked down on the heavy drug users—junkies, speed freaks, space cadets who took acid and smoked angel dust and the like. I drank my beer and rum and Cokes, smoked my weed, took pills, and tripped a few times, but I was mostly in the drug-dealing game for the money.

The third thing was my first love, a beautiful seventeen-year-old Italian girl named Gabrielle. She lived up the block from me and came from a good Catholic family. We dated from fifteen to seventeen years old, and I was head over heels for her. She had gone away to Long Beach Island with her family that summer. When she'd returned, I already had one foot in that drug and criminal world, and I was now living on my own.

Gabrielle didn't approve of my new lifestyle, which I tried to hide at first. We had met for dinner at an Italian restaurant in our neighborhood a week after the incident with Mark and Kenny and the speed. I stood outside under the red awning of the restaurant, to stay out of the rain, and waited for her. She turned the corner, holding an open umbrella over her head. She was my height and had long brown hair and big green eyes and a fair complexion. I was sure God had made her just for me. She was also a knock-around girl who played basketball for her girls high school. She wore jeans, sneakers, and her high school sweatshirt. As she walked closer, I could see she was upset.

"Hey, what's the matter?" I asked as I pulled her close.

"My parents forbid me to see you anymore, especially my father."

"What happened?"

"My mother ran into Officer Fielding the detective yesterday at the cleaners on Kingsbridge Road. He said they arrested a guy with a very large amount of speed, and the guy said he got it from you. And something about a guy overdosed on pills in an apartment you were in. My parents are completely freaked out."

"I'm sorry," I said as I hung my head.

"What happened to you? How could you do this to yourself?" She took a step back out into the rain, opened her umbrella, turned, and walked up toward the Grand Concourse. I stood under the canopy as the rain fell and watched her disappear around the corner. That would be the last time I would see Gabrielle as I had come to know her. We would see each other on the sly a few more times in the coming months, but her family got wind of it and flipped out. Soon afterward she and her family would move to upstate New York. It would be many years before I would see Gabrielle again. When the dark days came, it was those childhood memories with Gabrielle I would revisit for a moment of light.

In the following months, I continued selling pot and speed but made the fatal mistake of trying the speed. That would lead to staying up and partying for days in a row, which led to not thinking straight and carelessness, and an arrest. Not my first, but a big one. I was driving Snapshot's (a.k.a. Timmy D.) 1970 Riviera when the cops pulled us over on Fordham Road. There were four of us in the car, and we were still up from the night before. It was Saturday around 9:00 a.m., and the streets were crowded with people and traffic. A traffic scooter cop pulled up in front of us and stepped out. I looked behind me at the traffic and crowded sidewalks. There was nowhere to run. I reached behind me and pulled the gun from my waistband and shoved it down into the seat behind me.

"License and registration please," said the uniformed cop beside my window. His right hand was resting on his holstered gun.

Tommy reached into the glove compartment and handed me the registration, which I handed to the officer.

"I don't have any ID on me, Officer. I was just driving the owner of the car home because he's not feeling well."

He looked into the car, scanning all four of us, and pulled his gun.

"Everyone slowly get out of the car and put your hands against the wall," the officer yelled as a cop car pulled up. Timmy, Wally, Zef, from the Sinisters, who was now a good friend of mine, and I filed out of the car and stood facing the building with our hands raised. I stood there, my hands touching the cold brick building, a seventeen-year-old with long brown hair combed back, the cool hippy look, in my blue farmer jeans, T-shirt, and new blue suede Puma sneakers. I was just a young kid out driving his friend's car, until, while searching me, the cop came across the extra clip of bullets in the side pocket of my farmer jeans. They handcuffed us and hauled us to the station, where they put us in separate cells and tore the car apart looking for the gun. I still had three half grams of speed in my sock and four Tuinal pills in the small hideaway pocket in the front of my jeans. I flushed the speed down the toilet and popped the pills.

"If they find the gun, we're fucked," Timmy yelled from the cell to the left of me.

Timmy was the oldest of the four of us. An Italian guy from Villa Avenue, one of the last Italian neighborhoods in the Bronx. He stood around five foot nine, brown curly hair and thick mustache, always dressed sharp, a ladies' man for sure. Although we came from different neighborhoods and cultures, we had some things in common: We liked to drink, get high, and make money. Timmy liked the harder stuff. I wasn't there yet.

"Yeah, and I still have an open case. I'll be done," Wally yelled from the cell to the right of me.

"Fuck it. We'll handle it," Zef yelled from the cell across from me.

"Timmy, is the car clean?" I asked.

"Yeah, the registration and insurance are up to date, and my license is good," he answered.

"Well, rest easy, boys. If they find it, I'll take the weight for it. There's no point in the four of us going down for it, and it is my gun." No sooner did I finish the sentence and the arresting officer walked in with the gun dangling upside down from a pencil.

"We got it. Is anyone gonna cop to it, or is everyone going to Rikers tonight?" There was a few seconds of silence before I answered.

"That would be me, Officer. It's my gun."

"Okay, I'll get some paperwork for you to sign, and we'll start the process of releasing these guys."

I signed for the gun, and the boys were released. I had taken the four Tuinal pills before they were released, so I was passed out in my cell when they were leaving.

"Yo, Robby, are you okay?" Wally asked as he passed my cell. There was no response, as I lay on the metal bench. "Hey, Officer, you better check on him. I know he had some pills earlier, and he may have taken too many."

Wally was right, and they rushed me to the hospital and had my stomach pumped. When I awoke, I was in Central Booking on Third Avenue and 161st Street, and someone was calling my name.

"Are you Robby?" the young Puerto Rican with an afro asked.

"Yeah, that's me." I swung my feet off the metal bench and sat up. I was in a large holding cell in Central Booking, with about ten other guys. The young guy pointed to a window that was too high for me to see out of.

"Your boys are outside asking about you. You got some good friends there."

"Yo, it's Robby. Who's that?" I yelled up at the barred window.

"It's me and Zef and Timmy. Are you okay?" Wally asked.

"Yeah, I'm okay now. Just a little out of it," I responded

"The cops said you'll see a judge tonight, and they'll set bail, then they'll bring you to Rikers Island."

"Do me a favor—call Gary and see if he'll put up the bail, and I'll see him when I get out." I yelled back up to Wally.

"You got it, brother. We'll see you when you get out," Wally yelled back.

My bail was set at $1,000, and off to the Rikers Island I went. I was still out of it. I had been up for a couple of days before I got busted and took the downers, so I kept nodding off. I got to my cell on Rikers and slept the night away.

I was awoken by the clang of the heavy metal cell doors opening.

"On the chow," screamed the short, heavyset White corrections officer as he walked past the cells, keys jangling at his side.

I sat up and looked around, my head finally clearing. I was sitting on my bed, a single metal slab jutting out of the concrete wall, with a single plastic-covered thin mattress. There was a folded white single sheet and gray blanket that my head had been resting on. Three feet across from me was a small metal silver table and seat jutting out of the wall, and a silver metal toilet and connected sink sticking out of the back wall of the six-by-nine cell. I threw some water on my face and walked out of the cell.

I joined the herd of inmates walking toward the dayroom at the head of the cell block. I noticed right away that I was definitely in the minority. Out of the fifty or sixty inmates, I only spotted one other White boy. There were mostly Blacks and Puerto Ricans. I kept to myself.

I followed the crowd into the dayroom, where a group of inmates with head nets on were serving food behind a long steel counter. I picked up a plastic tray and stood in line. Guys were walking past me with trays that had small boxes of cereal, small milk containers, an orange, a couple of slices of bread, and some apple butter on them. My mouth watered. I was hungry and couldn't remember when I had last eaten. Before I could step up in line, a young Black guy stood right alongside me and put his right foot next to my left foot so that they were touching, right alongside my brand-new blue suede Pumas.

"Looks like they're my size, white boy," he said as I turned to face him.

The guys ahead and behind us took a step or two back.

"They're yours if you can take them, motherfucker," I snapped back as I slammed the side of the tray into the bridge of his nose, then charged him. We rolled around the dayroom floor as I got punched and kicked from other Blacks in line. It was broken up pretty quick by a few correction officers, also known as COs. The young Black man and I were cuffed and locked back in our cells. I wasn't beaten too badly, considering. Mostly kicks and punches to my back and the back of my head while I had him down between two mess hall tables. They got me, but I got him. I'd learned it always hurts less when you're fighting back.

This was not starting out too well. So far I'd been banged up and missed breakfast. When everyone finished eating and were locked back in their cells for the morning count, the yelling started. "You're fucking dead, white boy. That was a Black Spades' nose you broke. Now you gotta fight all of us."

"Well, line up, motherfuckers," I yelled back. The screaming, yelling, and threats continued for the next hour or so. I sat on my metal cot. *Well, this sucks. I'm definitely getting fucked up when they lock us out for lunch. If I could just make it out of here alive and not get my face cut, I'll be all right. No matter what, I'm not giving up my Pumas. Fuck that! Maybe I should ask God for some help? No, we haven't talked in a very long time.*

I could hear the footsteps and the jingle of the keys as the CO came walking down the corridor. He slowed as he approached my cell. A round white face with red cheeks looked through the small square opening in my cell door.

"Carney," said the voice.

"That's me."

"Your bail's been posted. Let's go. Open up twenty-seven," he yelled.

My metal cell door opened up with a clang, and I followed him down the corridor of cells to the yells of some of my new friends saying goodbye.

"The white boy made bail," came the first goodbye.

"You're fucking lucky, white boy. Those Pumas and that ass would have been mine by the end of lunch."

I heard more screams and threats as I passed the locked cells.

"Later, bitches," I yelled back as I passed the last cell and exited the cell block. The Rikers Island bus dropped me on the other side of the bridge to freedom. Wally, Zef, Timmy, and Gary were waiting at the end of the bridge. They greeted me with handshakes, pats on the back, a roast beef hero, and cold Heineken.

"Thanks, fellas. Your timing couldn't have been any better." That would be the one and only time I would make bail.

I got five years probation for the gun, with the help of the Fortune Society, an organization that supported successful reentry from incarceration and promoted alternatives to in-carceration. They were located in downtown Manhattan. I went there once a week for counseling and tutoring for my GED. They accompanied me to court for sentencing for the gun and helped me get probation instead of jail time.

I was leaving the Fortune Society after one of my weekly visits and ran into Vinny, one of the counselors there. Vinny was a big, tough, hard-looking dude. He was over six feet, with long, frizzy red hair and piercing blue eyes. He wore a small gold cross earring in his left ear and was tattooed up, wearing jeans and a T-shirt. The toughest hippy you ever met. I was following him down the metal staircase, when he stopped and turned to me.

"Hey, Robby, how are you doing?"

"I'm doing good Vinny. How about you?"

"I'm doing great. I'm heading over to a meeting. Do you want to come?" he asked.

"What kind of meeting?"

"Narcotics Anonymous."

I looked at him wide eyed and let out a chuckle.

"No thanks, Vinny. I'm good," I said matter of factly.

Vinny just looked at me with sad eyes and slowly shook his head back and forth. "Robby, you've got a long, hard road ahead of you, my friend," he said with his hand on my shoulder, then turned and walked down the metal staircase and out of the building.

I continued to deal drugs while on probation, but my constant smoking of weed and my sporadic days of partying and using speed took a toll on my dealing business. I was my best advertisement, because whatever I was selling, I was stoned on it. It got to a point where I couldn't even get a drug package fronted to me anymore because I couldn't pay it back. I would soon lose everything, and off to Brooklyn I went to be back home for shelter.

18

The Change Jar

My move to Brooklyn with my mother, sister, and stepfather was humbling, but I did have some hope that maybe I could have a better life. I had also given the probation department the Brooklyn address, so it kind of worked out. I got my own room upstairs in the back of the house. I still kept my job at Sultans on Fordham Road and commuted by train every day back to the Bronx, stopping at the schoolyard after work before catching the train home to Brooklyn. I was still selling nickels of pot, but the speed connection was gone, which was just as well.

Living in Brooklyn wasn't so bad in the beginning. We lived in a three-story home in the Sunset Park section. Donna and I both had our own rooms. She went to a new school and was making friends, and I kept my job and could pretty much come and go as I pleased. My mother seemed pretty happy at first. She was living in her dream home, at least during the day. The only problem with the whole setup was my stepfather, Fred. After a few months, it became obvious he didn't want my sister and me there.

It wasn't so much by what he said to us—it was what he didn't say, which was anything. It was also weird that when he looked at us, he seemed to be looking through us, as if we weren't there, never making eye contact. The only rule my mother laid down was if I was home during dinner, I had to join them at the dinner table. Dinner was served at 6:00 p.m., when Fred got home from work, and on the weekends too. It went like this after we were all seated at the table.

"Hi, Fred, how are you?"

"Hi, Robert," he would respond, while staring at his food.

I looked over at my mom and just shrugged my shoulders. She would just shrug her shoulders and shake her head, not having an answer.

My mother was doing very well at first with slowing down her drinking, but as her life in that house unraveled, she began drinking during the day, throwing up in the late afternoon, took a nap for a half hour, then sobered up and had dinner ready by six. Her new drink was vodka, always a pint hidden under the kitchen sink. My heart broke for her.

I continued to try and get my dealing business back to where it was, but the drinking, smoking pot daily, and now trying pills and some psychedelics would keep ending me up in the jackpot, broke. I wound up losing my job at Sultan's because of stealing. The money would always go to buy bigger packages of drugs to sell, but I never stayed sober enough to make a profit. Plus, not coming home for days at a time or at all hours of the night did not help the failed relationship between Fred and me.

You could almost cut the tension in that house with a knife. I had gone through all my money again, so one day when Fred had taken my mother and sister out to a doctor's appointment, I stole a change jar he had locked in a room downstairs. The reason the room was locked was because I had found his rolled-up silver quarters in a box in the basement and slowly started stealing them.

I had made up my mind that day that I was leaving that house to go and build up my dealing business and live on my own in the Bronx again, and I was taking the change jar with me for start-up money and never coming back. I justified it in my mind. *Okay, you don't want me here, so I'll leave, but it's gonna cost you.* Little did I know that it would not only be me who would pay the price for stealing that change jar but also my mother and sister. There was $1,800 in silver quarters in that big plastic green J&B bottle. I would get $3,200 cash for it. More than enough to start my weed-selling business up again. One of my many deals with the devil.

I was arrested a few days later outside the schoolyard for stealing that change jar and held for two days in lockup. When I appeared before the judge, I found out my mother had talked Fred into dropping the charges, so they released me, but the price I would pay was steep. I would be banned from living in that house forever. I was seventeen years old. I would continue to pay the price for that incident for many years.

The truth was, I'd robbed my family. I'd left my mother and sister to deal with the brunt of his screaming and anger for what I had done. Every time I drew a sober breath, that reality would hit me like being splashed with hot oil. For the next few years I tried my best to not draw a sober breath. With no home or home base to start from, life began to get hard and lonely.

19

Got My Wings

The money I had stolen from my family would eventually run out, along with my big drug-dealing days and dreams.

Around this time, I ran into Pete. A tall, thin guy with light-brown hair, in his late thirties. He drove a fancy green Karmann Ghia, had a beautiful brown Doberman pinscher, and had a gorgeous girlfriend, Pauline. She was thin and tall, with long black hair. Pete was a stickup guy who had gotten out of prison a year earlier. We met through mutual drinking and get-high buddies. On this Saturday we were hanging out in Poe Park, and I was trying to figure out a way to get money and re-up.

"Hey, Robby, you got some free time this afternoon?" Pete asked.

"Sure, what's up?"

"I wanted to show you something. Let me take Pauline home, and I'll be back in a half hour to pick you up."

"Okay, I'll be here."

He was back shortly. I slid into his little sports car, and we took off. "Where are we going, Pete?"

"Have you ever done a stickup, Robby?"

"No, it's really not my thing. I mostly just sell weed or whatever I can get hold of. Why, what do you have in mind?"

"I'll do everything. I just need you to drive the car when I come out with the money."

"I can do that." I looked up to this stickup guy, who had already done time. It was like that in my neighborhood, at least for me. It was a hot summer afternoon as he pulled up two car lengths from a Carvel Ice Cream store. Pete pulled a silver revolver from under the driver's seat.

"I'll leave the car running. When I get out, jump into the driver's seat. Just sit tight, and if the cops pull up, beep the horn two short beeps," he said as he lifted his shirt and shoved the revolver into his waistband.

He was in and out of the store in two minutes, carrying a white paper Carvel bag full of cash. He climbed in the passenger side, and I took off.

"How did it go?" I asked.

"Those places are easy. There's usually young kids behind the counter, and they don't want any trouble. They just give it right up."

I nodded, but thought, *A Carvel? I thought we were gonna rob a bank or something. What do I know? I'm just a drug dealer.*

"Pull over. I want to make a stop on the way uptown," Pete said as he was counting the cash in the bag. I pulled over, and we switched seats. He drove straight to Hunts Point in the South Bronx and pulled onto a rough-looking block. There were groups of Puerto Ricans drinking beer and listening to Latin music. Some were flying their colors, and *The Savage Skulls* was written on the back of their sleeveless dungaree jackets.

"Yo, Paco, you still got that Black Magic?" Pete yelled out of the car window at the crowd of guys on a stoop.

"Yeah, man, how many?" answered the older Puerto Rican with the white tank top and gold chains around his neck.

"Give me a bundle," Pete answered.

Paco walked over, leaned against the side of the car and my open window, and dropped a bundle of small glassine bags on my lap, ten glassine bags with a rubber band around them. I handed the small bundle to Pete, and he handed Paco the cash. In no time at all we were on the Bronx River Parkway heading uptown, and it was obvious he was in a big rush to get home.

"Yo, bro," I said. "We got a gun, drugs, and stolen cash from an armed robbery in the car. Slow the fuck down."

He slowed the car down a little but was still speeding.

We arrived at Pete's apartment, and he gave me the bag of cash to count. I sat down at the round wooden kitchen table and dumped the cash on it. Pete excused himself to the bedroom for a minute while I sorted through the bills and counted them. From my spot in the kitchen, I could see Pete sitting on the side of his queen-size bed, by the nightstand. He was tapping the side of an open glassine bag and pouring the white powder onto a metal tablespoon on top of the nightstand. He repeated that with two more bags, then took a syringe out of the wooden nightstand drawer, drew some water out of a glass, then squirted the water onto the spoon. He pulled a small piece of cotton from a Q-Tip and rolled it between his thumb and index finger and dropped it into the spoon. I stopped counting the money and just sat there mesmerized, and watched.

He took a Bic lighter from the drawer and flicked it on, passing the flame back and forth under the spoon a few times, then took the syringe and drew up the liquid in the spoon. He gently placed the full syringe between his lightly clenched teeth and pulled his belt off, wrapping it around the top of his left arm. He straightened his left arm, took the syringe from between his teeth, and poked his arm, injecting the contents of the syringe into his vein. Within seconds his whole body went limp. You could see the stress, worry, and tension leave him as he slowly placed the empty syringe on the nightstand, and the belt unraveled from his arm and fell to the floor. I was captivated by the whole scene and curious, to say the least. My half of the take was $150.

Three days later Pete pulled up outside the schoolyard in his sporty green Karmann Ghia and waved me over. I handed Wally a handful of nickel bags to sell and hopped into the car.

"Are you ready for another one?" he asked.

"Sure, Pete, but I feel like I'm not really contributing. Do you want me to go in this time?"

"No," he responded, as he drove to the next Carvel. "You just drive when I come out with the money, I got this."

"Okay." *Maybe he just doesn't want to do it alone.* The second robbery played out exactly like the first. He went in with the gun, while I shifted to the driver's seat and waited. A couple of minutes later, he emerged with another white paper Carvel bag full of cash. When we were a good distance away, we switched seats, and he took over the wheel. He drove directly to Hunts Point to pay Paco and the boys another visit.

"Hey, Paco, another bundle of Black Magic," Pete yelled out of the car window to the crowd of guys on the stoop, as we pulled onto the crowded and noisy block.

"Yo, Pete, get a couple of extra bags for me," I yelled as I grabbed a twenty out of the paper bag and handed it to him.

"No, you don't want to mess with this stuff," he said as he tossed the bill back to me.

"All right, I'll just get it myself," I replied as I opened the passenger door.

"Okay, okay," Pete shot back. "Just close the door. Paco, give me two more bags." Paco handed him the bags, and Pete paid him. Pete reached over and handed me the two bags, shaking his head back and forth.

We were heading north on the Bronx River Parkway, when Pete pulled over onto the grassy shoulder.

"What's up?" I asked.

"Nothing. I'm just pulling over for a minute." He then quickly pulled two glassine bags off the bundle, opened them, and dumped them onto a spoon he pulled out of a small black bag. Within two minutes he was shooting up in the driver's seat while we were parked on the side of the road. I sat looking out the side and back window for any cop cars as traffic whizzed by us.

"Holy shit, are you for real, man?" I looked at him questioningly.

"No worries. I'm done," as he pulled the belt off his arm and threw it in the backseat and pulled out into traffic.

When we arrived back at Pete's apartment, he was already flying high. I emptied the bag of money on the table and counted out $380. We figured out what we spent on dope and split the rest. I pulled out the two glassine bags I'd bought and held them out in my hand.

"Hey, Pete, I want to do this dope."

"Well, pour it on the table and sniff it up."

"No, I want to do it like you did," I responded.

"No way, kid. I'm not giving you your wings," he said as seriously as he could while scratching his nose, his eyes half-open.

"That's all right. I'll just go down to Decatur Avenue and give one of the junkies a few bucks to do it for me." As I gathered my money and dope and headed for the door, he yelled at me.

"All right, I'll do it, but don't ever tell anyone I did this for you." He got his small black leather bag and took out the syringe, blackened metal spoon, and rubber tubing to tie my arm off. Within minutes he was searching for a vein. I couldn't look, so I turned my head to the side. I felt the prick of the needle, and within seconds I thought my head would spin off, then a calm, warm feeling swept over my body. I stood up too quickly and almost fell back onto the kitchen chair.

"Yo, take it easy and sit for a minute. You may throw up, but you'll feel real good afterward."

"Thanks, Pete. I'm feeling better now, so I'm gonna head out. Come by the schoolyard if you need me," I yelled as I walked out of the apartment. I slowly walked down the three flights of steps. There was an open window between landings. Holding on to the wooden banister, I stumbled down the steps and stuck my head out the window and threw up into the backyard. I took a few deep breaths and felt better immediately and descended the steps without a worry in the world. I wasn't worried about my pending gun charge, or feeling guilty for stealing from my family, or ashamed of when I was sexually assaulted as a kid. No, I felt none of that, just a rush of euphoria throughout my body.

Yes, I had found euphoria, but there would be a price to pay, a very steep price. I exited the building into the afternoon sun and heat, rubbing my itchy nose and face.

20

Where Did Everyone Go?

The next eighteen years of my life were, for the most part, a living hell. My reign in the schoolyard had come to an end. The need to drink and get high would outweigh my drive to hustle and make money. I would end up trying to collect old debts, which sometimes turned physical, which would later cause me to be feared and disliked by some in the schoolyard and neighborhood.

I walked up to the entrance and looked into the schoolyard one Saturday morning, and it seemed a strange place, one I was unfamiliar with. I was eighteen years old. Most of my crew were gone. Even Wally had gone down to Decatur Avenue to deal for someone else. Most of the people there were from the younger crowd, and most of the older ones knew someone I had busted up. I stood there looking into the schoolyard from Briggs Avenue that Saturday morning, then just kept walking past the entrance, never to return.

I lost the furnished room because I couldn't pay the rent anymore, so I couch surfed between friends for a while. I started working pretty regularly for a moving company on the Lower East Side of Manhattan. It was the perfect job for the person I was becoming, someone who was drinking and getting high every day. At the end of each workday, I went back to the storefront on East First Street, where all the workers lined up in front of the boss's desk. Each man was paid cash for the hours he'd worked that day, and we almost always were tipped. Then I could walk two blocks in any direction and buy the best heroin in the city. It was just me, my alcohol, and my dope now.

Dave was the owner of the moving company, a heavyset gentleman in his fifties, with a white head of hair and a white beard. He had a white German shepherd that sat faithfully by his desk. He also owned the building and the storefront he operated out of. There were three floors, with two apartments on each floor above the storefront. Dave rented one of the apartments to me for $300 a month. It was an old New York building with two rooms in the apartment, a bedroom and a kitchen / living room. In the kitchen was a bathtub against the back wall. A small kitchen table and two wooden chairs and a small couch and television sat against the far wall. The bathroom consisted of a toilet inside a closet door, with the water tank up on the wall behind the toilet and a skinny metal chain that hung from it to flush with. The apartment was furnished, probably with furniture people wanted to get rid of from moving jobs. There was a bed and an old wooden dresser in the bedroom. The top drawer of the dresser was filled with old Off Track Betting slips and hundreds of losing lottery tickets. The old man who'd lived here and worked for Dave had died. He'd been a quiet, sad, older guy. I could see why now.

Dave also lived in the building on the top floor. He was married to a small, feisty blond German woman named Eva. The story goes that Dave was a homeless wino on the bowery and somehow hooked up with Eva, and she got him on his feet. He was a man of few words, but he did have a good heart.

Men would stand outside the office in the morning trying to get on a truck for the day, sometimes in the freezing cold in the winter. If there were men still out there after all the trucks had gone, he would buy them breakfast in the Polish restaurant on Avenue A. He was good like that. He was also well known for his yearly drinking escapades, which I got to witness once.

The driver was summoned back to the office immediately after we had finished a job one day.

"You have to go get him now. He's drunk and busting up a place on Eighth Avenue," Eva pleaded to the driver and us in her German accent as tears rolled down her face. She handed Mickey, the driver, a piece of paper with the address on it. We all jumped back on the truck and took off. Within minutes we were pulling up in front of a classy bar in the West Village, nothing like the bars we went to on the east side. There were customers and people looking in the window and door of the bar. We could hear Dave yelling and cursing from where we sat in the truck.

"Here's what we're gonna do," said Mickey, a tall, wiry Irish-man who also liked the booze but could carry an eight-draw-er dresser on his back up six flights of stairs all day long. "The four of us will go in and get him. We'll walk him out or carry him out. Don't worry about what he says or does. He'll forget everything by the morning. We'll get him in the side door of the truck, then lay him down on his back on some moving blankets. You two each grab an arm, and, Larry, you lay over his legs and hold him down. I'll drive back as fast as I can."

The four of us headed into the bar. It was becoming obvious that Mickey had done this before. There were barstools thrown about and two overturned tables. The bartender stood at the back of the bar with some ice in a cloth against the side of his head. Dave stood at the bar and poured himself another shot of whiskey.

"So she sent you little fuckers to come get me, huh? Well, let's go," Dave yelled.

All went according to plan. The four of us wrestled him into the back of the truck and laid him on his back on the blue moving blanket. I could see Mickey handing the bartender a business card and waving his arm around the bar, as if to say, *Let us know what the damage is.* The bartender shook his head and waved goodbye to Mickey. I could barely hold Dave's left arm down. He screamed and cursed and threatened me and everyone else. I just held that arm down and stared out of the opened side door of the moving truck, watching the passing cars and people.

We pulled up in front of the building, and Eva was standing in the doorway of the storefront. She strode toward the truck, and we all released our grip on Dave. He sat up and saw Eva approaching the side door, and he became very quiet.

"Upstairs with you," she said sternly as she pointed to the entrance door of the building. Dave did not let out a peep. He slid out of the side door of the truck and wobbled straight into the building, followed by her five foot, slightly plump frame. The next morning at work, it was as if nothing had happened. Yes, Dave was a strange bird indeed.

I had lived in the apartment and worked for Dave for just over a year. I liked living on the Lower East Side in the seventies, the cool people, the quaint shops and second-hand clothes stores, the Hells Angels Headquarters down the block, the drugs and drug addicts everywhere. It was the heroin capital of New York, for sure. There was a small Polish community, St. Marks Place, and McSorley's Ale House, where I nodded out over more than a few dark ales. I had become a daily heroin user. My life and the circle of people in it had become small. I was nineteen years old. It was a different, lonely time.

My days consisted of getting up at 6:00 a.m. and doing a morning shot of dope if I had saved one. Showered, shaved, and down to the storefront by 7:00. Out on the trucks all day, back to the office, get paid, and off to Avenue B and Fourth Street to cop my dope. Go home to get straight, then out to grab a sandwich or pizza and maybe a pint of rum, eat, drink, and nod out in front of the TV, wake up at 6:00 a.m. and do it again. That job, apartment, and neighborhood were the perfect place to not take a sober breath. My hiding place from the world.

Still, what stands out the most when living in the East Village was the loneliness. Less than two years prior, I was an asset to my family, I was in love with a beautiful girl, I was sur-rounded by friends, I had made a ton of money dealing weed, and the sky was the limit. I'd even enjoyed the reputation of being able to take care of myself with my hands, but that was all gone now. Only the thought, craving, and obsession for my next fix remained. Every so often, while loading or unloading a moving truck in Manhattan, I would glance at a young couple going by laughing or being romantic and intimate, or a family heading to a movie or dinner, clinging to each other, and I would ask myself, *What happened to me?* Then I would glance down at my watch and think of when I could get my next fix.

I'd push my young, strong body to the brink. Working as many hours as I could, and now stealing when I could. I would take a piece of jewelry here and there. I was sent to pack up apartments on Park Avenue and Madison Avenue, some very high-end clients. I would be faced daily with full jewelry boxes to pack. I would only take one small piece of gold when I thought it wouldn't be missed. It seemed to work, and gold was valuable in the seventies. I developed the thief's eye as my addiction gained momentum. It's when you first enter a room and quickly scan it for sellables.

I tried to keep up my appearance for work's sake. Always showing up showered, shaved, and reasonably clean clothed. I did the best I could for as long as I could. I became introverted, staying to myself most of the time. When the guys would gather in small groups in front of the storefront in the morning, I would stand off to the side with my coffee and cigarette, just waiting to see what crew and truck I was going out on.

For one thing, I didn't feel worthy of friendship, nor did I have the time for it. I was silently and tragically consumed with my need for the next shot of dope. Second, my constant weed smoking from when I was dealing for those few years affected my personality. I can see now how I began to get paranoid and became very self-conscious. I was okay speaking with someone one on one, but if two or more people joined the conversation, I would become quiet, afraid I would say something stupid.

At this point it was clear the alcohol and drugs had severely damaged me and had shaken my self-confidence. I clearly remember talking myself out of asking a girl who showed interest in me on a date, or asking for a raise, or promotion to driver at work. For a tough guy from the Bronx, I had certainly been humbled and broken by the likes of alcohol and drugs.

I did have one thing going for me: I was a good mover. I was strong, fast, and never had any damage. I could pad, pack, handle a two- or four-wheeler, or carry furniture or boxes up and down stairs all day long. My ability to work was never questioned, and I was reliable, so I always went out on the trucks. But after about a year working for Dave, the dope started taking its toll.

21

Another Morning Shot

I had gotten the day off, so I could sleep in, but I awoke startled, and my right leg was pounding. Feeling nauseous and sweat pouring out of me, I knew it was that time again. I glanced over at the nightstand, which was bare except for the empty syringe and blackened silver tablespoon with the tiny dried-out cotton ball in it.

"Shit!" I hadn't left myself a morning shot. I sat up slowly and swung my legs off the side of the bed and scanned the room for my jeans. They were hanging over a chair in the corner. I stumbled over some of the dirty clothes and glassine bags that littered the bedroom floor. I had become immune to my surroundings. Half-dressed, I made my way through the two-room tenement in search of a clean-looking T-shirt. I had the day off, no need to shave and shower this morning.

I punched my right leg a few times, trying to work some of the cramps and restlessness out of it. Leaning over the tub in the kitchen, I splashed some cold water on my face. Then I made my way to the bedroom window to see what I faced outside on this hot summer morning.

Pushing the sheet aside, I opened the window all the way up and stuck my head out and looked down on East First Street. The sounds of people and traffic below competed with the glaring sun at making my head pound. I could feel myself begin to heave. Pulling my head back in the window, I leaned on the windowsill and breathed slowly until it passed.

Sweat trickled down my back. I checked my face in the mirror above the dresser. I didn't recognize the person looking back at me. I ran a comb through my long, straight brown hair, trying to get the part as close to the middle as possible, to impress whom, I did not know. I only knew I had left myself short of dope this morning, and if I wanted to stop the nausea and pounding in my leg, I had to get going now. I felt for the roll of bills in my pocket and headed for the door.

Going down the long, steep stairs of my dimly lit building, I stopped on the second-floor landing and pulled the roll of bills out. I peeled off three twenties and put them into my front pocket. I took the remaining eight twenties and shoved them down the front of my jeans so they rested snuggly above my groin. *If the fucking vultures catch me out there this morning, they won't get it all,* I thought. I punched my right leg again, took a couple of deep breaths, then continued down the stairs and out into the summer morning.

The Lower East Side was fully awake now. Mostly young people on their way to work, dressed in the latest fashions. Black and loose seemed to be on the agenda this summer, and unique hairstyles that were created solely for that individual, while others not interested in style still had damp hair from their morning shower. People were rushing in every direction, trying to get to work on time. I tried to find myself among them somewhere, but the nausea in my head and stomach brought me back to where I was.

Turning left on First Avenue, I walked toward Houston Street. My eye caught the back of a bright, bouncy blonde disappearing down the subway steps. A year ago I might have caught up with her to ask directions to anywhere in hopes of getting her phone number, but not today. My shaky, restless legs carried me across Houston Street. Another young girl caught my eye as she turned the corner of Eldridge Street. Her long black hair hung stiffly against her pale complexion, and a quick step took the place of whatever bounce she may have once had. As the distance between us closed, our eyes met.

"Hey, sweetheart, what's good this morning?" I asked as we passed each other.

"Red tape is what I got, but you better hurry. The block is packed, and it's gonna get hot over there," she replied, recognizing the sweat rolling off me and the despair in my eyes. She then pulled her clenched fist to her chest, holding the glassine bags of heroin sealed with red tape, and made her way through the traffic on Houston Street.

I turned the corner. Eldridge Street was packed for that time of the morning. Four social clubs stood almost in a row on one side of the street, while the other side was packed with anxiously awaiting people, mostly young and White and from Jersey, but definitely all races mixed and from different parts of the city. The social clubs looked abandoned, boarded up as they were, except for the young Puerto Rican steerer in front of each club yelling.

"Blue tape, red tape, ten more for green tape, let's move it" came their yells from in front of each storefront. The color of tape defined that social club's brand of dope. The sidewalk across from the clubs were filled with people. I joined the crowd who stood across from the club selling red tape and waited my turn with the rest of the runny-nosed desperate addicts. We all concentrated on the steerer across the street, waiting for him to call the next ten.

Everyone looked up as the door to the red-tape club opened and ten eye-darting people filed out and quickly dispersed in different directions. I inched my way to the curb, making sure I would be in the next ten to get in. Hands shaking, I wiped the sweat from my forehead and stepped off the curb as the steerer yelled out for ten more.

"Red tape, ten more, let's go. Okay, that's it," rang out as we reached the other side of the street. The steerer knocked twice on the thick metal door, his eyes searching up and down the block for cops as the door to the club opened. One at a time we entered the dark storefront and formed a line in front of the pool table.

"Get your money ready," yelled the scar-faced Puerto Rican who bolted the door behind us. His nine millimeter protruding from the top of his jeans, no one questioned him. Arms crossed, his back to the door, he stared at us through squinted eyes as everyone pulled their money out.

"How many, girl?" asked the guy from behind the pool table. There were two paper bags on the pool table on either side of him. One held glassine bags of dope, and the other held glassine bags of coke.

"Give me four dope and two coke," replied the young Black girl at the front of the line. She laid her money on the pool table as she fidgeted with the blond wig she wore. The guy dropped the glassine bags on the table and scooped up her money. She grabbed the glassine bags with their red tape on them and walked to the front door of the club and waited for everyone to make their sale.

"Hold up, José" came the doorman's voice from behind us.

"Yo, my man," he yelled again, pointing to the third person in line, a tall White guy in his thirties.

The White man's head spun around, swinging a ponytail behind it. He seemed to fit in with us well enough, with his long hair, worn-out army shirt, and jeans, right down to his dirty white sneakers.

"What's up?" replied the White guy.

"I haven't seen you around here before. Let's see some ID."

"Huh?" the White guy said.

"Roll up your sleeves, motherfucker," said the scar-faced doorman as he moved toward the white guy, his gun now drawn and hanging at his side.

Shit, not now. The aching had worked its way into both my legs now. I breathed deeply and slowly to keep my composure as the sweat rolled off me. I stood there watching.

"Everything's cool. My money's right," pleaded the White guy as he held a handful of bills for the doorman to see. A desperate look appeared on his face, but no sweat rolled off him.

"I said roll up your sleeves, motherfucker." Before the doorman finished the sentence, he had the White guy's head pulled back by the ponytail, pushing the pistol into the back of his neck.

"Okay, okay," pleaded the White guy as he pulled up his shirtsleeves. He turned his arms upward. They were milky white and not a sign of a needle mark on them.

"Hold him there, Chino," screamed the guy from behind the pool table, pulling his own pistol from the back of his waistband. The White guy stood there shaking, his arms still turned up and extended in front of him, while Chino gripped his ponytail tightly.

"Let's not do anything stupid. Everything's cool," the White guy said.

"You fucking pig," the dealer said through his gold teeth. "Clasp your hands over your head slowly, or I'll blow your face off right here."

Dropping the crumpled bills to the floor, the man lifted his arms up slowly, clasping his hands above his head. From the back of the line, I spotted the bottom half of the handcuffs hanging from his belt, which were no longer concealed by the long army shirt.

Chino pulling him by his ponytail eased him off the line and to the door.

The manager came from behind the pool table, keeping his distance but carefully covering the cop with his gun, made his way to the door, looked out the peephole, then slowly turned from the door.

"Get this piece of shit out of here, Chino," he said as he spun from the door with his gun pointed at the cop's face.

"Just remember, everything's cool, fellas. You don't have to do anything stupid," the cop pleaded, knowing he was exposed and vulnerable.

The manager swung the door open, and Chino shoved the cop out with force so that he landed hard on the sidewalk. The cop regained his feet quickly and sped across the street, disappearing into the crowd of people waiting to buy dope. Chino slammed and bolted the door as the manager made his way back behind the pool table.

"How many?" echoed the guy's voice behind the pool table.

"Two and two," replied a watery-eyed, sniffling older Black man.

Chino took his place back at the door and directed everyone who made their purchases to one side of the darkened storefront.

"Six dope," I said, wiping my nose on the back of my forearm as my turn in line finally came. I placed the three twenties down on the pool table. One at a time the small glassine bags bounced on the green felt in front of me. I snatched them all up as the sixth one hit the table. When I had all six stacked neatly between my thumb and forefinger I joined the others near the door.

As the last person in line scooped his glassine bags up off the table, I carefully placed mine in my mouth, clenching down on them with my front teeth so my tongue wouldn't touch them and get them wet. I closed my mouth to hide them and waited for the doorman to let us out. My aching body shook at the thought of what could be waiting for us on the other side of the metal door.

If the cops are waiting for us outside, I could at least try and swallow the bags while they searched me, and if the vultures are looking for a mark and surprise me, I'd have my hands free to go for my knife and fight them off while I try to make a run for it.

"Are you ready for the next ten, Paco?" yelled the doorman.

"Yeah, let's go." Chino peeked through the small hole in the door, then cracked it open just enough to stick his head through. Satisfied by the signal he got from the steerer on the sidewalk, he opened the door and motioned us out.

I blocked the glaring sun with my hand as I followed the others into the street. Through squinted eyes I looked up and down the block, then quickly crossed the street and pushed my way through the crowd. Halfway down Eldridge Street, I made a right into a parking lot and came out on Allen Street and made a left onto Houston Street, then down the subway stairs, constantly looking behind me to make sure no cops or vultures were following.

The coolness of the subway station felt good against my overheated body as I made my way under Houston Street, only to reemerge on the other side. I came up out of the subway on the northside of Houston Street, thinking, *God, only one more block and I'm home free.*

Walking up First Avenue to East First Street, I made a right at the corner and jogged toward my building, looking behind me one last time. I entered the dimly lit hallway, leaned against the closed door, and spit the glassine bags into my hand. I made it to the staircase and balanced myself against the railing, trying to catch my breath, then took the steps two at a time up to my haven.

Reaching the third floor, I fumbled with my keys, keeping a tight grip on the six glassine bags in my hand. When the door was open, I raced for the bathroom. I lifted the toilet seat and dry heaved. Some yellow bile made its way up and out and into the toilet. I caught my breath and pulled the long chain that hung from the water tank.

Stepping onto the toilet seat, I felt along the top of the doorframe for the used syringe I had placed there the night before. My fingers found it. I stepped down off the toilet seat and went into the bedroom and shot my dope.

A warmness enveloped me. My head spun as the aches slowly left my legs and that familiar taste made its way up my throat and into my mouth. I sat staring at the ray of sun that made its way through the slit in the sheet that hung from the window. I placed the needle on the nightstand and watched the belt fall from my arm. Yes, this was it. This was what I had given everything up for. I closed my eyes and leaned back on the bed, the pain, worry, and shame replaced with silence and numbness.

22

A Moment of Clarity

The night went by quickly. I faded in and out of a hero-in-induced sleep, watching whatever was on the television when my eyes opened for a few seconds. The alarm went off at 5:00 a.m. I pushed myself up and off the bed, showered, shaved, and dressed. I made a cup of instant coffee, then prepared my morning shot of heroin. It was gonna be a good day. I had saved myself a bag of dope for the morning. *Hopefully I will get some good hours in today, or maybe a pack job on Fifth Avenue and slip a piece of jewelry in my pocket.* I skipped down the stairs.

Stepping out of the building and into the morning light, there were nine or ten guys standing around in small groups outside the storefront, waiting to get some work on the trucks. I leaned against the lamppost, lit a cigarette, and waited for the boss to come out with his clipboards and tell us what trucks we'd be working on. Dave stuck his head out the doorway, looked in my direction, and waved me into the office. I followed him in as he made his way around the white shepherd by his desk and plopped down into his work chair. I stood in front of his desk as he looked up at me with sad eyes.

"Robby, I gotta let you go," he said in a monotone voice.

"Really? Why? I'm one of your best workers."

"You know why," he said as he straightened his left arm and tapped the inside of his forearm with his index finger. "If you're doing that, you'll steal, if you haven't stolen already. I'm gonna need you to clear out of the apartment by the end of the month also."

"Okay, Dave," I replied, with my head hanging down, staring at the floor and lost for words. "I'll be out of the apartment by the end of the month." I knelt and petted the shepherd one last time. I stood, looked at Dave, and said, "Thank you for everything. I appreciate it," then turned and walked out of the office and through the crowd of guys waiting for work.

Did someone see the tracks on my arms, even with my long-sleeve shirts? Or maybe because when I'm high, I always nod out on the way to unload the truck? It could also be that my withdrawal symptoms toward the end of a long day are becoming more noticeable. Or maybe because it's been over a year now and I've gone from dipping and dabbing to becoming a full-blown strung-out junkie. Yeah, maybe that's it. I headed straight to Eldridge Street to buy more dope. If I wasn't working, I would stay high for the rest of the day.

The next morning brought me a moment of clarity.

I opened my eyes and scanned the bedroom. The sun had made its way in where the hanging sheet didn't cover the window. It was hot. I sat up on the edge of the bed in my underwear. The place had become my own private shooting gallery.

I dropped my face into my hands. My world was getting smaller and smaller. I had used up most of the people in my life who cared about me. One thing was certain—my right leg was becoming restless, and I had to go get straight. I jumped in the shower, threw on the cleanest clothes I could find, and hurried out the door. I was down to my last $100. I made a left on Second Avenue, and that was when the moment of clarity hit me.

"Cabby, cabby," I yelled at the sea of yellow cabs whipping by. One pulled over, and I slid in. "Metropolitan Hospital on Ninety-Sixth Street and First Avenue," I yelled to the cab driver. I had heard that they had a detox for heroin there, and I could feel the walls starting to close in on me. It was time to at least try to get off the stuff.

I walked into the hospital and was sent upstairs to speak to someone in the detox unit.

"How can I help you?" asked the older Black nurse behind the counter.

"Good morning. My name is Robert Carney, and I'd like to get into the detox," I answered.

"Did someone tell you to come in today, or do you have an appointment to speak to someone in intake?"

"No, ma'am. To be honest, I don't even know what I'm doing here. I have $90 burning a hole in my pocket, and it's taken everything in me to just get here instead of going to cop dope this morning."

"Okay, young man, relax. You're in the right place. Have a seat over there, and I'll have the doctor talk with you in a few minutes."

I sat in the orange plastic chair, stared at the clock, and kneaded the top of my restless thigh with my knuckles.

"Mr. Carney, come in and have a seat," said the older doctor, who was tall, with glasses and big, bushy gray eyebrows. He reminded me of a tall Groucho Marx, but I was in no mood to laugh or even smile.

"I heard you guys had a detox here, and I'd really like to get off the heroin," I answered.

He sat down in his long white jacket, crossed his knees, and placed his entwined fingers over his top knee.

"How old are you, Mr. Carney?"

"I'm nineteen," I replied, with a shrug.

"How long have you been using heroin?"

"About a year now, but every day these past few months."

"Do you sniff or inject it?"

"Inject it." I pulled up my sleeve.

"Where do you buy your heroin, Mr. Carney?"

"On the Lower East Side, Doc."

"When you heat it up in the water, does it turn light red?"

"Yes, it does."

"Well sure enough, you have a heroin habit, Mr. Carney. We've heard about the heroin down there, and it's extremely potent, which has caused a lot of overdoses. We just got a free bed, so we'll admit you today. You can expect to be here for a couple of weeks."

"Thanks, Doc," I said as the nurse unlocked the door to the detox ward and led me in, locking the door behind her. A wave of relief fell over me. *Maybe this is it. Maybe there is a way out.*

I followed the nurse to a room I would be sharing with another guy, who was sleeping at the time. She handed me a set of light-blue hospital pajamas, a robe, and a pair of orange Styrofoam slippers in a clear plastic bag. She also handed me a plastic bag of toiletries so that I could brush my teeth, wash, and shave.

"Your family or friends can drop stuff off at the front desk for you. Stuff like books, cigarettes, or sweats and T-shirts to wear while you're here," said the old Black nurse in a soothing voice.

"Thank you," I replied. "I have an aunt and some cousins nearby, so I'll do that. I hate to ask, but I haven't had anything since last night, and I'm starting to get sick. Do you know when I'll get medicated?"

"They'll be giving out medication in about an hour, so just hang in there, okay?" She said softly, looking at me with sad eyes.

I changed into my hospital pajamas and slippers and sat in the main room next to the medication window. One hour and eight minutes later, the wait was over.

"Medication time," yelled the nurse. All the patients in the detox ward came out of their rooms and shuffled up to the medication window. I was second in line. I glanced at the other patients in line, and it was a mixed crowd, for sure. I counted thirteen patients, eight men and five women, any-where from eighteen to sixty, but mostly in their twenties and thirties, Blacks, Whites, and Latinos. It was obvious that alcohol and drugs do not discriminate. I was next in line for meds.

"Name?" asked the White middle-aged male nurse.

"Robert Carney," I replied anxiously.

"Hmmm," he murmured, as he scanned the chart for my name. My eyes widened as I watched his every move. *I'll have to get out of here and get straight if they can't help me.*

"Carney, Carney ... Okay, there you are." He handed me a small paper cup with orange liquid in it and a second cup with two blue pills in it. "These pills are to calm your nerves, and the methadone will help with your heroin withdrawal. Drink up."

I swallowed the bitter-tasting methadone, followed by the pills.

The medication window was in the back of the main room, which had two black leather couches and a dozen colored plastic chairs to sit in, along with a television sitting high along the front wall. After everyone had taken their meds, most of the patients made their way to the couches and chairs and lit up cigarettes. I went and sat in one of the empty plastic chairs.

"Yo, my man, when did you get here, and haven't I seen you around Fourth and B Street, copping?" a young Puerto Rican guy said as he lit up a cigarette.

"I just got in an hour ago, and yeah, I cop on Fourth and B, but mostly on Eldridge Street. You look familiar too. Can I bum one of those smokes off you? They held on to my open pack when I came in."

"Sure." He handed me a cigarette. "If you can spit those blue pills out without the nurse catching you, that White chick over there with the blond hair will give you a pack of smokes for them. Her name is Sue. I know her from the street. She's crazy and she got money. Anyway, my name is Pablo." He stuck his hand out.

"Thanks for the smoke, Pablo. I'm Robby." I shook his hand, then scanned the room, and Pablo gave me a rundown on all the patients there. A wave of warmth came over me as the methadone and valium kicked in. My restless leg relaxed, and my shoulders dropped as the stress and tension melted away. It wasn't a shot of dope, but the methadone was doing the trick. I had never done it before, and the nurse said they would start me on a high dose and wean me off it before I was released.

I called my cousin Paddy, who lived with my aunt Francis and six other siblings on Ninety-Third Street and Second Avenue. Aunt Fran was my mother's sister who had gone through foster care with her. Of all my cousins, Paddy and I had gotten along the best and we would party sometimes. He was an Ironworker and union guy. He liked to party too, but he stayed away from the hard stuff, and unlike me, he hadn't crossed that line yet and could stop when the party was over. I still hadn't burned that bridge in my relationship with him yet, and would do my best not to.

I called Paddy from the social worker's office, and he came to visit me. He brought me a carton of smokes, some underwear, sweats, and flip-flops. The nurse had led me into the conference room just outside the locked detox ward. There was cousin Paddy, sitting at the long conference table by himself with a big smile on his face. His red afro, big nose, and thick glasses only added to his always-funny demeanor.

"What's up, cuz? You okay?" he asked with half a grin.

I shuffled over to him in my hospital pajamas, robe, and Styrofoam slippers. We hugged and patted each other on the back. Paddy wasn't used to seeing me like this. I was always his tough cousin from the Bronx. We were either drinking, gambling, or hanging out with his friends in the bars on the Upper East Side and getting into fights with guys from other neighborhoods.

I sat down at the conference table across from him. I could hardly look him in the eye. I was clearly broken.

"What happened to you, and why is the ward you're in locked down?"

"Everyone in there is detoxing from alcohol or one drug or another, so they don't want you to just walk out. If you want to leave, they want you to talk to a doctor first."

"Can you leave anytime?"

"Yes," I answered.

"Then get your shit and let's go. You don't have to stay here. I got you."

"Thanks, cuz, but I gotta stay here for now. I've been messing with heroin for about a year now. The reason I haven't been around for the last six months is because I've been getting high every day. I'm strung out. If I leave now with you, I'm afraid I'll go right back on it. Besides, I literally have nowhere to go." I looked down at the long wooden table.

Paddy's usual witty, sarcastic humor went silent. He leaned on the table and looked me in the eyes. "Listen, cuz, don't worry about anything. Stay here until you feel you're ready to leave. If you need anything, just call me. I bought you some smokes, clothes, and toiletries."

"Thanks, Paddy," I said quietly.

He looked across the table at me, and his eyes came alive and that big grin appeared. "You call me when you're getting out of here, and we'll get you set up. I got some money put away, and I can always borrow some money from Bobby G. He owns the after-hours club on Fifty-Eighth Street, and he lives in our building. We're good friends. You don't worry about a thing. You're a good worker and hustler. You'll be back on your feet in no time."

I stood and gave him a hug, then he went off, and I shuffled back into the detox ward.

It was like that with my long battle with drugs and alcohol. When things would get really bad and I had nowhere left to turn, I would say a foxhole prayer and try to get myself off the street and get some help. Help would always appear. God would send his angels in many different forms. Looking back, I can clearly see that now.

It had been three weeks since I entered Metropolitan Hospital to detox, and my time there was complete. They had started me on a high dose of methadone and slowly brought me down to almost nothing. I was feeling awake, alive, and full of energy. It felt good to feel human again. Myself and two other patients, Darryl and Clarence, were waiting outside the social worker's office to talk with her and get released from the hospital. Clarence and Darryl knew each other from Harlem and had gone through the detox before. Clarence was in his thirties and dressed sharply, silk sharkskin slacks, alpaca sweater, and black suede shoes. Apparently he was a dealer who liked to test his product too often, but he was always a gentleman and respectful to me during our stay in detox. The same for Darryl, who was an old-time dope fiend, and a good guy who would give you the shirt off his back, if he wasn't getting high. Darryl had track marks from shooting up on his arms, legs, hands, neck, and any visible part of his body. He had been in the game a long time. We waited patiently for the social worker.

"Where are you going from here, Robby?" Darryl asked.

"I'm not really sure. I've burned most of my bridges, but I do have a cousin here in Yorkville that offered to help me if I needed it. I might give him a call. Where are you guys off to?"

"We're off to welfare. If you get on the methadone program, they automatically get you a place to live and pay the rent, give you food stamps, and a check for about $150 every month," Darryl answered with a straight face.

"No fucking way," I replied. "What if I don't want to be on the methadone program?"

"Then you can't get on welfare." Darryl added, "All you have to do is get on the program. It doesn't mean you have to take it. You show up at the methadone program here every morning, drink the methadone in front of the nurse, but don't swallow it, then walk out the door and spit it back in a small bottle. Depending on how many milligrams you build up to, you can get $30 to $60 a day for it. You make out all around," he said, smiling.

"Man, you guys got the system down. If you don't mind, I'll tag along with you to welfare after I let the social worker know I want to get on the methadone program."

"Sure, white boy, we'll show you the ropes. By this afternoon you'll have $150, food stamps, a dirty single-room occupancy to live in, and you'll be buzzed on the forty milligrams of methadone they start you off with." Clarence laughed.

Darryl was right on all four counts, and I did have to take the methadone that morning and was pretty high for the day. So much for feeling energetic and alive again. I went to welfare and got the check for $150 and the food stamps, and they sent me over to Ninety-Fifth Street and West End Avenue to a single-room occupancy welfare building. The room was no bigger than any cell I had ever been in. There was a single bed and a dresser and a shared bathroom down the hall. I sat on the bed for a second and watched a roach appear from behind the dresser and climb up the wall.

I never did spend one night in that room, but I did go down to the hotel once a month to pick up my check and food stamps. I sold the methadone for about six months to a beautiful, dear friend of mine. Sometimes she had the money and sometimes she didn't. She was trying to stay off the heroin herself. I watched the drugs transform her over the years. She used to be such a beautiful young woman, but she never lost the sparkle in her eye or her good heart.

I moved up to Inwood in upper Manhattan, where I had some friends. I managed to stay off the heroin for over a year. I began dealing weed again, in Inwood Hill Park this time. On a Friday night you could find well over one hundred kids hanging out in the park and partying. I had found a new home. Inwood and the people in it had given me a second chance at living any kind of a normal social life, even if it was surrounded by alcohol and drugs. All I had to do was stay away from the needle and drop the tough-guy routine. I found that having people fear you has its advantages, especially in the drug-dealing world, but when someone you know is formulating a list for his girlfriend's birthday party, if you are violent and unpredictable, you are usually not on that list, and life begins to get very lonely, so I toned it down and kept my hands to myself.

23

Zapped

I had just turned nineteen. I was living with my friend Skino and his mom and two younger sisters in Inwood. I was working at a printing shop downtown and selling weed in Inwood Park on the weekends. I was staying off the hard stuff, but I started taking pills, and one weekend when I was high on reds (Seconals), things went bad. I stole a car. I was heading south on Broadway when I saw the blue lights in the rearview mirror. I looked up. I had just passed Twenty-Third Street. I moved over to the next lane in hopes they were trying to get by me, but it was me they were pulling over. I hit the gas, speeding down Broadway, weaving in and out of traffic.

"I think you lost them, Robby," Larry yelled as he clutched the headrest and continued looking out the back of the car window. We had just driven down from Inwood, the northern tip of Manhattan, heading to the Lower East Side for some heroin. The stolen car wasn't supposed to make the hot sheet for another twenty-four hours. It must have been my erratic driving. After all, I had been high on reds (Seconals) and alcohol for two days now. I made a sharp screeching left turn onto Fourteenth Street, heading east toward the FDR Drive. As we sped across Fourteenth Street, I ran a red light at Avenue C and got hit by another car on the passenger side.

The car spun and skidded onto the sidewalk. Two police cars pulled up behind us, lights flashing and sirens blaring.

I opened the driver's door and ran for it. Larry couldn't open the smashed-in passenger door, so he jumped into the backseat and exited the back passenger door, where he was met by a police officer who had drawn his gun.

There was a ten-foot wooden wall about thirty yards from me, the kind you might see around a construction site. I ran straight at it as fast as I could. I heard the cops screaming stop as they chased behind me. When I reached the wooden wall, I ran up it with my right foot first and leaped as high as I could. My fingers just grasped the top of it. I pulled myself up and over. I could hear the cops cursing on the other side.

Once I hit the ground, I looked for an exit. There were power lines and what seemed to be huge generators everywhere. I started running through them, still hearing the cops yelling through the wall.

The next thing I remember, I was lying there on the floor. It felt so comfortable and warm. It was like having to get out of a warm bed on a cold morning when you had to go to school. You still felt tired, and it was cold outside the blankets. It felt so comfortable, you would do anything to just stay there for just a few more minutes. It took everything in me to push myself up off the floor. I stood and looked down at myself. My clothes were burned off, and parts of my body were black. I had been burned badly. I remember walking down some steps and through a door. There was a man behind a counter. He looked at me and was noticeably startled.

"Excuse me. I think I hit a wire," I said calmly, probably in shock. Then I collapsed, and everything went black. I don't know how much time passed, but the next thing I remember was hearing my mother's and Aunt Fran's voices. *Are the lights out? Why are we in total darkness?* I wondered.

"Mom," I mumbled into the darkness.

"Yes, Robert, I'm right here. Aunt Fran is with me. You've been in a very bad accident."

"Well, I know I'm blind, because I can't see anything."

"Your body and face are swollen from all the electricity that went through you. Your eyes are swollen shut."

"Mom, am I going to die?"

"No, you are going to live, but you're in pretty bad shape. Listen to me, Robert. When you get out of this hospital, I want you to find a nice, tall building and jump off it, because they'll only find you dangling from some clothesline. Stop trying to leave us. God is not done with you yet." I could feel her take my hand, then all went quiet.

I awoke from the sound of doctors talking above and around me. I squinted, barely opening my eyes. I could see them in their white coats, standing around my bed.

"This is Mr. Carney, the one I was telling you about. He came in contact with thousands of amps of electricity and survived. He flatlined on us when they first brought him in, but we paddled him back."

I looked at the older doctor talking to the students and tried to form a question, but the doctor began talking before I could.

"Hello, Mr. Carney. You've been in a very bad accident and are lucky to be alive. Do you remember anything?"

"Hi, Doc," I mumbled in a low voice. "I just remember feeling really comfortable lying there and not wanting to get up. I really had to push and force myself to get up off the floor, then I walked into an office and talked to a guy, then blacked out. I remember seeing myself pretty burned up. Then I think I talked to my mother for a minute, then I blacked out. How long have I been here?"

"Just a couple of days, but you have some severe burns from the electricity. Your left hip, inner left arm, a part of your chest, and the inside of your left leg are burned. You'll be with us for a while, but we'll fix you up. You're very lucky, Mr. Carney. There are people who have come through this burn unit that have been hit with a fraction of the electricity that went through you, and have either not made it or lost limbs. Yes, someone is looking over you, Mr. Carney."

"Thanks, Doc. I understand," I said.

They all left the room and moved on to the next patient. I lay there alone. I pushed off the sheets and blanket and opened my hospital gown. My twenty-year-old body was a mess. Wherever the electricity entered or exited my body were burns covered in white cream. I would later learn that white cream was Silvadene. Silvadene and morphine would be the only things between me and excruciating pain for the next two months.

They had arrested Larry and held him for two days until court. He was charged with grand theft auto and released. He was later sentenced to probation. They had a cop guarding my room for the first three weeks. They tried to cuff me to the bed, but the doctors wouldn't allow it because of infection, and I really was in no shape to go anywhere.

The hospital staff in that burn unit and some of my friends in Inwood helped me keep my sanity while getting through that ordeal. Skino, my good friend from Inwood, had brought some weed to the hospital, at my request. Skino stepped off the elevator as I wheeled myself out of the room to meet him.

The uniformed cop sat at the end of the hallway near the elevators.

"Who are you here to see?" the cop asked Skino, who was nineteen, stood about six foot, and had blond hair.

"I'm here to see Robby Carney," he answered, looking surprised.

"What's in the bag?"

"Just some cigarettes, candy, and a magazine." Skino opened the plastic bag and showed him.

"All right, put the bag down and stand with your hands up against the wall." Skino set the bag down, put his hands on the wall, and looked sideways at me as I sat in the wheelchair up the hall. My mouth hung open as I raised my hands and shook my head back and forth. I had no idea they were searching my visitors.

The cop patted him down, seemed satisfied, then pointed toward my room.

"What the fuck, bro?" Skino said as he entered my room, laughing.

"I didn't even know they were asking people who they were visiting, never mind frisking them," I answered.

Then he pulled a half ounce of weed out of the front of his jeans, rolled up in a plastic sandwich baggie.

"I flattened it behind my garrison belt or he would have felt it. It's Thai weed. You'll love it. Anyway, I hope this makes things a little easier."

"Thanks, brother. I owe you."

Every four hours I would press that buzzer for my morphine shot. Then I would wheel into the shower room, turn on the shower, and take a few tokes off a joint, then blow it out of the air vent. The weed would amplify the morphine, and I would be stoned for a little while anyway. They would apply the Silvadene three to four times a day. After a few hours the Silvadene began to dry, the air would get to the burns, and I would be in unbearable pain until they applied that white cold cream on me again. Yes, Silvadene was my friend.

After a month of having a cop posted near my room in the burn center, they held a bedside arraignment. They held court right there in the hospital meeting room. I could walk now, so I shuffled into the meeting room in my hospital gown and orange Styrofoam slippers. The judge, district attorney, my court-appointed lawyer, and the court stenographer all sat around the long wooden conference table. I sat next to my lawyer.

He leaned over and whispered, "Just plead guilty to the grand theft auto and illegal trespassing, and you'll get forty-five days time served."

"Sounds good to me."

The Judge and DA agreed I had suffered enough. All went as planned. The court proceeding took about ten minutes.

The judge looked over at me and said a few last words. "Mr. Carney, I hope you realize how fortunate you are to have survived that ordeal, and hopefully you've learned something from it?"

"I certainly have, Your Honor. Thank you." I looked above his head at the clock on the wall. It was 11:15. Only forty-five minutes until my next morphine shot.

Now that I wasn't under police guard, I got a visit from a bunch of the boys from Inwood Park. There were eight or nine guys, so the hospital staff let me use the same meeting room I had the bedside arraignment in. Only now we passed a joint and a bottle of Jack Danels around the conference table. The visit would be cut short because of the noise and smell of the weed.

My second month in the burn unit would take its toll on me. The few visits I'd had stopped, and depression and loneliness set in. I shuffled around the burn unit one Sunday morning. Most patients were getting visits from family and friends. I had traded all my relationships with family and friends for drugs and alcohol. I pushed in the glass folding door of the wooden phone booth on the floor and sat on the wooden seat. I called my mother.

"Hey, Mom."

"Hi, Robert. How are you feeling today?"

"Not so good today, Mom." Then the tears came. I hadn't cried in years, not this tough guy.

"What's wrong?"

"I don't know, but I can't seem to handle this anymore. I don't know what happened to me. I just turned twenty, and I'm in this hospital with my body all burned up. I'm alone and with no place to go when I get out." There was quiet for a minute while my tears fell.

"Don't worry, Robert. I will try to help you when you get out."

"Can I come home, Mom?"

"I can't have you here. Fred won't allow it since you took the money jar, but I'll try and find you a place to stay."

"Thanks, Mom." I hung up the phone and wiped my eyes and nose, then shuffled back to my room.

The next morning I lay staring at the clock outside my room in the hallway. It was 9:45. Only fifteen minutes before they came to get me. The process of skin grafting the badly burned areas of my body had begun. They came for me at 10:00 a.m. promptly. The nurses wheeled me into a room and laid me on a plastic board that lay across a round tub. A shower hose hung above me.

"Good morning, Robby," nurse Andrews whispered., "Do you want your shot now or after we're done?"

"After is fine, because it does nothing for this pain," I answered.

"Okay, we'll give it to you once we get you back to your room. It will help calm you down and relax you. Okay, now off with the robe, and lay on the board please," the nurse said.

I had come to know her and the other young staff well at this point. I believe they got a kick out of me. I'm sure they all knew I was smoking weed in the shower room.

I disrobed and lay naked on the cold plastic board over the tub. I stared up at the shower-head hose that hung above me. The three staff members smiled and said it would be over quickly. Nurse Andrews placed a small piece of rubber between my teeth to bite down on. One staff member held my arms down above my head, and another held my feet down.

"It's very important you try and stay as still as possible," Nurse Andrews said softly as she picked up a pair of surgical scissors and tweezers and stood above my naked, burned body. She then began to cut away at the burned skin on my hip, leg, chest, and the side of my bicep. I screamed as my body tensed up. They put all their weight on my arms and legs so I would remain still. I begged her to stop, then I began to threaten them.

"If you don't stop, I will fucking kill you when this is over. I swear, you and your whole family." Then I let out another scream. Those ten minutes seemed like an eternity. When she grabbed the hose above my head and began washing away the dead skin, I knew she was almost done. She then applied some cold Silvadene cream to the open wounds, and my body began to relax as they loosened their grip on my arms and feet. After a minute I stood up, put my robe on, and sat in the wheelchair. The four of us exited the room together.

"Hey, guys, I'm really sorry about all the cursing and threats. I know it has to be done."

"No worries, Robby. We know you don't mean it. Now let's get you back to your room and give you your shot so you can relax."

This would go on for a week until all the dead skin was removed. If there really is hell filled with pain, I'm sure I have time served. Once that process was complete, they applied pigskin on the open wounds for a few days in place of Silvadene, then they performed the skin graft procedure. They put me under, then took skin from my right thigh and patched up my left hip, arm, leg, and chest area. I walked out of New York hospital two weeks after the skin graft procedure, two months after I was electrocuted.

My mother set me up in a studio apartment a block from her house in Brooklyn. She really tried to help me. Two weeks later I felt good enough to party and went up to Inwood for a night out. I would end up getting drunk, high, and stealing a car that night. It ran out of gas at 7:00 a.m. on the Fordham Road bridge the next morning. I walked away. That would be my last grand theft auto. My physical wounds would finally heal, but my emotional and spiritual wounds had a ways to go.

I found a second home and friends that would last a lifetime. Inwood Hill Park covers the tip of Manhattan and spans to the Hudson River. You would almost not know you were in New York City, and the people were just as beautiful.

As hard as I tried, with all my great plans, I could never get it together in Inwood, where I could have my own place. I worked on and off with moving companies and printing shops and selling nickel bags in the park at night and all summer long. I was always staying with someone for a while until I got on my feet. My good friend Skino (everybody had a nickname in Inwood) shared his room at home with me for a year or more. He had two single beds, and we shared a dresser. When he heard I had nowhere to stay, he said no problem and brought me home. He lived with his mom, Rita, and two sisters, Chrissy and Carey. They treated me like family. All Rita wanted was $35 a week, and sometimes I couldn't pay that on time. I lived on and off with friends and girlfriends for years in Inwood. Of all the years I hung out in Inwood without my own place, I never spent a night on the street.

I put the needle down but was selling and smoking weed on a daily basis again, then the pills came along, but the killer was the weekends at the neighborhood bars. It was the late seventies, the bars were hopping, the music was blasting, and the dance floors were packed. The beer and liquor flowed, and everyone was doing blow, including me. The party would start Friday night at the Sloop and end Sunday night at Gary Owen's after a softball game, with me wondering what happened to all my money again. One thing is for sure about Inwood—it was a partying neighborhood.

I was heading into work early one Saturday morning at a print shop on Eighteenth Street and Fifth Avenue, to get some overtime. I was early, so I stopped in Union Square park to smoke a joint with my coffee before work. There was an older Black gentleman sitting on the park bench across from me, having his coffee and reading the paper. I noticed from the lettering on his shirt that he worked for a printing company.

"Good morning. What kind of press do you run?" I asked.

"The 2650 Multilith." Then asked, "How about yourself?"

"The 1250 Multilith," I answered, then raised the joint and offered him some.

"Sure." He joined me on the park bench. It was a gray and cloudy morning as we sat on this wooden bench in this sea of grass and trees, surrounded by concrete buildings, sidewalks, black paved streets, cars, and noisy traffic.

"The weed is pretty good," he said.

"I have a few nickels on me, if you're looking."

"Sure. I'll take a bag." He handed me a five-dollar bill. We talked about the printing companies we worked for and different printing presses we'd worked on, then the topic turned to drugs and I told him how I'd just got over the heroin addiction.

"You seem like a nice young man with a good head on your shoulders," said the older Black man. "But I do have one piece of advice for you. Whatever you do, don't ever, and I mean ever, shoot cocaine." By the sound of his voice and the look in his eyes, I felt every word and knew he meant it with all his heart. "Tried it when I was a little older than you are now, and boy, I surely let the devil in. The cost of my relationship with that drug and the needle has cost me any chance of having a family, any real friends, any chance at a real life, and my mind is consumed with thoughts of using. So heed my warning, boy, and stay clear of it."

"Yes, sir, I certainly will, and thank you for the warning." I hopped off the bench and down the stone steps to the sidewalk and off to work.

God had sent me an angel to warn me, but the day soon came, and I let the devil in.

I started doing heroin again but became obsessed with the rush from shooting cocaine. Just like the old man said, it took over everything, especially my mind. Lying, cheating, and stealing had become an everyday occurrence. It would not be long before the inevitable. I would be up for a couple of days shooting coke and dope and run out of money, then become desperate enough to commit an armed robbery, for which I would serve five of a twelve-year prison sentence.

Part Three: Corrections

24

6 Block

"On the chow," yelled the CO, followed by a loud clang as the long tier of cell doors slid open. I stepped out of my cell and immediately went on high alert, while appearing as cool and calm as a White guy in Rikers Island could be. *Show no fear, baby—that's the name of the game in this place.* Six Block is one huge concrete and steel jungle, broken into A and B sides, three tiers high and forty cells to a tier. A metal staircase divided the block in half, twenty cells on either side of the staircase. There was another staircase at the front of the block. The guard booth was just outside the metal bars at the front of the block. My cell was on the second tier in the back of the block.

I looked down off the tier as we all walked toward the staircase, then down the stairs to the flats and up to the front of the block to the dayroom for breakfast. I picked up a plastic tray and was handed a metal spoon by the CO, which I would have to produce and drop in a metal bucket in front of the CO as I exited the dayroom. Down the line I went as my fellow inmates served us breakfast. These inmates worked on the house gang, where they served food, swept, and mopped the cellblock. Each house gang member would be assigned a certain job by the house gang corrections officer. If you worked on the house gang, the jail paid you a small stipend, maybe $20 a month, that would go on your books to be used to purchase commissary (smokes, snacks, toiletries) every two weeks. If you were fortunate enough, you had family or friends who would send you money to be put on your books.

The Blacks had the house gang sewed up. Which meant they could look out for their homeboys if they were serving something good for chow. I got on the house gang at one point and was the token White boy. I heard some crap from the White guys for doing that, but once they saw I would look out for them on the chow line, and that I managed to stash commercial-size cans of peanut butter, jelly, and some bread for snacks at night, was when the talk of being the only White guy on the house gang stopped.

Breakfast that morning consisted of a small box of cereal, a banana, and a couple of slices of bread with butter and jelly. It did the trick, and I was grateful to have an appetite back. It had been a few months since I had gotten busted and landed in the Men's House of Detention on Rikers Island, also known as The Blocks. The physical craving for heroin had been gone for a while now, and I was starting to feel human again. The mental obsession for heroin and cocaine, however, would take much longer.

I finished breakfast, cleared my tray, and dropped my spoon into the metal pail. The overweight, red-faced CO stood in his blue uniform and nodded as the spoon clanged into the metal pail. I exited the dayroom and walked through the crowd of inmates gathering on the flats after breakfast. I was always aware of my immediate surroundings. They had already carried three inmates out of this block recently, so I knew shit could pop off any second.

Heading back to my cell, I nodded to a couple of the White guys in the block—we were the obvious minority and stood out. The jail population was 60 percent Black, 30 percent Latino, and 10 percent White. We had a few more White guys in our block than most, so we tried to look out for each other and stay together.

"On the count" bellowed out of the loudspeakers mounted throughout the walls of the block. This meant get back to your cell and get locked in until the head count was cleared. They did this four times a day, and it usually took a half hour. After the count cleared, the cell doors slid open with a clang, and I headed to the dayroom to get a morning workout with one of the White guys, Anthony. The dayroom was used three times a day to feed us. The large room with its fifteen metal picnic tables was also used to play cards, do some push-ups and sit-ups, or just hang out in between meals.

There were also four metal picnic tables on the flats, two in the front of the block and two in the middle of the block. A television hung in front of both sets of metal tables. The Latinos had control of the television in the front of the block, and the Blacks controlled the television in the middle. There were no signs up; it's just the way it was. If I watched any TV, it was with the Blacks, because it was in English, and I stood back behind the benches.

Anthony and I worked out for a good hour, push-ups, sit-ups, and dips off the metal bench. He was a young Italian guy from Brooklyn in his mid-twenties. Anthony was a straight-up dope fiend, and a young crazy dude. He had just gotten out a month ago and was back again. He had lost about twenty pounds and was trying to eat, work out, and bulk up. Anthony was short, like me, about five foot seven, but after being locked up for a few months, he would bulk up pretty good. He had just gotten arrested again a week ago.

We finished working out.

"Anthony, how long were you out this time?"

"Not long, just a few weeks. I had some bad luck."

"What did you do when you got out a month ago?" I asked.

"As soon as the bus crossed the bridge and let me off in Queens, I walked into the neighborhood, found a house where no one was home, kicked the door in, and robbed it. It was a pretty good score too. I got some cash, a gun, and a shitload of jewelry."

"How did you know nobody was home?"

"I knocked first," he answered matter of factly, then we both cracked up.

We left the dayroom, and I headed back to my cell to get ready to shower. Anthony stopped to talk to Midtown Manny. Manny was the oldest of us ten White guys in 6 Block. He was in his late forties and had been in and out of these places his whole life. Just another dope fiend who hadn't died yet. He was about five foot ten and skinny, with a chiseled face. He had long black hair and a thick mustache. Manny was from Hell's Kitchen on the westside of Manhattan, and he knew his way around Rikers Island. If you had any questions about what was on Rikers, he was the guy to ask.

The shower room was located at the front of the block. The door to the shower room was right next to the phone line. There were two phones just outside the bars at the front of the block. A house gang member ran the phones. You were allowed five minutes per call, unless you were friends with the guy running the phones. There were always two lines of guys waiting in the phone line along the shower room door, maybe five to ten guys on each line.

In my cell I gathered up my plastic soap dish, shampoo, and towel. Still in my gym shorts and T-shirt and now my shower slippers, I walked down the metal stairs and along the concrete flats, through the guys on the phone line, and into the shower room. The heavy metal door closed behind me. I put my stuff down on the concrete bench, stripped, grabbed my soap and shampoo, then walked into the shower area and turned on one of the six showers. I was alone in the shower room. I looked over and could see the outline of a face peering through the small wired metal window in the shower room door. Then there were some whistles and kissing sounds you might hear when a woman walks by a construction site in the city. I made a mental note to remember who was on the phone line when I walked into the shower room.

I finished showering, dried off, and put on some clean shorts and a T-shirt, then gathered up my stuff and started back to my cell. As I walked out of the shower room, I noticed one of the White guys on my tier was waiting in the phone line. Johnny B., a guy from Staten Island in his mid-thirties. He was heavyset, stood about six feet tall, and had blue eyes and a crew cut. I heard some Blacks refer to him as the Blue-Eyed Devil. John had just copped out to fifteen years to life for a murder. Johnny was yet another dope fiend just trying to get a fix. He was a burglar, and during his last burglary, the homeowner's son came home and walked in on him. Things went south quickly, and Johnny stabbed him, ending up here with a murder rap. He seemed to handle the fifteen-to-life murder rap well and was just waiting to go upstate now.

I climbed the metal steps up to the second tier and entered my open cell. I put my shower stuff down on the small metal table and hung the wet towel off the empty top bunk, then I kicked off my shower slippers and put on my socks and sneakers. I reached over the bottom bunk and ran my fingers under and along the back of it. There was a quarter-inch space that ran around the edge of the metal bunk bed. It was there that I hid my homemade shank.

I had broken one of the ten-inch metal slats off an air-conditioning vent in one of the bullpens on Rikers, coming back from court one day. I'd bent it in half to make it more sturdy, then sharpened it to a point on the concrete floor of my cell. I pulled a long strip off the edge of my bed sheet and wrapped it tightly around the bottom of the shank to make a handle that would fit tightly in that space around the edge of the bunk bed.

I stood in my cell, staring at the shank in my hand, knowing what I had to do. Making those kissing noises and whistling at me in the shower would not go unnoticed, or my reaction to it. While in the shower would not have been a good time to react, but now I was prepared. I slid the blade down the slit I'd made in that strip of cloth in front of my zipper in my denim shorts, so only the handle with the sheet wrapped around it was visible. I pulled my T-shirt down over the handle and left my cell to see who was making the noises while I was showering. I saw Johnny coming back from his phone call. I caught his eye, nodded, and approached him.

"Hey, John," I said in a low but clear voice. "Did you see who was making all that noise at the shower door when I was in there?"

"Oh yeah." He nodded toward the metal picnic tables under the television the Blacks watched. I glanced over my shoulder to see a few Black guys sitting on the two tables under the television, *Soul Train* playing on the TV overhead. Four of them sat at one table, and the other sat on top of the second table. They were laughing and singing along to Smokey Robinson's "Just to See Her."

"It was the heavyset Rasta with the dreads and gold teeth, sitting at the first table against the wall."

"Thanks, John."

"Are you good?" John asked.

"Oh yeah, I got this." I turned and walked toward the middle of the block, stopped, and took a few deep breaths, then walked directly over to the television and tables. I stopped between the first and second table and looked directly at Mr. Gold Teeth. They stopped laughing and singing and looked up at me. There I stood, this skinny White boy who was five foot seven and weighed 150 pounds, with brown hair, too long for this place.

"How are you?" I asked Mr. Gold Teeth, with a smile. "Are you the one that was making all those kissing and whistling noises when I was in the shower earlier?"

"Ya, mon, that was me." He smiled, eyeing me up and down.

"Do you want to kiss me?"

"Ya, mon," Gold Teeth replied with a big smile, while the other four sat there quietly.

"I'll tell you what, kiss this, motherfucker." I lifted my T-shirt, grabbed the handle of the shank, and with two long steps, I was behind him with a handful of dreadlocks in my left hand, pulling him backward, his legs caught under the metal table. Blood spurted from his arms as he tried to ward off the stabs. He thwarted my third thrust with the shank with his arms, and it hit the metal table and bent. He let out a blood-curdling scream as he pulled himself under the table and crawled out the other side. He got to his feet and ran to the front of the block, bleeding from his arms and screaming through the bars for the COs to open the gate, that someone was trying to kill him.

I stood there with the bent shank in my hand and a handful of dreadlocks in the other, blood splatter on my T-shirt and shorts. The other four guys had scattered after the stabbing started. The flats had become deserted in an instant. I shook his hair from my hand and slowly walked to the staircase in the middle of the block. I ran up one flight of stairs and dropped the shank down an opening between the two sides of the block. It was a space that housed the mechanics who opened and closed the cell doors. Then I ran up the second set of steps to the first tier and made a right toward my cell. I looked off the tier at the empty flats and the blood splatter on the floor and table just below me. I walked in my cell and sat on my bunk, waiting for the COs to come and get me and march me out of the block in cuffs.

Midtown Manny stuck his head in my cell. "Are you good?"

"Yeah," nodding my head up and down.

"I'll be right back," he said. "Take those bloody shorts and shirt off." He returned in less than a minute with a paper bag.

"Give me those clothes, then wash up and put some clean clothes on."

I did as he said. He stuffed the bloody clothes in the bag and walked toward the stairs in the middle of the block. A few seconds later a loud voice came over the speakers in the cellblock.

"All inmates return to your cells. Six Block is locked down until further notice" echoed throughout the block. Whenever there was an incident or any violence, the COs would lock everyone in their cells until they sorted it out and things calmed down. Midtown Manny had returned from the stairwell empty handed. He glanced into my cell as he passed and put his index finger in front of his lips to say "Shhh," then pushed both palms toward the floor to let me know to just stay quiet and try to relax. He then walked toward his cell to lock in. Within a minute the sound of metal hitting metal clanged and the cell doors slid across and slammed shut.

I sat there quietly, waiting for only my cell door to slide open and the COs to come rushing in, cuff me, and march me out of the cellblock. The minutes turned into an hour, and still nothing. I sat there wondering what would have happened if the shank didn't bend and I killed him. I could have expected to spend the next twenty to twenty-five years in prison. I would be out by the time I was forty or forty-five, so I would still have some time left. I could also end up spending the rest of my life in these joints. After all, this was where the tough guys usually ended up. The hour turned into two hours, then three.

The loud clang of the cell doors startled me. "On the chow" bellowed throughout the cellblock as the doors slid open. I stepped out of my cell and looked up and down the tier. Everything looked okay. I blended in with the crowd of inmates and headed down the stairs and up to the dayroom for dinner. Walking into the dayroom, I picked up a plastic tray and was handed a fork by the CO at the door, then I moved to the chow line. I did notice that I had about two feet of space in front of me and behind me in the chow line. I glanced around the dayroom and could see some of the inmates whispering to one another and nodding in my direction.

I sat with a few of the White guys to eat.

Midtown Manny sat next to me. He looked straight ahead and spoke in a low voice. "I think you're good. If they haven't come for you yet, they're probably not coming." He stared straight ahead and then down at his food.

At least Gold Teeth didn't rat on me, but I will definitely have to watch my back for a while.

25

4 to 12

Finally, after ten months in Rikers Island and back and forth to court, I had to file my plea.

"To the count of forcible theft armed with a deadly weapon, how do you plead, Mr. Carney?" the judge asked.

I looked over at my court-appointed lawyer, this young, short, curly-haired Jewish guy, and he shrugged and nodded yes.

"Guilty." I looked down at the stack of overstuffed white folders on the table in front of us. I peered back over my right shoulder and searched for the cab driver I had robbed. Our eyes met. He was an older White gentleman standing next to his wife in the third row. "I'm really sorry," I said, waiting for a response. There was none, just a cold, blank stare. I hung my head and looked back at the judge.

"You are hereby sentenced to four to twelve years in the New York State Prison," the judge said sternly. The court officers then approached the table to cuff me and bring me back to the bullpens to await transport back to Rikers Island.

"Take care of yourself," my court-appointed lawyer said as he stuffed his briefcase with the white folders on the table.

I nodded goodbye to him as they led me back to the cells.

Within a week I was bused up to Ossining Correctional Facility, also known as Sing Sing. The transition from county jail to state prison was quick and to the point. On arrival at Sing Sing, we were taken directly to the barber shop.

"Can you crop the top and give me a short fade on the sides and back?" I asked the inmate with the buzz cutter in his hand.

"Sure." He laughed. "Would you like a shave with that?"

"Let's move it along," said the CO, standing in the doorway. There were six barber chairs, and each was full with guys who came from Rikers with me. There were about twenty of us. The six inmates with the buzz cutters in their hands went to work, and everyone got a crew cut.

In the next room, we were given our state greens, three pairs of underwear and socks, along with new black leather state boots. I moved through the line, told the COs my sizes, then stood to the side, holding my new state wear. The green button-down, short-sleeve shirt bore my name, R. Carney, and my new state number, 81A1964. Later, all the old inmate dope fiends would tell me that 1964 was a good year for heroin.

At the next station, we had to give up all our personal clothes. The CO handed me a brown paper bag with my name and number on it and told me to strip and put everything in the bag. Then naked, we were taken three at a time into the next room and told to stand on these twelve-by-twelve wooden blocks in the middle of the room. I was one of the first three.

"Cover your mouth and nose, and close your eyes when I spray you down with this bug and lice killer. Then wait five minutes until I tell you to hit the shower behind you, then put your new greens on," said the uniformed CO as he sprayed down the first inmate to the right of me.

I looked around as I stood naked on that small wooden block with my new crew cut. There were COs walking around everywhere, giving out clothes, handing out paper bags, both men and women COs, while we stood there on display waiting to be sprayed down with bug spray.

"Here we go," said the young CO. I covered my mouth and nose and closed my eyes as I was covered with the smelly, cold, wet liquid spray. When he finished spaying, I stood on the wooden block for what seemed like an eternity. *Okay, this is it. I've been stripped of everything–no hair, clothes, friends, family, weapons, drugs, money, reputation, nothing. It's just me now. It's time to find out what I'm made of. God help me.*

I spent the next two weeks in Sing Sing, then I was shipped to Downstate Correctional Facility to be classified. There are three types of prisons: maximum, medium, and minimum. Downstate is where they decide which type of prison to send you to.

Downstate was much stricter than Sing Sing. You spent much of your time in your cell. Whenever you locked out for meals, you marched two by two in silence from the cellblock to the chow hall and back. Downstate was a newer, modern prison. There were no bars. The cellblock consisted of three cells to a landing. Up one set of stairs and down one set of stairs to each landing. There were maybe six landings to a cellblock, and the CO sat behind a thick window, where he controlled the cell doors on the middle landing.

During my six to eight weeks at Downstate, my head cleared. Going from county jail (Rikers) to state prison was a big change. There were plenty of drugs on Rikers Island, and I'd gotten high when I could. I would buy heroin with postal money orders that I asked people to send me for commissary, or buy a joint for three packs of cigarettes. If you had money or plenty of commissary, you could get whatever you wanted in Rikers, but you also had to watch your back all the time. If there was drugs, there was violence.

Being away from the drugs and the violence, I began working out in my cell every day and reading any books I could get my hands on. I even began writing letters to the few friends I felt I had left. I sat on the edge of my bunk between push-ups and sit-ups and thought of where my life was going. I was twenty-one years old.

I tried to keep my nose clean while I was in Downstate, in hopes of getting classified medium security so I would end up in a place with just a fence around it and closer to the city, in case someone wanted to visit me.

Every Saturday was GI day, which meant the COs did a general inspection of all cells, and everything had to be clean and tight. When we returned from chow on Saturday morning, the cells were left open for an hour so that the upstairs and downstairs landings could each share a broom and mop and mop bucket to sweep and mop our cells out. Everyone on our landing had swept, and we were waiting on the mop bucket. We had fifteen minutes left, so I went down to get it.

"Hey, guys, we're running out of time, so I'm gonna grab the mop and bucket for our cells upstairs," I said as I walked down the second set of eight steps to their landing. The mop bucket sat in the middle of the landing, not being used.

"Yo, my man, I'm not done with it yet," the young Puerto Rican said, whom I recognized from Rikers. He was part of a small crew of guys who would prey on any new guys coming in, if they had jewelry or anything of value on them. They would beat or stab them if they didn't give it up. I saw one guy they went after jump off the third tier and run up to the gate. I don't know how he survived the jump.

"Well, use the mop now, and I'll wait for it. We're running out of time," I said.

"Fuck that. I'll mop it when I'm ready."

"I don't think so." I went to grab the mop bucket.

He stepped out of his cell and smacked my hand away. I looked up the stairs to where the CO sat behind the glass. He was watching everything. I landed four quick shots to the Puerto Rican's head and face. The first shot to the temple knocked him out, and the next three shots held him up. He leaned back against the wall and slid down to the floor. I looked to the right, and the CO had made it to the top of the stairs. I took a step back and raised both hands over my head, then turned around and put them behind my back to be cuffed. My impolite friend lay there bleeding from the top of his left eye and mouth.

The CO cuffed me and locked me in my cell. I remained in my cell for the next few days, and they slid my food under the door. I was then brought before the Adjustment Committee. There were four higher-ranking COs, in white shirts, who sat behind a long table and decided your punishment for breaking the rules.

"Have a seat, Mr. Cooney," one of the white shirts said.

"That's Carney," I replied as I sat down.

"That's not what we heard," replied the lieutenant, as all four white shirts laughed. It then occurred to me that Gerry Cooney would be fighting for the Heavyweight Championship that year, 1982. Once again I would be praised for my act of violence, only to pay dire consequences later.

The guy I had the problem with was brought to an outside hospital and received stitches over his left eye. I got ten days locked in my cell. At the end of the ten days, I was scheduled to meet with the prison counselor to find out how I was classified. I was escorted to the counselor's office and told to take a seat. The prison counselor wore civilian clothes and was a short, balding man in his fifties.

"Good morning, Mr. Carney. How are you today?" he asked.

"I'm okay, but curious as to what I was classified."

"What do you think we classified you, Mr. Carney?"

"Since it's my first felony conviction, I would think you classified me medium security."

"Max A, Mr. Carney."

"Really?"

"Oh yeah, but don't you worry. You'll handle yourself just fine up there," he said with a slight snicker.

The CO escorted me back to my cell.

Max A security meant walls and gun towers, steel bars and concrete, the worst of the worst, from murderers on down. I would have to call on all my survival instincts, street smarts, and courage to make it through where I was going. My biggest fear was that I would have to kill someone in there to survive, and never get out. I hadn't asked God for help yet.

Three days after I was classified, my cell door slid open, and the CO stuck his head in.

"Pack it up, Carney. You're heading up north today."

"Do you know where I'm going?"

"You'll find out when you get there. Now let's move it," he barked.

I put whatever little stuff I had in the net bag with my name and number on it and was escorted to a holding cell where a dozen or so inmates waited. Within an hour we were all handcuffed, shackled, and on the prison transport bus. There was plenty of chatter coming from some of my fellow inmates. We had all heard how tough max A prisons were.

"Fuck these state COs," said the Black fellow in the seat in front of me.

"Yeah, these motherfuckers ain't scaring nobody," said another inmate across the aisle. There were a few more mumbles from the back of the bus, about coming from Spanish Harlem and not taking any shit from anybody. I looked up at the two COs sitting beyond the wire mesh at the front of the bus, and they just smiled at each other. I kept my mouth shut and looked out the bus window at the passing cars on the freeway and rainy morning, trying to enjoy the view, not knowing when I would see the outside world again.

A few hours later we exited the freeway and rode along the back-country roads for a couple of miles. The bus finally came to a stop at a guard booth. Beyond the guard booth was a big green perfectly mowed field that led to a huge gray wall with gun towers every couple of hundred feet. There were two big, tall steel doors in the middle of the wall, which as the bus pulled up to, they opened inward. I looked back one last time as the bus rolled through the steel doors and beyond the walls. The inside of the bus went completely silent, except for the CO unlocking the wire mesh gate that separated us.

"Welcome to Great Meadows Correctional Facility, boys, also known as gladiator school." Both officers laughed. "When you get off, line up right alongside the bus, and I will uncuff and unshackle you," he continued.

I had heard about Great Meadows prison and how it was referred to as gladiator school. It was where they would send all the violent felons and fuckups from other prisons.

There were four state COs in their gray uniforms standing at attention off to the side of the bus in front of us, with what looked like long wooden axe handles in front of them, that their hands rested on. They were all over six foot and two hundred pounds. Another CO walked back and forth in front of us, waiting for us to all be unshackled before beginning his speech.

"Welcome to Great Meadows Correctional Facility, gentlemen. Before you take one more step, we're going to get a few things straight right now. You are no longer on Rikers Island. You are in my fucking house now. You will do what you're told, when you're told. When you address myself or any other officer here, you will address us as *sir*. Am I clear?" He went from one inmate to the next, screaming "Am I clear?" six inches from each of our faces.

"Yes, sir," we all replied. Not one peep out of anyone. We were handed our net bags and marched off to our cells. Great Meadows Correctional Facility opened in 1911 and now housed over sixteen hundred inmates. It was much like the blocks on Rikers Island, steel and concrete. All the COs were big, straight faced, and White, unlike Rikers or even Sing Sing. My cell was one of forty on the second tier of a block. Showers were once a week on Thursday evenings. The shower was at the front of the block. The CO opened one cell at a time for your five-minute shower. On my tier I noticed one other White guy, in the front. A big White dude with short blond hair, in his twenties. He was in shape—you could tell he worked out with weights. I kept to myself and was keenly aware of my surroundings at all times. After three days I was allowed to go to the yard after dinner.

The yard was very interesting. On the other side of that big gray wall, it was sectioned off into handball courts. These handball courts were sectioned off by three-inch white lines on the blacktop. The inside of the big gray wall is used to play handball against. These handball courts are also considered real estate. Different ethnic groups from different parts of New York claimed them. There was the Hillbilly Court (White guys from upstate New York); the Puerto Rican Court (guys from Spanish Harlem); the Black Court (Black guys from Harlem and around the city); the Brooklyn Court (mostly White guys from Brooklyn and around the city); the Jamaican Court; etcetera. These particular groups owned these courts, and you were not allowed on them unless you were invited. In fact, if you were walking the yard and stopped at the top of one of these courts, you would be told to keep moving. If you didn't, you would deal with the consequences. This was the newest man on the court's job. If you didn't belong to a court, you walked the yard.

I walked the yard for the first couple of weeks. At this point I had no one sending me any money for commissary. I ran into a friend I had made on Rikers Island a few years earlier. A big Irish fella named James. I remember it was my first trip to Rikers, and I was only there for a few days, but it was on my eighteenth birthday. James had been my cellmate. I'd woken up on my second day there and told James it was my birthday.

"Did you tell the CO it was your birthday?" he asked.

"No, why would I do that?"

"Because if you tell them, they will have a cake for you tonight at chow."

"Really?" I asked him.

"No, I'm just fucking with you. Happy Birthday," and we both had a good laugh. James was a good guy, and we'd watched each other's back on Rikers, and he'd hooked me up with some smokes while I was there. James was six foot one and 250 pounds, with short red hair and a red beard. He reminded me of a large leprechaun. I spotted him a mile away as I walked the yard in Great Meadows.

"James, how are you doing, man?" I stopped to shake his hand.

"I'm doing okay," he said, "but let's keep moving." Apparently we were standing at the top of the Jamaican court. "When did you get here?" He could tell from my crew cut and new greens and boots that I was brand new.

"I got here earlier this week, but they just let me out into the yard yesterday."

"Did they program you yet?"

"No, I haven't spoken to anyone yet."

"Well," he said, "when they set you up with a program, take the typing class. I take sports bets here. Cigarettes are money. You can type up the football tickets for me. I'll pay you a carton a week. Do you have any smokes now?

"No, James, I got nothing."

"Well here, take these for now." He handed me a just-opened pack of Marlboros. "And I'll bring you out a few packs tomorrow to hold you over."

"Thanks, James, I appreciate that."

I saw the counselor a few days later and took typing in the morning and plumbing in the afternoon. James would give me the handwritten games and odds on Tuesday, and

I had until Friday morning to type up as many as I could. The classes were two hours long, and I became a fast typist.

26

The Brooklyn Court

In my third week at Great Meadows, I came back from the yard and locked in for the night. I sat down to write a letter to my sister Donna, when I heard singing coming from the next cell, loud and off-key. The guy in the cell to the left of me had his earphones on and was singing along to a song out loud. There was no way I could write a letter, read, or sleep with that going on. I banged on the steel wall that separated us.

"What's up, man?" a loud voice yelled from the next cell.

"Yeah, I'm trying to write a letter. Could you keep the noise down?" I knew that all the other inmates within earshot could hear us, and that could be bad.

"Yo, Darnell, I don't think he likes your singing, man" came a loud voice from a few cells down.

"Fuck you, white boy. Move to another neighborhood if you don't like it here," Darnell responded.

More laughs and similar remarks came from other nearby cells. I was the only White guy in the back of the tier. I sat on my bunk, shaking my head, then responded.

"I'll tell you what, my man. I don't want to argue with you through the bars because I really can't express myself, so I'll see you in the morning on the lockout."

The laughing and taunting came from many of the surrounding cells now.

"Sounds like that White boy's coming for you, Darnell" came a voice from the tier above us, along with other voices.

"That White boy ain't gonna do nothing but get fucked up," Darnell yelled through the bars of his cell. I sat on my bunk and stayed quiet, and the singing resumed. I knew what I would have to do. One of us would have to go.

I hardly slept that night, and I was up, dressed, and ready to go when the cells opened for breakfast. I stood at my cell door, like a caged bull waiting. As soon as the cell doors clanged and slid open, I rushed out of my cell and into the cell next to me. Darnell was half-dressed and still sitting on his bunk when I rushed in swinging. I didn't give him a chance to get up. He was a tall, thin guy in his thirties. I landed a few good punches, but I was getting punched in the back and head from behind from other inmates. I threw punches wildly, trying not to lose my footing and go down and get stomped. Suddenly a big arm wrapped around my neck from behind and dragged me out of the cell. When I looked up, it was the other White guy from the front of the tier. There was a lot of yelling and screaming, and a crowd was forming outside that cell.

"Look at me," yelled the White guy. "Calm down and start walking down the tier with me toward the steps. The COs are already on their way down here. Don't even look up at them—just keep walking," he said as three of them ran by us with their axe handles in hand. He looked over at me as we headed to the mess hall, and he laughed. "You crazy bastard. What happened?"

"The guy in the cell next to me started singing loudly last night, and I asked him to quiet down. There's no way I could handle that shit every night."

"Me neither. You did the right thing. My name is Billy. Welcome to Great Meadows."

"Thanks, Billy. That cell you ran into was getting crowded." And we both laughed.

That night there was no singing. The following morning Billy waited for me at the front of the tier to go to breakfast.

"Good morning, Robby. How was the singing last night?" Billy asked.

"No singing last night," I answered.

"Good. Listen, I was talking to some of the guys on the Brooklyn Court last night, and I'm inviting you on if you want. We play handball, hang out, bullshit. Come by on the lockout after chow tonight, and I'll introduce you to all the guys."

"Thanks, Billy, I appreciate that." It occurred to me that, unlike the outside world, violence at times could serve me here or get me killed. It was nice to be able to step on the Brooklyn Court and play some handball. Billy introduced me to the cast of characters. It was nice to be around some like-minded fellows. I met with Jimmy the next day and was walking the yard with him.

"Hey, Jimmy, they invited me onto the Brooklyn Court. Do you hang with any of those guys?"

"I know a few of them, and they're okay, but I had a beef with a friend of one of theirs a few years back on Rikers. He turned out to be a snitch, and I caught him in the blocks and whipped his ass good, so I'm not too popular on the Brooklyn Court." He shrugged.

"Really, well, fuck them, Jimmy. I'll walk the yard with you."

"No, Robby, you stay on the Brooklyn Court. There's some good guys on there, and it's good that you're part of a group. I don't come out all the time, mostly to take bets and collect my cigarettes." He laughed.

"All right, Jimmy." I handed him a stack of typed-up betting slips.

I spent over a year in Great Meadows Correctional Facility. Billy and I became good friends, as did Jimmy and me.

One night Billy told me to stay out in the yard for the last go-back, 7:30 to 9:00 p.m., because he had a surprise for me. It was a cold winter night, and we walked the yard.

"Look what I got." He pulled out a joint.

"Nice," I said. "It's been a while for me, almost a year." It was harder to score drugs in prison the farther north you were, and the security in max A was tight. It was harder, but not impossible. We waited until we passed a gun tower, and Billy lit it up.

Billy was in his early twenties and was sentenced to fifteen to life for murder. They said he killed a kid in a Brooklyn Park who was dealing drugs. He was nineteen when that happened. We walked the blacktopped yard and smoked the joint as "Sultans of Swing" by Dire Straits echoed from the speakers along the wall. There were a few guys in the weight yard still working out, the visible cold air blowing out of their mouths and noses as they pumped the steel weights. There was a game of three one three on the basketball courts and a few guys playing handball and talking on their courts.

The music sounded much better after I felt the effects of the joint. The yard looked different, even the lighting, not so menacing and cold. I relaxed for a moment.

"Hey, Billy, I have a question for you."

"What's up, Robby?" he asked with that big grin.

"How do you do it, brother?"

"Do what?"

"You got fifteen to life, and you always walk around with a smile on your face. You're a good guy too. I see you looking out for these new White guys coming in, just like you did for me. How do you stay so positive with all that time?"

"I'm gonna share something with you that stays between us, okay?"

"Sure, Billy, what's up?"

"It doesn't matter now because I'm in it, but I didn't even do this fucking crime," he said, shaking his head. "Before this arrest, the only trouble I was in was a ticket I got for an open container, drinking some beers in the park with my friends."

"Why were you arrested and charged for it?"

"I was in the area of the park when it happened, and a fourteen-year-old kid picked me out of a lineup. It's crazy. I never saw that kid in my life. Check out the picture of my prison ID when I first got here three years ago." His blue eyes had big black rings around them from lack of sleep, and his face was completely drawn in. "After I was sentenced, I couldn't sleep for three weeks straight. I couldn't believe this happened to me."

"Wow, Billy, that's crazy." I stood there stunned.

"My parents have stuck by my side from the beginning, which makes it much easier on me. I got almost four years in, and eleven to go, so I'm just gonna stay positive." He smiled again.

"Not that it matters, Billy, but I believe you. I can tell you don't belong in here. Me, on the other hand, I'm guilty as sin," and we both cracked up.

"On the go-back" blared out of the speakers and echoed throughout the yard. We headed back to our cells.

I spent just over a year in that max A prison. I became friends with Billy and Jimmy and made a few acquaintances with some of the guys on the Brooklyn Court. I played pinochle with three older guys two nights a week in the yard. There was Vinny, Jerry Bones, and Anthony—we played on the bleachers.

I found out that the guys you really had to watch out for were not the big mouths but the quiet and polite guys—they were the real killers. I remember when I first started playing pinochle with these fellas. My pinochle partner, Vinny, asked me a question in the middle of a game.

"So, Robby, tell me, what was your beef and how much time did you get?"

"I did an armed robbery and got four to twelve."

"Ahh, he's just visiting for the weekend, fellas," Joey Bones said, and they all started laughing.

I looked over at Vinny. "How about you, Vinny?"

"Twenty-five to life."

I looked over at Joey Bones and nodded.

"I got eighteen to thirty-six," he said.

Then I looked toward Kyle. An old, quiet, respectful, and kind Irishman.

"I got life, no parole." The old man threw a card down and yelled hearts. I didn't ask them what they did, but I had an idea. I became a decent pinochle player. It's all about signals.

After fourteen months in max A, I was transferred to a medium-security prison in Warwick, New York. I had just over two years to go to the parole board.

27

Penn State to State Pen

The prison transport bus made two stops at other prisons before we arrived at Mid-Orange Correctional Facility. Although I was handcuffed and shackled, being outside the prison walls and catching a glimpse of the outside world, people driving, families traveling together and laughing, if only through the bus window, was exhilarating. The world was still there, only without me.

Once inside the barbed-wire fence, the bus rolled to a stop, and the gate slid closed behind us. Six other inmates and I exited the bus and lined up, and the COs uncuffed and unshackled us. I rubbed my wrists and looked around. This was not what I had become used to. From Rikers Island to Sing Sing, then to Downstate and Great Meadows, there were metal bars, concrete walls, and blacktop. There were no walls here, just tall silver fences you could see through, topped with barbed wire. This place was grass and trees and a small concrete path that led to all the small red brick cottages.

There were twenty or so one-level cottages and a couple of two-story buildings. There was a lake right outside the fence, where half a dozen ducks had just taken flight, causing the still surface of the lake to ripple and the sound of quacking off in the distance. I had been transferred to a medium security prison. I took a nice long breath and let it out slowly.

"Okay, fellas, grab your bag and follow me, and we'll get you processed and assigned a cottage and cubicle," the tall, bearded CO said.

We followed him along the small concrete path. We arrived at one of the cottages, and I was assigned to cottage D, cubicle eleven.

"Hey, Carney," the bearded CO yelled. "You can leave your bag here and go over to J cottage and call your family to let them know where you are."

"Great, where is J cottage?" I asked. The CO walked outside with me and pointed to a cottage up a grassy hill about a quarter mile away.

"When you're done with your call, come back over, and I'll take you to the cottage you're assigned to," he said, then he walked back inside.

I stood outside for a moment by myself, unsure what to do. There was nobody around except me. I had not been alone except when I was locked in a cell, never mind out in the open. It was midmorning, so most inmates were at their morning program. I scanned the grounds, then walked over to J cottage and made my first weekly call home.

Medium security was a big change, especially my sleeping arrangement. I was assigned to D cottage, cubicle eleven. Say what you want about the most violent criminals in max A security prisons, when you are locked in your cell for the night, you could relax, if only for a short while. In these new dorm-style cubicles, you were not locked in, and you were vulnerable when you slept. It took me about two weeks and some yoga to finally get a decent night's sleep.

I met this Italian guy named Tony, whom I had seen standing on his head and doing some other stretches in a room off the gym, in shorts and a T-shirt. He was in his thirties, around five foot ten, and in shape. He had thick black curly hair and always looked like he hadn't shaved in three days. He was part of the pizza connection back in the eighties. They were importing heroin in dough from Italy, which was being transported to pizza shops in New York. Tony was one of the very good fellas I met when I was there. We were standing in line for chow, when he struck up a conversation with me.

"So what joint did you come from?" he asked.

"Great Meadows up in Comstock," I replied.

"Don't they call that place gladiator school?"

"Yes, and for good reason. They send all the fuckups there." I laughed.

"How are you liking it here?" he asked.

"I like it. I can breathe. The only problem I have is sleeping. I'm used to sleeping in a locked cell. This dorm and cubicle thing is gonna take some getting used to."

"I'll tell you what," Tony said. "Come down to that room off the gym tonight after the 6:00 count, and wear something comfortable, like gym shorts and a loose T-shirt. I'll show you some exercises that will help you relax."

And that was my introduction to yoga and a good friendship with Tony. After an hour of holding the stretched poses that Antony showed me, I slept like a baby that night. Yoga was one of the tools I used to help me cope with being locked up for years at a time.

Each cottage in Mid-Orange had about twenty cubicles in a large dorm room, and a few two man and single rooms. The longer you were there, the closer you got to a single room. Medium security was a much more relaxed atmosphere. Most guys just wanted to stay out of trouble, do their remaining time, and get out. I found my small crew of White guys that I ate and worked out with. Every night after the 6:00 count, we would meet at the weight shack and pump some iron. One night we would do arms, then back, legs, etcetera. This big Italian guy, Steve, from Throgs Neck in the Bronx, knew his stuff about body building, and he instructed us. There were four of us: Steve, Kyle—an Irish guy from Yorkville in Manhattan—myself, and Barry from Queens.

I was in Mid-Orange about two months, when I heard about the college program. Mercy College from Dobbs Ferry offered an associate's degree program. They came into the prison at night and taught classes from 6:00 to 8:00 p.m. I thought, *How good would that look at the parole board?* There was a semester just starting, so I enrolled.

I had gotten my GED through the Fortune Society when I was trying to beat the gun charges, so I was eligible to enroll, but my lack of education had me worried. I did well that first semester, two As and two Bs. I began to assert myself and chased the good grades the way I chased the drugs and alcohol. I learned much in the college program, especially about myself. I had taken a creative writing course, and the teacher and I did not see eye to eye on certain topics.

Mr. Cohen was an English teacher from Mercy College, in his late thirties. He was about my height and was slightly pudgy, sporting a ponytail and short beard. He wore jeans, penny loafers, a shirt and tie, and a corduroy jacket most of the time. Mr. Cohen taught English and creative writing.

Mr. Cohen's teaching methods made me uncomfortable. In fact, he held class on Columbus Day, when all the other classes had the day off.

"Good morning, class," he said as he was writing on the board. "In case you're wondering why we're having class today, it's because I don't believe Christopher Columbus was a hero. Oh no, he was no hero, and there's no reason he should be celebrated. When he arrived here the Natives swam out to his boats bearing gifts and welcomed them. He, in turn, butchered them and made slaves of them. No, he was no hero, and the White man would eventually wipe out most of the Natives of this country.

"Is this guy for real?" I whispered to Hector, sitting at the desk next to me. He just shrugged his shoulders and looked puzzled like the rest of us.

Mr. Cohen constantly criticized the White government, as he would say. Because I was the only White guy in the class besides him, I began to take his criticism of the White man personally. Since I was not well equipped educationally, I could not immediately argue his points, but I would do some research during the week and respond during the following class.

"The Blacks and Latinos have the highest unemployment rates because the city and state have a reputation for discriminating against minorities when it comes to hiring," he said once during class, when the subject of employment came up.

I worked in the prison library in the mornings and had the first crack at the city newspapers that came in.

I found an article in the *New York Post* that said that the NYPD was actively seeking minorities to work at desk positions in the precincts, but none would apply. I cut the article out and brought it into class the following week. We spent fifteen minutes debating employment, minorities, and the welfare system during that class. I always tried to do some research before I opened my mouth, and I debated with him when he brought up the cruel and unjust White government, except one particular day.

"Yes, the White man and government have been suppressing the Black man and other minorities for over two hundred years now," he said as he turned from writing our homework on the chalkboard. Once again, I felt his rhetoric about the White man was offensive, and my hand flew up.

"Yes, Mr. Carney?" he asked.

"Yes, Mr. Cohen, may I ask you what you are?"

"What do you mean?"

"I mean, can you describe yourself, Mr. Cohen?"

"Yes. I am a White Jewish male and college English professor. And now I have a question for you, Mr. Carney. Can you tell me what the Bill of Rights is and describe the Declaration of Independence?"

"Well, um"—I coughed—"not right off the top of my head."

"No, you can't, Mr. Carney, and you know why you can't? Because you're ignorant. That's why you're sitting there and I'm standing here," he said in a deep but low voice while looking down on me.

"Oohs" and "ahhs" came from around the room. I felt as if I had been kicked in the stomach and punched in the throat. I had two choices: jump up and snatch him up by the neck, or sit back and sink into my chair because he was right. I sank into my seat. I led with my chin, and I paid for it. As the bell rang and we were leaving the class, I heard it from the other guys.

"You won't be getting any A in this class, Robby," said Davis, a tall older Black guy who also got good grades.

"You'll be lucky to get a passing grade from him, Rob," said Hector, who also does well in school.

That week I got all the information I could dig up in the library on the Bill of Rights and the Declaration of Independence and wrote a paper on each, which I presented to Mr. Cohen the following week. I arrived at class a few minutes early.

"Good evening, Mr. Cohen," I said, then set both papers on his desk and slid them across to him. "I did these papers, each describing the Bill of Rights and the Declaration of Independence. If you have any questions about either, feel free to ask."

He looked at the papers, then up at me. "I'll look them over," he said, then went back to grading papers.

I continued to question most of his liberal political remarks and debate him, but only when I could back it up with intelligent facts, which I had to work for. I also learned that once I let my emotions dictate the debate, or raised my voice or cursed, I'd lost the debate. My fellow felon inmates continued to insist that I would flunk his class, and I was starting to believe them. At the end of the last English class that semester, Mr. Cohen called to me as we were all leaving the class.

"Mr. Carney, may I have a word?"

"Oh shit," Davis said as I stopped in my tracks, then turned and walked back to Mr. Cohen's desk.

"Yes, Mr. Cohen?"

"Mr. Carney, I just wanted to let you know that it's been a pleasure having you in my class this semester, and I've enjoyed our debates."

"Really?"

"Absolutely," he replied. "I could tell this whole class that the moon was made out of blue cheese, and they would all nod in agreement, but not you. I knew your hand would fly up to question me. Questioning is a sign of intelligence. Anyway, it's been a pleasure having you in my class this semester, and you're a very astute student."

"Thank you Mr. Cohen. It's been a very challenging class, and I've learned a lot." Then I ran back to my cottage to look up the word astute, to make sure he wasn't dissing me.

Astute: "Having or showing shrewdness and an ability to notice and understand things clearly, mentally sharp or clever." That compliment was better than any A I had gotten while attending college. Mr. Cohen gave out two As that semester, Davis and myself.

I began to write short stories after that class.

Another course I needed for my associate's degree in science was Introduction to Philosophy. One subject we discussed was predestination versus determinism, and it got me thinking. Was my life already predetermined, was everything already laid out, or did I have some choices in the matter?

The likeness and comparisons made between my father and me, by my family and older friends of his, had stayed with me through the years. I once walked into a bar in the Bronx, and an older gentleman asked me if Raymond Carney was my father.

"Yes," I'd replied.

"I could see it the minute you walked through the door. You're old man was a crazy bastard," the older gentleman had said.

Somehow I came to believe that I would follow in his footsteps (except for drugs ... he hated junkies) and that I would eventually end up just like him, a violent death at an early age. He'd died at thirty-five years old. But if my life was not predetermined, then maybe I had some choices on how it unraveled. Both my parents had good and bad qualities. Perhaps, like in a buffet, I could take and use the qualities I liked and bypass the rest.

As hard as my mother was, she always had a soft spot for those who had less and would try to help them. She was a prankster at times and liked a good laugh. She also liked a clean house, which I definitely inherited. On the other hand, she could be violent and unemotional. I'd take the first three and leave the rest, thank you.

From the stories I'd heard of my father, he was a good friend, would put his life on the line for you if you were his friend. He could also handle himself physically in a fight, which served me well in the places I'd ended up, and he had a big heart. On the flip side, he had a bad temper, was violent, and was unpredictable. On my tray leaving the buffet line will be a big heart, a good friend, and handle myself well, to be used only in emergencies. *Now where's the checkout line?* Until I had taken that class, I never realized I had a choice in how my life might turn out. That may very well have been the beginning of my recovery from that life and lifestyle.

Two years and sixty-three credits later, I graduated from Mercy College with an associate's degree. I had been locked up almost four years now and had been in weekly phone contact with my mother and sister. My mother had even gotten a ride up to the prison to attend the college graduation ceremony. I was brimming with pride and a sense of accomplishment. It had been a long time since I had done anything to make her feel proud of.

28

High Inside

Officer Franklin sat at his desk in the storehouse, where I now worked full time. He peered over his newspaper and yelled at us as we came through the door for work that morning.

"Hey, Carney, you made the local newspaper. It says here, in the *Record*, local area resident Robert Carney graduates Mercy College with an associate's degree in science."

"Are you serious?" I walked toward his desk.

"It says it right here." He handed me the paper.

Sure enough, it mentioned me and one other person who resided in the Warwick-Middletown area.

"Well, Carney, you *are* a local resident," he said, laughing. "Now get back out there and help those guys finish unloading that Entenmann's truck, and don't forget my donuts." He cut the article out and gave it to me.

CO Franklin was a decent guy whom I worked for in the storehouse for about two years. He was in charge of the storehouse, where everything was brought into the prison. The inmates' job was to help unload the trucks and put the stuff in the freezer or rooms it belonged in, in the storehouse. It was a good gig, and CO Franklin looked out for us.

I had a deal with each of the food truck drivers who delivered to the prison and whom I got to know. We could see their trucks coming a half mile away. I would tell them that we would have coffee and lunch waiting for them when they backed into the dock, since the storehouse was next to the kitchen and we had a fridge, and we'd have their truck unloaded in record time while they ate, if they let me enter the back of the truck and take two or three things for myself and the two other inmates. Otherwise, it could take a while and no lunch. They all agreed, and it worked out well. We were allowed to cook in our cottages, so there was no shortage of rice, vegetables, and fruit. Although we did have to hook up CO Franklin when the Entenmann's truck pulled up.

Officer Franklin and I had become friends, but we both knew our places. He was around five eight and slightly overweight, a blue-eyed, black-haired, and pale-skinned Irishman in his late forties. He was married to a nurse and had no children. He was also a member of the Ancient Order of Hibernians in that area. He would tell me about the normal life of a CO living in upstate New York, and I would share some crazy stories of an addicted and alcoholic criminal who lived in the city. We had a few laughs. I believe he looked out for me on more than one occasion.

At that point of my incarceration, I was doing better physically, mentally, and socially than I ever had, both in and out of prison, but there was still one demon remaining. I was back to smoking pot again. As I mentioned, the closer the prison was to the city, the more drugs were available. I was smoking pot at least twice a week there, sometimes more. The only reason I could still function well was because I couldn't smoke it the way I wanted to—all day, every day. The thought never entered my mind to just stay clean and not smoke it. For a time in that last year or two, I began smoking pot more frequently and even dealing it in there for a while, especially after school was over. The insane part is, had I got caught with it on me, I would have had to pay with years of my life, literally. In fact, I was within four months of the parole board when this happened.

I opened the door to the room I shared with one other inmate, and startled another inmate who was in our room, a young light-skinned Black guy, a bit bigger than me. He was kneeling down in front of my locker with the door open. He had pulled out five packs of cigarettes, two cans of tuna, and an unopened jar of Tang so far. I stepped in and closed the door behind me.

"You got in, asshole. Now you have to get out," I told him, looking squarely into his eyes.

We both squared off in the small room, with our hands up. There was nowhere to move with the two beds and lockers crammed in there, so I rushed him, swinging wildly for his head, and caught him with one good shot above his right eye, which started bleeding. On the way in, he hit me hard in the chest and grazed my head with a left. We crashed into the lockers and rolled around the room, throwing punches. Within a minute two COs entered the room, pulled us apart, and handcuffed us.

I stood with my hands cuffed behind my back and a CO holding me by the arm as they walked the other handcuffed inmate out of the room past me. Blood was dripping from the cut above his right eyebrow. He was taken to an outside hospital for stitches. I wondered if I would get an assault charge with only four months to go to the parole board, but that was not my biggest problem.

In my left sock were three balloons full of weed. They were small enough to swallow if I could get to them. An assault charge, along with a possession of an illegal substance, could cost me another four to six years and back to a max A prison. It was a cold, cloudy February day, and I took a deep breath as the CO led me along the cement path through the brown grass and bare trees to the infirmary, where they had some holding cells.

The heavy set gray-haired CO opened the door to the holding cell and uncuffed me.

"All right, Carney, I want you to stand in front of the bunk and strip down, handing me each piece of clothes as you take it off, so I can check it," he said as he stood just outside the door of the holding cell.

I had a couple of layers of clothes on. I took off my sweat-shirt and handed it to him. He shook it, then ran his hands along it, then handed it back to me. I folded it and put it neatly on the bed. To the left of the bunk was a metal toilet and sink combination protruding from the wall. *When I get down to my socks, can I make it to the toilet and flush the balloons before he gets to me?*

The silver button to the toilet was just above the sink. I took my state boots off and handed them to him, and he shook and searched them and handed them back. I placed them on the floor to the left of me. Then my long-john undershirt and pants. I stood there with only my long-johns and socks on. As he checked the pockets of the pants, I bent over and slid both socks off, holding the balloons inside the sock, folded them in half, and stuffed them into the boot to the left of me. When I stood up, he handed me the pants. I threw them on the bed and quickly pulled off my long johns and handed them to him, standing there naked with my arms up in the air.

"Anything else, sir?" I kept my hands in the air as he finished checking my long johns and handed them back to me.

"No, Carney, you can get dressed now. You'll be going to the Adjustment Committee in a couple of days." He then took a step back and closed and locked the wooden holding cell door.

I sat down on the bunk naked and took a long, deep breath and let it out slowly. I dropped my face into my hands and thanked God the CO hadn't asked to see the socks. After a minute I stood and walked to the toilet to pee, then pushed the silver button to flush it, and the water in the sink came on. Had I tried to flush the balloons, I would have pushed the wrong silver button and gotten caught for sure. The flush button was out of my sight and to the left of the toilet.

Later that day a CO had come by and dropped off a pack of cigarettes and some reading material my friend Jimmy D. had asked him to give me. Mid-Orange was nothing like max A. The COs treated you okay if you weren't a knucklehead and gave them problems. I was glad to get the smokes. I emptied some tobacco out of a couple of the cigarettes and stuffed some weed in there, smoked it, and blew the smoke out of the barred window in the holding cell. It helped the lockup time go by a little easier. Two days later, I was brought in front of the Adjustment Committee, back in front of the white shirts.

"Good morning, Mr. Carney. Have a seat," said the young lieutenant at the table, joined by the two other white shirts.

"Good morning," I answered.

"Would you like to tell us what happened in your cottage on Monday between you and inmate Wright? He had to be taken to an outside hospital for six stitches above his right eyebrow."

"I hit him, sir."

They all started laughing.

"We're well aware of that, Mr. Carney. We would like to know why you hit him. Did he hit you first?"

"No, sir, we just had a disagreement and I took a swing at him."

"Did you invite Mr. Wright into your room, Mr. Carney?"

"No, sir."

"Well, we understand your locker was open and some cigarettes and food were scattered on the floor, so we have a good idea of what took place, and Mr. Wright has been in this situation before. We're gonna send you back to work, Mr. Carney. I want you to know that you can thank Officer Franklin for your good fortune today, he put in a very good word for you. Just so you know, there will be no mention of this when you go to the parole board in May. Have a good day, Mr. Carney, or should we call you one-shot Carney?" and they all laughed.

"Thank you, sir," I said as I followed the CO out of the office. I was back working in the storehouse that afternoon.

"Thank God you're back, Carney," Officer Franklin yelled from his desk as he peered over his newspaper and glasses. "We've been starving over here. These guys don't know how to handle these truck drivers." He laughed.

The guys in the cottage were glad to see me back. Apparently, this wasn't the first time Mr. Wright had done that, but it was the first time he had to pay for it. I got slaps on the back that time, but it could have gone bad, very bad.

May finally rolled around, and I was counting the days, minutes, and hours until I sat before the parole board, and I was prepared for them. I had my college degree and my certificate for attending a Twelve Step meeting for six months. (Somehow the prison thought you could graduate from a Twelve Step program after six months.) I also had my Alternatives to Violence Certificate, for which I'd had to freely fall backward in hopes that the other felons in the class would catch me, which they did. This sweet little old lady ran the class. I brought all this and my most angelic smile to the parole board.

I was called in and led to a straight brown wooden chair and sat before the four parole officers, who sat behind two long wooden tables.

"Good morning, Mr. Carney," said the slim, middle-aged White woman, who had a very serious face. I was unsure if she was even capable of smiling or, God forbid, laughing. She took a minute to flip through the folder in her hands, which I assumed was mine.

"You seemed to have used your time in the prison system well, Mr. Carney. What are your plans when and if you're released?" She asked as she peered over the folder at me through small, squinted eyes.

"Thank you, ma'am," I said with a smile. "I plan on staying with my sister in Brooklyn and pursuing employment. Once I'm on my feet, I'd like to continue college and get a bachelor's degree in occupational therapy."

"That all sounds great, Mr. Carney, and you've done quite well in the associate degree program they've offered here. I see you've also accumulated a number of positive workshop certificates. It's very impressive. You seem to do quite well in a structured environment. The problem is, when you are out in society, you are a menace. Drugs, guns, violence, theft … Do you see my point, Mr. Carney?" She stared at me with those beady eyes.

"Yes, ma'am," I answered, staring at the floor.

"Very well. You'll have our answer by mail in a week or two." She put my folder on a pile and picked up another one.

I followed the CO out of the room, all the air stolen from my sails.

I received their answer nine days later. I was to report back to the parole board one year from the date I had seen them. That was good and bad news. The bad news was I had not made parole. The good news was, because they had only hit me with one year and not two, I was sure to be released in a year. The parole board can only hit you with a maximum two years each time you go, but they can do that until your sentence is complete, so if you're hit with less than two years, you know you're getting out next time. I would be getting out if I kept my nose clean.

The insanity is, I knew I would be released in a year but still continued to smoke and sell pot and get into minor scuffles, but never caught. I was released from Mid-Orange Correctional Facility in June of 1985 after serving five years of a four-to-twelve-year sentence.

Part Four: The Insanity of It

A Day At a Time Publishing

29

Back to Earth

I walked through the silver-fenced gate that sunny summer morning, almost in a dream state. *Was it true? Was I free?* My beautiful friend Lisa had come up from Florida to pick me up. Her curly blond hair and soft blue eyes rested atop her slim five-foot body. She stood beside the waiting taxi, with a bottle of champagne and a white sign that said, "Congratulations, you're FREE!" She was a sight to behold. I pinched myself to make sure I wasn't dreaming.

Being locked up for five years, then being released back into the world of people (especially women), food, animals, choices, opportunities to come and go as I pleased, or choose when to eat or sleep, is a feeling I cannot compare to anything I've ever experienced. It was as if I had been plucked from planet Earth and taken to live in exile on another planet that was cold and lonely. But now I had returned.

Lisa and I took the cab into town, then a bus into Manhattan. I went directly to report to my parole officer on West Fortieth Street. Then we walked over to Central Park, my receptors overloaded from all the people, traffic, and noise. We made it to the park and found a nice spot to lay in the grass alongside a lake, and smoked a joint. There were kids flying kites with their parents and playing with motorized toy boats in the lake. I could hear The Who singing about a teenage wasteland from someone's radio across the lake. I glanced down at Lisa lying next to me in the grass and tried to take it all in. It was great to be alive and free. We hung out for a couple of days, then she went home to Florida and I tried to start my new life.

The next three years started with a great takeoff, climbing high, then smoothing out and leveling off, then hitting some turbulence, and I then began to lose altitude, only to ultimately spiral downward and crash. While I was locked up, I'd done my best to prepare myself for the outside world. I got an education. I was in great physical shape. I'd worked on socializing with people through mail (letters), visits, school, and getting involved with some sports activities. I'd believed I had my bases covered and was ready to hit the real world running.

My dreams and expectations were to keep my freedom, be accepted and a part of society, earn a good living, have a good woman and home, friends, family, and maybe a dog. You know, the American dream. In the next three years, 1985 to 1988, I can see now the two key elements I was missing to achieve any of those goals.

The first was my defense against alcohol and drugs. The second was that I did not have a God or Higher Power in my life to ask for help with a problem I did not fully realize I had. I was lost. No matter how successful I would be in those three years, whether it be in gaining employment, romantic relationships, family and friends, it would all come crashing down around me as a direct result of alcohol and drugs, every time. It was heartbreaking.

Not long after being released, I pursued a young and beautiful woman from Inwood, whom I had always had a crush on. Now, with much more confidence in myself, I pursued a relationship with her. Her name was Penny, and she had a seven-year-old daughter named Angela, an absolute angel. I moved in with her. Her sister and mom, who both lived in the neighborhood, accepted and welcomed me into their family circle.

I got a job through a friend working for the Sandhogs, building subway and water tunnels for New York City. I shaped up on the swing shift. It was tough work, and I welcomed it. The tunnel I worked in was just off the FDR Highway and Dyckman Street in Manhattan, walking distance from Penny's house in Inwood. I joined one of the neighborhood bar's (Gary Owen's) football team and was making some good friends. My relationship with Penny and her daughter was great. I was in touch with my mother and sister, even visiting the house in Brooklyn when my stepfather was at work. Life was good and getting better than I had expected.

30

I'm Different Like That

Then like a thief in the night, the alcohol and drugs stole away any joy, happiness, or success I had earned. I just wanted to hang out after the football games with the guys and have a few beers. But once I had a few beers in me, I would get these great ideas, like, "Let's get some coke!" The same would happen on the weekends. It was the eighties—going out to the bars, drinking, dancing, and sniffing coke was what we did. It was a lot of fun, until it wasn't.

I was able to hang out for a few months and play that game, but it soon took me over and would own me. I had many friends in Inwood that partied hard, but when the night was over, they went home, went to work, handled their households and responsibilities, and took care of business. I also knew some who didn't.

I remember coming home with Penny one Thursday night around 3:00 a.m. from the bars after drinking and sniffing coke all night. We both had work the next day, and she always made it to work.

"Robby," she said. "Just lay on the bed next to me, relax, and breathe deep. You'll fall asleep," she said caringly, trying to keep me from losing it.

"You keep breathing, and I'll be right back," I said as I watched her lying there, then I headed out the door to get more drugs and alcohol.

Penny was about my height, long brown hair and brown eyes, and pouty lips. She was a head turner for sure. She was beautiful inside and out. She could dance, cook, make me laugh, and everything else you'd want in a woman. She was also a girl who liked to party, but with the help of her mom and sister, she could manage a job and a household. Penny, her sister Josie, and their mom will forever be in my heart. I enjoyed every minute with Penny, but as the alcohol and drugs took over, she would soon take a backseat, and I would be gone for days at a time. Because just drinking and sniffing coke were not enough for me anymore, I began to shoot coke again. The devil knocked, and I let him in. I would go off on my own at those times.

I headed down to Hell's Kitchen, where a guy I had done time with was dealing coke. Not many people knew or could buy from them. They only sold to a select few, and you couldn't buy less than an eighth of an ounce. There was a phone booth on the corner of Forty-Sixth and Tenth Avenue.

"YO, it's Robby. I'm downstairs."

"Okay, I'll drop the key now" came the response over the phone. *Clang.* The key attached to the round silver key ring bounced off the sidewalk outside the phone booth. I picked up the key and let myself in the front door of the old tenement building on Tenth Avenue. I climbed the three long flights and tapped on the door. Diego peered through the peephole, then opened the door.

"Que pasa, Diego?" I said as I stepped into the apartment.

"I'm doing good, white boy, how about you?"

I'd met Diego in Rikers Island a while back. He didn't appear to be your usual drug-addict criminal. He was in his mid-twenties and looked like the college type, very clean cut. He'd been caught with six ounces of cocaine in the trunk of a private cab he was driving. He'd been confident he would beat the charges and be out soon. We'd become friends and had watched each other's back while we were in Rikers. We'd exchanged numbers. He'd gone to court one day and never returned. I had saved his number.

"What do you need?" he asked.

"An eight ball to start," I answered.

There were two more guys in the kitchen. One weighed out an eighth of an ounce on the silver triple-beam scale, then scraped the white powder off the scale with a playing card onto a piece of tinfoil.

I paid Diego the $150 and headed out. "See you soon," I said as he locked the door behind me.

I stopped at a bodega and bought a box of tinfoil, then got a cheap motel room on Forth-Sixth Street between Eighth and Ninth Avenues. I tore the tinfoil and made fifteen $20 pieces of coke and had enough left for a few shots for myself. The thought of shooting it made me want to dry heave. I gathered my folded tinfoils up and headed over to Irish Eyes West, a bar on Fiftieth Street and Ninth Avenue. It was Friday afternoon, and a lot of White boys from Jersey would be coming over to Hell's Kitchen to buy coke, among other things. I approached a couple of Puerto Ricans guys I had gotten high with.

"Yo, fellas. I got $20 pieces of some good coke. I'll be sitting at the bar at Irish Eyes West right near the window. When either of you have five pieces sold, tap on the window and I'll come out. I'll give you $20 apiece for each five you help me sell."

I sat at the bar near the front window that looked out onto Ninth Avenue and ordered a beer. Ten minutes later there was a tap at the window. It wasn't long before I was back at the phone booth on Tenth and Forty-Sixth and climbing the stairs back up to Diego's apartment for a quarter ounce of coke. Then back to the hotel room to make up some more twenties of coke. Only this time I stopped and brought a couple of syringes and began shooting up, which was what I had been wanting to do from the moment the thought had entered my head that morning and had been haunting me until that minute. I bagged up more coke, did a few shots, then back to the bar to make more money.

This would go on for a couple of days, without me hardly eating or sleeping. Once in a while, I would bring a girl back with me to get high with and hang out, but sooner or later I would not be able to stop drinking and shooting coke long enough to make more money. These two- or three-day trips downtown, when I cut out on Penny, never ended well.

I came back to Penny's one time after another three- or four-day coke run. I was broke, exhausted, and with my tail between my legs because I had done it again. The memory of the last coke rush was so strong that it overwhelmed me, and I had grabbed my stashed money and taken off, not thinking of the consequences.

The train ride back uptown to Inwood and the walk to Penny's house was horrible. I felt ashamed and guilty, and I hated myself for being such a piece of crap. I walked into the apartment, and she was doing dishes in the kitchen. Her daughter was watching television in the living room. They had just finished dinner. She looked up from the sink with those sad eyes and just shook her head back and forth.

"I'm sorry," I said, barely able to make eye contact with her.

She grabbed the dish towel and dried her hands.

"What the hell is wrong with you? This is like the fifth time you've disappeared for days at a time. We don't know if you're dead or alive, and you look horrible. I bet you're broke again?"

"I am." I looked at the kitchen floor. I was also exhausted and starving. I hadn't eaten or slept for three days.

"How could you do this to us and yourself? You're fucking crazy," she said, shaking her head.

"I'm crazy?" I asked. "What about you? I've done this over and over, and you keep letting me back in your house and taking care of me."

"Do you want to know why I keep letting you back in?" she asked. "Because there's a good, decent guy I fell in love with in there somewhere," she said as she pointed at my chest. "I'm just waiting for him to come back," and tears rolled down her cheeks.

That statement crushed me and helped me in so many ways. It let me know that I was still in there, that good and decent guy, and that I was redeemable. It was the drugs and alcohol that had taken over. I might have a chance if I could fight my way back.

I tried, I really did. A few weeks, a month, I would stay clean and sober and things would go well for a while, then the thoughts, followed by pictures in my head, then the obsession would kick in, and I would be off again. In my years of dealing with alcoholism and drug addiction, what I've learned is that for the active alcoholic or addict, it never gets better, only worse, and it did. I would eventually steal from Penny, her sister Josie, and borrow money from anyone who would lend it to me, with the promise of paying it back. I couldn't even look at myself in the mirror. The old man in the park was right. I'd let the devil in.

31

Recovery in Hell's Kitchen

Eventually Penny had enough, as did my aunt Anna in the Bronx, whom I could always go to and crash on her couch. I agreed to go into rehab. It was the National Recovery Institute (NRI) on West Fifty-First Street in Manhattan, in Hell's Kitchen. Penny helped me find the place and get into NRI, a men's drug and alcohol rehab. It was run out of a three-story townhouse on West Fifty-First, by an old, short Black fellow named Herman. He was a family man from Harlem and knew the drug and alcohol game well. Along with Twelve Step meetings, we had weekly house meetings that Herman would sometimes attend and speak to the participants.

"Gentlemen," he would say as he walked back and forth on the hardwood floors, in his jacket, shirt, and tie, with his hands behind his back. "I smell dope in this house," which meant he believed someone in the house was drinking or getting high. "If the person or persons do not approach and talk to me about it before my shift is over tonight, you will be gone tomorrow. Okay, gentlemen, have a good night."

Herman and the other drug and alcohol counselors were helpful, but Herman himself had some sort of gift. It was as if he could see right inside you. I always tried to avoid making eye contact with him, afraid of what he might see.

After completing thirty days at NRI, I was eligible to seek employment. I bought the *Village Voice* newspaper and began looking for jobs. I called and got an interview with the Lion Agency on Seventy-Second and Broadway. The job was for a placement counselor. It entailed taking job orders for maids, butlers, nannies, baby nurses, cooks, and chauffeurs. It also entailed interviewing applicants for those jobs and setting up interviews.

Having been clean and sober for thirty days helped my confidence slowly return. I arrived for the interview in a pair of khaki pants, penny loafers, and a long-sleeved button-down shirt. All my clothes were borrowed or given to me at the rehab. I carried my associate's degree and some of my certificates in a manilla envelope. I entered the office building on Broadway, checked in, and took a seat in the waiting room. There were two gentlemen there before me, awaiting an interview. I sized them up and immediately felt out of my league.

They were in their twenties, like me, but they wore dress slacks and jackets with shirts and ties. They also carried their résumés and credentials in slim leather carrying bags. As I checked them out, I thought, *What am I doing here? I can't hang with these guys. They're probably well educated, have experience, and are dressed for the job. I'm not gonna embarrass myself, I'm out of here.*

"Hey, did you guys see a bathroom on the way in here?" I asked them.

"Just past the elevator," said the older one, giving me the once-over, with disdain, I thought.

I walked toward the elevator. I pressed the Down button, and it lit up. I stood there looking back into the waiting room at the two fellows sitting there. I stood there staring at them. *What do they have that I don't have?* I thought to myself as I looked down at my attire and manilla envelope. Yes, they were dressed better and probably presented better than me, but could they have gone through and survived what I just went through? Living with killers and criminals for five straight years. Making my way through minefields of dangerous people and situations, standing my ground when I had to. *I could survive Penn State, but could they survive state pen?*

I brushed off my khaki pants, straightened my shirt, and with my chin held high, walked back into the waiting room. I figured, if nothing else, I would go on my first real job interview and get some interview experience. The two gentlemen in front of me took five to ten minutes each, and I sat in the waiting room alone now.

"Mr. Carney, come on in," said the owner, a nicely dressed young man in his thirties. "Have a seat. Would you like some coffee or water?"

"No thank you." I scanned the walls and desk of his office. There was a Boston Celtic banner on the wall behind his desk. There were also pictures of his wife and two small children on the wall. One picture was taken in front of a diner I knew in Riverdale in the Bronx.

Mr. Lion leaned back in his big brown leather chair. I slid my résumé across the desk to him. He laid it on a pile with the others.

"So have you ever done any work like this, Mr. Carney?"

"No, sir, mostly I've done physical labor. I've worked for moving companies and as a sandhog, building water and subway tunnels for the city. Also I've done some demolition work. I recently attended Mercy College in the evenings and acquired an associate's degree. I would like to try and apply that now."

"What makes you think you'll be good at this work?" he asked.

"Having worked in the service industry, I have a feel for what qualities people are looking for in hiring people. I also do quite well with people in general. How do you like those Celtics? Larry Bird, McHale, Danny Ainge, Parrish, they're like a well-oiled machine." We spoke of the Celtics and the Riverdale Diner. Turns out we both grew up in the Bronx. He called two days later to meet with him and his wife for a second interview, and I got the job.

I was doing well at NRI. I was making meetings in and out of the rehab. I was excelling at matching employees with clients, and I began to take Penny and her daughter out on the weekends. We'd go out for a meal or ice skating in Central Park. I was trying my best to make up for not being there for them. My only secret was that I had been spending money on them on the weekends that I should have been saving in my bank account. I had made a verbal agreement with a counselor at NRI on how much I would save.

I watched Herman chew a few guys out for different things. Mostly for being irresponsible or lazy, so I made sure to cover all my bases. You never knew when Herman would stop you as you were walking by to see how you were doing, then peer into your soul with those piercing eyes. He hadn't looked my way in over a month, but the day came.

"Mr. Carney," he said as we were passing in the hallway. I always looked down as I walked by him, hoping he wouldn't see me. "It's been a while since we talked. How are you doing? You're looking much better, and I heard you have a new job."

"Yes, Herman, things are going well."

"You know what I like about you, Rob? You're always ready for me. You always have the right answers and your bases covered. Don't forget why you came here," he said in almost a whisper, and patted me on the back.

"I won't, Herman," I said as he walked off.

He turned back. "Oh, and by the way, Rob, how's that bank account coming along?" He smiled as his office door closed behind him.

How could he have known that? No one had asked about or looked at my bank account. It was the one base I hadn't covered. They had left that responsibility to me. I got back on track after Herman's remark.

32

Forgive Me, Father, For I Have Sinned

Something happened to me in my third month at NRI. Outwardly everything was going well, but inside, my heart hurt. As my head cleared, all the crappy things I had done to Penny, Josie, the money I'd borrowed or had stolen, some from friends, all the people I had hurt and lied to, and all for the sake of feeding my addictions, bubbled up to the surface. I felt more and more like a worthless piece of crap as the memories presented themselves. I knew it wouldn't be long before I was off and running again, drinking and getting high to mask the shame. That vicious merry-go-round, drink and get high, hurt people, stop, shame sets in, drink and get high to mask the shame, hurt people. The merry-go-round goes round and round.

I passed a church on West Forty-Ninth Street every day on my way to and from work. Sometimes I would stop in to say a prayer on my way back to the rehab. On this day I saw a young priest entering the church and followed him in.

"Hey, Father, do you have a minute?"

"Sure, what can I do for you?" answered the young priest, in his mid-thirties, with an Irish accent. He was tall with red hair and blue eyes above his white collar and black shirt.

"I was wondering if you had a few minutes to talk? I'm in a drug and alcohol rehab down the block, and I really need to talk with someone. My head is about to explode, and I don't want to do anything stupid."

"I'll tell you what," he said. "Tomorrow is Saturday. Come around 1:00 p.m., when I'm done with confessions, and I'll give you a half hour."

"Thanks, Father. See you then," I said, feeling slightly relieved already.

The following day I entered the quiet and dimly lit church from the noisy city streets. The priest was walking up the aisle, past the rows of wooden pews, carrying two metal folding chairs. I stood staring at the ten-foot picture of Jesus painted on the backdrop of the altar behind him. Jesus held a bright-red heart in his hands, set ablaze by a bright light shining on it from the floor of the altar.

The priest opened and set both chairs about six feet apart behind the last row of pews and in front of the confessional booths.

"Have a seat. I'm Father Weber. Now how can I help you?"

"I'm Robert Carney." I shook his hand, then sat in the folding chair. "Thank you for taking time to see me today."

"Are you a Catholic, Robert?"

"I am, Father, and I've been Baptized and Confirmed as a kid, but never really a part of the church, except to stop in once in a while and pray for help with my battle with addiction. I'm twenty-seven years old, and I've been drinking and doing and selling drugs since I was sixteen. I've also spent five of those years in prison for armed robbery. I'm in rehab on Forty-Ninth Street now, but with no drugs or alcohol for the past three months, my conscience is getting the best of me. I'm trying to stay clean and sober, but the guilt and shame are getting to me now."

"Tell me exactly what it is that you're ashamed of and what is bothering you," Father Weber said.

"Well, I've been out of prison for almost two years now, and things were going well for a while, until the drugs and alcohol got hold of me again. So many people from my neighborhood in Inwood have stepped up to help me, and I've failed them all, and myself. They've opened their homes to me, loaned me money, gotten me jobs. I've been living with a woman and her young daughter for the past year and a half. I've lied and stolen from her and have not been able to be there for her or her daughter, and it's killing me, Father."

"I have a question for you, Rob."

"Yes, Father?"

"Were you high or drunk, or trying to be, when you couldn't be there physically, emotionally, or financially for the woman and her daughter?"

"Yes, Father."

"What about when you stole from them or others?"

"Yes, Father, I was."

"How about when you lost your jobs and lied to friends and family who loved and cared about you?"

"Yes, Father."

"What about now, Rob, now that you're clean and sober?"

"No Father, I wouldn't do anything like that. In fact, I'm trying to make up for it and see that it doesn't happen again."

"I can see that. Rob, I know you've taken advantage of those people because of your addiction problem, but they all chose to be in a relationship with you because they saw something in you that was good, and they also got something out of the relationship. I want you to do something after our talk here."

"Yes, Father, what's that?"

"For your penance I want you to pray and ask Jesus to forgive you for not using the gifts he's given you."

"Really, Father, that's it? What gifts are you talking about?"

"Jesus has blessed you with many gifts. Just in our short talk here, I can see that you're very well spoken and have a good heart, to name a couple of things, but there are many more."

"Thank you, Father. I really appreciate your time and for listening to me."

He then blessed me and sent me on my way.

Leaving the church and heading back out into the sunlight and sounds of people and traffic, I felt lighter and in better spirits. It was as if I had just cut my shame and guilt in half and left it in the church by just talking about it out loud and sharing it with someone. Father Weber's feedback also gave me some things to think about. Me, and me on drugs and alcohol, a clear distinction. The gifts were still in question.

33

The Insanity of It

Once again I would do very well in a structured environment. I progressed while at NRI, with my job and savings, and repaired a couple of damaged relationships, including Penny and her family. Things were going so well that I left NRI and moved back in up to Inwood, against the advice of Herman and the staff there. They warned me that going back there could easily lead me to relapse.

They were right. I held out for about three weeks, until I joined the party again. I had that first beer, and all bets were off. Before long I was right back where I'd started. I lost my job at the Lion Agency. Apparently they were sensitive about employees shooting cocaine in the office bathroom. I remember thinking, *If I could only get the job back, everything would be okay.* I had no clue. Penny once again said I had to leave. This time because I had taken some of her sister Josie's jewelry. She had left it in the house, and while on a three-day coke run, I took it and traded it for more coke.

"How could you?" Penny said, sitting on the bed cross-legged and crying. "Now you have to leave, and I can't see you anymore or my family will call the cops on you."

"I'm so sorry." I sat next to her on the bed. We both held each other tightly and cried.

I gathered my few things and left. Alcohol and drugs have no mercy.

I headed back down to Hell's Kitchen, got a cheap hotel room, then walked over to the phone booth on Forty-Sixth Street and Tenth Avenue to call Diego. It wouldn't be long before I could turn off the guilt and shame with a few drinks and some coke.

I lasted for a few days, until the money ran out, like it always did. This time I got desperate. On one of my more reckless attempts to get more drug money, I walked into a supermarket on Eighth Avenue to see what I could steal. There was a display of cases of Heineken beer about eight feet high. There were five cash registers, and all were being used except one, the fifth one. I took a case of Heineken off the stack and stood in line at the fourth register. When it seemed no one was paying attention, I took a step to the left and walked through the empty register and out the door. I was able to trade the case of Heineken for a half gram of coke. I went back later that morning and walked out with two cases. Early that evening on my fifth trip to the supermarket, the stack of cases was only about five feet high—they had finally caught on, and this time they chased me down Eighth Avenue. I dropped one case but managed to hold on to one and get away by running through traffic.

The point being, when I was high and wanted more drugs, I sometimes thought I was invisible. I would also run a situation into the ground, as I did with the cases of Heineken. If I hadn't been caught, I would have taken them until the stack was gone. The same goes for people. If someone could help me get more booze or drugs, I would use that person until they were used up and useless to me. Then on to the next person, and the more they cared about me, the more I would use them.

It's hard looking back at those times with sober eyes. Now it's okay to look back when I'm helping someone, but not to stare. My three years out of prison would come to an end soon.

I got very desperate on one of my coke runs and attempted to strongarm a guy for his money and jewelry. I showed up for my monthly parole visit, and the female parole officer called me into her office from the waiting room. When I stepped into her office, two male parole officers slammed me down on her desk and cuffed my hands behind me.

When they stood me up, I took in and let out a deep sigh of relief. It was over. I could not stop on my own, I was partly relieved. I was picked out of a lineup and charged with attempted robbery in the third degree and sentenced to one and a half to three years in state prison. After a short stint at Rikers Island, I was headed back upstate. I ended up at Ogdensburg Correctional Facility near the Canadian border and alongside the Saint Lawrence River. Because there was no violence or weapon used during the crime, I was sent to a medium-security prison.

It was suggested by a counselor in the prison that I work in the prerelease office. Prerelease is a program for inmates who have made parole and are getting prepared for the outside world. It was done through a series of workshops hosted by the three inmates who worked in the prerelease office. The workshops consisted of going on job interviews, family reintegration, AIDs awareness, and the like. Also, writing to different agencies to try and get guys temporary housing or employment when they were released. Of course I accepted the job, thinking how good it would look at the parole board.

In my second month working in prerelease, an old man, a civilian, walked into the prerelease office.

"Hey, fellas, the name is Ed McDonogh," said the old white-haired man in the gray saggy suit that hung off him. "The counselor in the front office told me to come and talk to you guys. I want to start a Twelve Step meeting in the prison, and maybe one of you guys could help me." He held his gray fedora in his hand.

My two fellow inmate coworkers barely lifted their heads up from their work, but I gave the old man the once-over. *Wow, wouldn't that look good at the parole board.*

"Are any of you guys familiar with Twelve Step meetings?" the old man asked.

"I've been to a few of those meetings," I answered. Every time I went to a detox or rehab, I had to attend the Twelve Step meetings. Or the many Twelve Step meetings I went to in Rikers Island to meet up with some of the boys from other parts of the jail to exchange drugs and cigarettes. "Yeah, I can probably help you with that," I answered.

"Okay, and you are?"

"Rob Carney."

"Okay, Rob Carney, we need thirty guys to sign up, and we'll meet on Thursday nights for one hour, between 7:00 and 8:00 p.m. They showed me a room in the gym we could use. The office said if a guy attends the meetings for six months straight, they'll give him a certificate to bring with him to the parole board. Get the list together, and I'll be back next week to see how many guys you got to sign up." Then the old man shook my hand and put his fedora on. "Have a good day, gentlemen." He turned and walked off.

I got the list together within a few days. Most of the guys were in there for drug- and alcohol-related crimes and could use that certificate to bring to the parole board. One week later we had our first Twelve Step meeting. Thirty guys showed up at the room in the gym on Thursday night at 7:00, along with Mr. McDonough, who stood at the front of the room with me. He handed me a packet of pages to have the guys read to open the meeting, then gave me a pat on the back.

"Okay, Rob, you guys have a good meeting, and I'll check in with you in a couple of weeks," he said as he shook my hand goodbye.

"Wait a minute, Mr. McDonough. Aren't you going to stay here and run the meeting?" I asked as panic began to set in.

"No, this is your guys' meeting. Everything you need is in the packet I gave you. You'll be fine," he added, as he turned and slowly walked out of the room.

I looked at the thirty fellow inmates who sat in the metal folding chairs, and I took a deep breath. "Okay, fellas, this is the deal. We meet here one night a week for one hour, and we get our certificates in six months to bring to the parole board. The CO will be sticking his head in the room once in a while to check on us, so let's act like we're having a meeting. Can we do that?" There was some mumbling and wisecracks but mostly heads shaking yes.

"All right, this is how it works. I'll need a couple of volunteers to read some stuff to open the meeting. Then I'll need someone to volunteer to tell their story for about fifteen to twenty minutes, then we'll go around the room and you can raise your hand and say a few words if you want. And remember, the CO will be checking in on us."

Two guys raised their hands to read something, but no volunteers to share their story. I stood there in silence looking over the room full of my fellow felons and tough guys. No volunteers.

"Okay," I said to break the silence. "I'll share this time, but we're gonna take turns doing this over the six months." I took a deep breath and began.

"My name is Robby, and I'm an alcoholic and a drug addict, and this is what happened to me." Something happened in that room that night. For twenty minutes I let my guard down and let those guys see who I was. I put the hard, tough-guy role away for a while and was honest with them. Honest about what alcohol and drugs had done to me. I shared some of the fears I carried with me. The room got quiet, and I noticed a lot of heads nodding in agreement with me. We then went around the room, and many of the guys shared some of their experiences of what alcohol and drugs had done to them. We actually had a meeting!

That following week I was approached by two of the guys who had attended the meeting. Each one approached me on a different day as I was walking around the dirt track, cooling down after a run. The first was Luis.

"Hey, Robby, wait up. Do you have a minute?" he yelled as he ran down the grass hill to the dirt track.

"Sure, Luis, What's up?" I slowed down to let him catch up. Louise was a tall, skinny Latino, a quiet guy.

"I didn't share at the meeting, but I wanted to thank you for being honest. I didn't know other people thought about drinking and drugs like I do, especially in the outside world." Luis and I walked and talked for a half hour that day.

He did raise his hand and share at the next meeting. A couple of days later, a young Black guy named Gary, in his early twenties, who'd attended the meeting, joined me on my jog around the track.

"Yo, Rob," Gary said as he jogged alongside me. "I didn't talk at the meeting, but I just wanted to tell you we have a lot in common. The single parent, drinking, and people coming and going from your house, welfare, and feeling different around other kids. Anyway, I'll see you Thursday night at the meeting," and off he jogged to his cottage.

I had only agreed to do the meeting because it would look good at the parole board. In fact, I was still smoking pot when I could get it. It was scarce this far up north, but I got my hands on some occasionally. And then there was the jailhouse hooch some guys who worked in the kitchen would brew up.

After we had our second meeting, and having some more guys share some stuff with me, I couldn't drink or get high in there and look those guys in the face again. I stayed clean and sober for one year and four days. I ran the meeting for six months, then handed the reins to the next guy but continued to attend. The old man, Mr. McDonough, would stop by the prerelease office to chat and drop off some literature once a month.

I was paroled on December 14, 1989, after eighteen months of incarceration. Working in the prerelease office and being part of the Twelve Step meeting, which helped me stay clean and sober in there, had aided me tremendously. My release from prison this time was different.

The prison van dropped me off at a corner bus stop on a cold and snowy winter morning around 8:00 a.m. I looked around as the prison van drove off. The snow was falling, and the area was desolate, except for a few small commercial buildings that were closed and an occasional passing car. I stood shivering under the bus stop awning and waited. An hour later the bus pulled up, and I climbed on and found a window seat in the back. Off to New York and once again paroled to my little sister's apartment in Brooklyn until I could get on my feet.

When I got on that bus that snowy morning, there were a few things I was certain of. I was an alcoholic and addict, and it felt great to be free, and clean and sober, for one year and four days. I had a plan when I got to New York. I would call and find out where the Twelve Step meetings were in my area and make a meeting every day. It was also suggested I get a sponsor right away to do the Twelve Steps and secure my sobriety. Yes, I knew what the problem was, and I would fix it.

The bus ride to New York took the better part of seven hours, plenty of time to think. I knew my sister and her boyfriend smoked pot, but that didn't mean I had to. Four hours into the ride, thinking hard and left to my own devices, my thoughts slowly changed. *I just did eighteen months. I can at least smoke a joint to celebrate. I don't want to seem weird to my sister and her boyfriend. And besides, I never did an armed robbery to get more pot.* All my resolve had gone out the window in that seven-hour bus ride, left to my own devices.

34

Marijuana Maintenance

I arrived at the port authority and took the subway to Donna's one-bedroom apartment in Brooklyn. Donna and her six-year-old daughter lived there. I got to stay on her couch until I got on my feet, and was grateful for that. Donna's home was always open to me. She was twenty-seven, she worked, she partied, but she held it together. I smoked a joint with her and her boyfriend, Danny, to celebrate my release. Danny, a young Puerto Rican in his late twenties who worked in the neighborhood bakery, pulled me to the side.

"Hey, Robby, why don't you go down to Third Avenue and get yourself taken care of," he said under his breath as he handed me $50 and his car keys.

"Really?" I looked down in my hand at the money and keys.

"Yes. I know it's been a long time for you." We walked outside, and he pointed his car out to me. "And don't catch anything." He laughed as he pulled a condom out of his pocket and tossed it to me.

"Thanks, Danny. I'll see you guys in a little while." I drove toward Third Avenue and began my search for a hooker. There were a few walking underneath the Gowanus freeway, but I spotted a young girl in her twenties turning the corner on Fortieth Street. I slowed down and pulled up alongside her.

She slowed up and looked at me. "Are you looking for a date?" she yelled over.

"Sure," I yelled back, and slowed the car to a stop. She jumped in and gave me her rates. She was a slim brown-haired White girl who didn't look like she had been on the streets too long. I spotted the tracks on her arms right away, along with the pain in her eyes.

"How old are you, and how long have you been out here?" I asked, genuinely concerned.

"I'm twenty-two and have been out here for a few months now. Look, mister, do you want a date or not?" she asked impatiently. She looked at me with those big brown painful eyes, then crossed her arms and lowered her gaze to the floor.

"Look, I know you need to get high, and you don't want to hear any shit, but I just got out of the joint after eighteen months because of that dope and coke. Is there any way I can help you? I could bring you to a detox or a meeting?"

"I just need to make some money right now, so just pull over and let me out."

"Okay. Just tell me where to drop you, and here's $20 to get straight. I'll give you my sister's number, where I'm staying. Call if you want some help." I dropped her off on Thirty-Fifth and Fifth and headed back to my sister's place.

Amazingly, I stayed clean and sober for the next couple of months. I began going to my Twelve Step meetings the next day. At my first Twelve Step meeting, they asked if anyone was new, and I raised my hand and introduced myself. An older fellow approached me after the meeting.

"How ya doing? My name is Chicken Charlie." He shook my hand. "I'm glad you're here, and you keep coming back."

He handed me a business card with his number on it and a picture of a chicken on a rotisserie.

"Thanks, I appreciate that." I stuffed the business card into my pocket. As I walked to the bus stop to get back to my sister's place, I pulled the card out of my pocket and read it. *That was my first meeting outside, and Chicken Charlie gave me his card. I'm in.* I smiled to myself.

I was thirty-two years old, staying on my little sister's couch. I was ten blocks from my mother's house but not allowed there when my stepfather was home. I didn't know anybody in Brooklyn and was feeling kind of by myself, so when Chicken Charlie gave me his card, I lit up and was looking forward to the next Twelve Step meeting.

The next night, at my second meeting in a different location, there were all new faces. When it got around to me, I told them who and what I was and that I had just gotten out of prison for the second time. Again, at the end of the meeting, a gentleman approached me.

"Hey, Robby, my name is Tommy Time. You know why they call me that? It's because of all the time I've spent in the joint."

"It's nice to meet you, Tommy." I shook his hand.

"I'm gonna be your sponsor," Tommy said matter of factly. Tommy was an Italian guy in his mid-fifties. He stood about five foot ten and was in good shape. "Here's my number," he said. "Call me every day, and I'll meet you at a meeting most nights." Then he gave me a ride to my sister's house in his sharp black Cadillac.

I met Tommy the following night at a meeting he had recommended. The speaker shared, then it went around the room, and everyone shared for a minute or two. I shared something, then a guy shared. It sounded like he shared just the opposite of what I'd said, or so it seemed. I felt that maybe he was intentionally trying to belittle me. I got angrier and angrier as the meeting went on. At the end of the meeting, I pulled Tommy aside.

"Hey, Tommy, you see that guy over there in the green sweater?"

"Yeah, what about him?"

"Did you hear what he said when he shared?"

"No, what did he say?"

"Well, I think he's trying to make me look bad. Now I don't want to disrespect the meeting, but when he gets about a half a block away from the meeting, I'm gonna give him a smack so hard you'll be able to hear it for three blocks in every direction."

Tommy's eyes widened, and he took a step back, then he busted out laughing.

"What's so funny?"

He took a step closer and put his hand on my shoulder. "I'm gonna say something, and I don't want to hurt your feelings," Tommy said, still smiling.

"What?"

"That guy in the green sweater doesn't even know you're in the room," he answered with a straight face.

"Are you sure?"

"I'm positive." He laughed again. "Don't worry. You're in the right place. C'mon, let's go get some coffee and pie and I'll drive you home. It's freezing out there."

That was the beginning of me realizing I'm not that important and to not to take myself and others so seriously. Also, after all these years sober, I've come to realize that most of my troubles and worries are like the guy in the green sweater—they began and ended in that space between my ears. Probably 95 percent of my problems began and ended in my head. The 5 percent that did materialize were solved with the help of God, the Twelve Steps, and my clean and sober friends. Looking back, I wish I would have laughed more and worried less.

After being out of prison and at my sister's place for a couple of weeks, I got a job delivering repaired TVs and electronics out in Brighton Beach, in Brooklyn. I had heard someone talking about the job opening at one of my Twelve Step meetings, and I inquired. It felt good to be able to give my sister a little something and start saving for a place of my own.

One night after attending a meeting on my own, a bunch of the people from the meeting were cramming into a van to go to a nearby coffee shop and hang out for a while. I had just enough money left for carfare and lunch that week, so I walked off.

"Hey, Robby, where are you going? Come join us for some coffee and pie," yelled Kevin, a friend I had just met at the meeting.

"I gotta get up early for work," I responded.

Kevin walked after me and herded me back to the van.

"C'mon, we're only gonna be an hour or so." He gently pushed me into the van, then sat down next to me. On the ride there, he slipped a five-dollar bill into my hand.

I nodded to him. *How did he know?*

The coffee shop was great. I got to meet some new friends and enjoyed the company.

That Friday when I got paid, I put $5 aside. When I saw Kevin outside the meeting the next week, I made a beeline toward him.

"Kevin, here's that $5 I owe you. Thank you. It really helped."

Kevin took a step back and put a hand up to stop me. "No, Robby, someone gave me that $5 when I was new. Now you have to find someone new who could use it."

"Thanks, Kevin, I will." I put the five back in my pocket. I began to see how this thing worked. The meetings were going well, and so was the delivery job. I worked with a younger guy named Sal. We delivered to every borough, and we'd stop and play a game of handball at almost every handball court we passed. Sal was a good kid, but he liked to smoke pot the way I used to. I asked him to please not smoke it in the van because I was trying to stay clean.

I had saved up enough to get a furnished room not too far from my sister's apartment and my mom's house. I worked and went to meetings all week, but on Sunday mornings I would meet my mother and two younger sisters from Fred at Mass.

One Sunday my mother held my hand tightly during Mass and whispered to me. "Robert, this is all I've wanted and prayed for. That you would be here with us, healthy and doing good."

I was truly taken. I didn't think she gave me that much thought. After Mass we walked down Eighth Avenue until we reached Forty-Third Street, where they would make a left toward their house and I would continue on the ten blocks to my furnished room. It had been seventeen years since I had been banished from that house for stealing the change jar.

After a couple of months of meeting them at church, I wondered if and when I would ever be allowed back in their house. I grew impatient. On our walk back from church one Sunday, I asked the question.

"Hey, Mom, when are you going to invite me over for breakfast after Mass?"

"I don't think Fred is ready for that yet, Robert," she answered.

"Mom, are you sure it's Fred?"

"Yes," she answered. "Let's give it more time."

I kissed my mom and hugged my two little sisters goodbye and said I would see them next Sunday. I walked the ten blocks back to my furnished room and brooded. I called Tommy Time before I got too depressed.

"Hey, Tommy, how are you?"

"I'm good. How was church with your mom and sisters?"

"It was good, but I asked my mother when she would have me over for a meal when my stepfather was there, and she said he wasn't ready yet and to give it more time. Can you believe that?"

"No, I don't understand," he answered. "It's not like your behavior hasn't worried the woman sick for the past seventeen years. The overdoses and calls from the police stations and hospitals. Any call after nine at night she probably thought this was the call, you're gone. Then there was that change jar. No, I don't understand why she would be weary."

The phone went silent for a minute, then I started laughing. "Oh yeah, then there's all that," I said. "Thanks, Tommy, I'll call you tomorrow." I pulled out my Twelve Step meeting book and found a meeting for that evening. It was a lonely time. I could still visit the house when my stepfather wasn't there, but it wasn't the same.

People at the meetings would ask how much clean and sober time I had, and I would say, "I'm not sure, because of the prison time, and all." The truth was, no I hadn't drunk or shot any dope or cocaine, but I had smoked a joint the first night I moved into the furnished room. There were just some nights I couldn't bear going there and being alone with myself. I was okay in prison with people around, at my sister's house, or at meetings and with Tommy, but I was not okay by myself, alone. So I started buying a joint or two off Sal at work to smoke in my room and listen to music or zone out with television. The truth was, I had no clean and sober time. I was smoking pot, but that was my little secret.

At one point I thought, *Maybe this could work out. I'll go to work, go to my Twelve Step meetings, smoke an occasional joint, and stay away from the hard stuff.*

35

The Man in the Cage

After being out of prison a few months, the entrepreneur kicked up in me again. I started doing personal training. From working out in prison, I was in pretty solid shape. I started putting work-out programs together for some of the people I met in my Twelve Step programs. Then my boss at the electronics repair shop hired me as his personal trainer. We met three times a week before work, and he was showing results. So I put an ad in the *Village Voice* in Manhattan, had some business cards made up, and boom, I was in business. Within a month I had five steady clients, mostly in Manhattan. I let go of the delivery job and started training people full time. I would design a work-out program that included aerobics, calisthenics, light weight training, and some yoga, all depending on the client's needs. I started to get more clients from referrals.

Within a few months I was bopping around Manhattan in a running suit, gold chain around my neck, and a sports bag over my shoulder. I saw six or seven clients three times a week at $35 a session at their homes. My bank account was growing, and so was my head. In fact, my head got so big I could hardly squeeze it through the door of a Twelve Step meeting. The more clients I took on, the less meetings I went to. My calls to Tommy Time would get further and further apart.

I also met a young lady downtown Manhattan who thought I looked cute in my running suit and gold chain. We began dating, and I pretty much thought I had arrived.

Smoking an occasional joint became an every night thing when I got back to my furnished room in Brooklyn. Then things turned quickly. I began smoking pot three or four times a day, and I stopped going to meetings and calling Tommy altogether. It turns out, for a guy like me, all that pot smoking made me thirsty, and a cold beer sounded good. After my sixth or seventh beer, a shot of heroin and cocaine sounded even better, and I was off again.

Out of prison six months, a small place of my own, the beginnings of a relationship with my family, a thriving personal training business, all gone in two weeks. I lost it all again. I had gone on a drinking and coke-shooting run that lasted two weeks and ended me up in a detox in Brooklyn. I sat there in the TV room of the detox, in my hospital pajamas and paper slippers, with my head in my hands, asking myself, *How could I have let this happen again? I can't take this anymore."*

I lied to the nurses about how long I had been on heroin so I could get some methadone to calm my nerves. This detox was like all the other detoxes I had been to, except for two things. One, I called Tommy Time and told him where I was and that I could use some help when I got out. He assured me he would be there for me.

The second was something the speaker from one of the Twelve Step meetings, who came into the detox, had said. He was a well-dressed, young, and smiling Black gentleman who seemed to be enjoying the fruits of a clean and sober life as a result of the Twelve Steps. He told us who and what he was, then something that perked my ears.

"I know you guys are having it rough right now, but if you hang in there and get involved in a Twelve Step program when you get out, you can have a life beyond your wildest dreams. There is something I want to share with you guys that I deal with on a daily basis, and this is just me. It might sound crazy, but it is my story." Then the young man stopped for a moment and scanned the room.

"I have this little gremlin-like man that lives in a cage in my chest. His job is to kill me, but he will settle for making my life as miserable as possible. He's locked in his cage right now so he can't hurt me. He can only hurt me when he's out, and there is only one way he can get out of his cage. If I take a drink, a snort, a puff of pot, a shot of dope or coke, or willingly take any mind-altering substance, the cage door swings open and he's out. Once the little man is out, it's very hard to get him back in." The young man stopped talking for a few seconds and looked at the floor, as if remembering the little man's last escapade. Then he continued.

"Once I start drinking or using, that becomes more important to me than my job, family, or friends. That little gremlin-like man has me causing all kinds of havoc. I began avoiding my responsibilities, lying to people who love and care about me, even cheating and stealing from them and others. There have been times I've felt so bad I wanted to take my own life, but by some miracle, and with the help of others, I got him back in his cage. So long as he's locked up, he can't hurt me. The one problem I have is, although he's locked in his cage, he can still talk to me when I'm alone. He's quiet when I'm in a meeting or with my sponsor or here with you guys—he runs off and hides in the corner of his cage. It's when I'm alone that he starts chatting it up, especially when I'm having a weak moment. He tells me lies, like I'm not good enough, I don't deserve a sober life, I'll never amount to anything, people don't like me, and on and on. If I listen to him long enough and start believing his lies, a drink or drug starts looking good.

"He's a very slick and deceiving little bugger too. He once promised me up and down that he would get back in his cage if I let him out for just a short while, three beers and a joint. Sure enough, after I drank three beers and smoked a joint, he skipped back into his cage and even closed the door behind him. A couple of weeks later I received a substantial amount of money I had been waiting for. My little gremlin-like friend had been quiet for a while, but he began to rattle his cage door.

"'Pssssst, hey, Gary, that's a lot of money we got there. Can we at least celebrate with a couple of beers?' he asked.

"'I don't think so,' I told him. 'I could really hurt myself with all the drugs and alcohol this money could buy.' The man in the cage was quiet for a moment, then started rattling his cage door again.

"'Hey, Gary, c'mon, man. Didn't I keep my promise last time? We had a couple of beers, smoked a joint, and I got right back in. I know you got that Twelve Step thing going, but who has to know—it'll be between you and me.' So I let him out for a couple of beers, and the little liar would not get back in his cage. Two weeks later I ended up in this hospital from a heroin overdose. I blew through most of the money, lost my job, and broke up with my girl. He almost got me that time. I've had him locked in his cage for two years and four months now. In fact, he started whispering to me when I was home and getting ready to come here tonight.

"'Pssst, yo, Gary,' he whispered. 'Don't push yourself so hard. You put a hard day of work in. Take a break, relax, and watch the game tonight. They won't even miss you.' I just smiled and looked down at my chest and said, 'Shhh, not tonight. Those guys at the detox are waiting for me to bring a meeting to them. I have work to do.' Yes, he tries to catch me at a weak moment. In fact, if you ever see me walking along the street and I look down at my chest and yell SHUT THE FUCK UP, you know who I'm talking to."

It's been many years since that young man brought that Twelve Step meeting into the detox that night. He gave me an insight into what I was dealing with and that I had a choice in the matter. That would be the last of many detoxes I had visited. I had spent all my savings on drugs and alcohol, lost the room I was renting, and hadn't contacted any of my personal training clients, so that was gone. I called Tommy and asked for help before I was released. He said I could stay on his couch for a few days but that I would have to take his suggestions. I agreed.

36

Pittsfield, Mass

I stayed on Tommy's couch for three days. Then at his suggestion, I went to a rehab in Pittsfield, Massachusetts. I called my parole officer and got honest about my situation, and he gave me permission to go out of state for the rehab stay. Tommy loaned me an old green army duffel bag to carry my few possessions, gave me $50 and a carton of cigarettes, then drove me to the port authority in Manhattan. He waited until I boarded the bus and it departed. I'm glad he did. The man in the cage had been whispering to me on the quiet ride down there.

Some notable things took place in that rehab that were a first for me. The first group I attended was an investment group. They gathered the group of us in a room and sat us in a circle of chairs. Pete, the young, skinny counselor from Brooklyn, led the group.

"Today everyone in this circle is going to share one thing they are ashamed of or consider a deep, dark secret. We must all agree that it will never leave this room. The idea is to form a bond of trust between us so we can easily share what's eating at us while we're here. Okay, who's first?"

The circle sat quiet for the longest two minutes ever, then Pete broke the silence. "Okay, I'll make the first investment. When I was using drugs, I broke into my parents' home and stole all their jewelry, cash, and valuable coins. I made it look like a burglary. They were devastated. Some of what I took held sentimental value. It broke their hearts. I have told them and since made my amends to them for that. It's not something I'm proud of or would normally tell anyone."

The room went quiet for a moment, then a hand raised. "Hi, group. My name is Gloria. My last run included getting hooked on heroin, and I began turning tricks to get my next fix." Then she began sobbing, and the older woman sitting next to her put her arm around her. Gloria gave me some courage.

"Hi, group. My name is Robby. When I was seven or eight years old, I was sexually abused by an older male friend of my mother. I've never said anything to anyone about it, and it kills me to think of it. I don't know why, but I feel really ashamed of it."

And so it went. The pile of secrets in the middle of the room grew. There were some tears, anger, and shame, but we made it around the circle. We all left that room a little lighter and closer to each other. The anger, embarrassment, and shame from my sexual assault had been exposed to the light and had been cut in half. Especially after hearing others who had gone through similar or worse ordeals.

Another group that I was part of and that left an impression on me was the candlelight group. The room was dark except for one candle burning. The group formed a circle and set a chair in the middle of the room. Since I was the newest member, it was my turn. They sat me in the middle of the circle.

"Okay, group," said Felicia, a female counselor in her fifties. She was tall and slim with long graying hair. You would never know it, but she had come from the streets and had been in prison. She was an easy person to talk to.

I took my seat in the chair. It got quiet, and Felicia asked me some questions.

"Good afternoon, Robby. How are you feeling today?" She gave me a warm smile.

"I'm good, Felicia, how are you?"

"I'm doing fantastic. Are you ready?"

"Yes," and complete silence fell over the room as the light from the candle flickered on the faces in the circle.

"Okay, Robby, close your eyes, take a couple of deep breaths, and let them out slowly. Now, I want you to go back in time and describe to me who you were before you ever took a drink or a drug." A few moments of silence passed as I pictured that adventurous, hustling little kid.

"I was a pretty good kid. I was always trying to hustle up money to help my mom and little sister. I would come up with all these jobs, shoeshining, helping people home with their groceries with my mom's shopping cart, bringing in the garbage cans for buildings on my block. I always gave my mother half the money and looked out for my little sister, Donna. If there was a special doll she wanted for Christmas, I made sure she got it. Although I did steal on occasion, especially clothes to stay warm or food to eat when I was hungry.

"I was adventurous too. I would walk to different neighborhoods by myself, or sneak on the trains and get off a stop further from my house each time. I didn't really fit in with the kids my age, and felt different, but older people seemed to like me a lot. I think that's about all I have for now."

"Thank you, Robby," Felicia said. "That kid you described. That little hustling, caring, and adventurous kid. That's who you are. That's Robby. The problem is, once you add alcohol or drugs to that kid, you are no longer yourself. You are now the Robby on drugs and alcohol."

That made sense to me. Almost everything I had ever done that made me feel less than or ashamed of myself was a result of alcohol or drugs.

During my stay at rehab in Pittsfield, I became friends with a girl named Maggie, who was also a patient. Maggie was in her early twenties, short blond thin hair, about five foot six, and on the thin side, but was cute in a country-girl way. She was from the area, and we had been staring at each other much too long those last few days before she was released. It's amazing how the mind and body come back once the alcohol and drugs leave it. We exchanged numbers, and she came back to meet me the day I was released. We hung out for a day and promised to stay in touch, then back to New York I went.

A month had gone by and I was staying clean and sober. Maggie invited me to spend Christmas with her and her family in Monson, Massachusetts. I accepted her invitation and spent the Christmas holiday with her and her beautiful family on the side of a mountain in Monson. It was a great few days. They reminded me of the TV show *The Waltons*. When I was leaving, her grandmother pulled me aside.

"Robby," she whispered, "if it gets too tough staying on the straight and narrow in New York, you know you can always come back here. We have a place for you here." She hugged me goodbye.

Maggie drove me to the bus station, and I promised her I would give Gram's offer some thought.

Though back in New York, I stayed in touch with Maggie and her family. I managed to stay clean and sober for two months while staying at a friend's apartment, assembling lockers (my job), and going to meetings, then I relapsed. I got the man back in the cage after a few days. Then one more month and a second relapse. I called Maggie to see if the offer was still open.

"Of course," she responded.

I called my parole officer in Brooklyn and asked if I could transfer my parole to Massachusetts, because I had a good opportunity. To my surprise, he got back to me the next day and gave me the green light. I was to report to the Springfield parole office and check in when I arrived there, then check in with my Brooklyn PO every two weeks to see how the transfer was progressing.

37

Gram

I tossed the green duffel bag that held all my worldly belongings onto the pile of luggage that was being loaded into the belly of the Greyhound bus. I boarded the bus at the port authority in New York that spring morning, off to start the next chapter of my life in Monson, Massachusetts. I was thirty-three years old. Maggie and her family were heaven sent, giving a guy like me a new start in life. God knows, New York had chewed me up and spit me out more than a few times already.

The bus rolled out of the darkness of the port authority terminal and into the morning sun of Manhattan. The sirens and beeping horns were everywhere. I was relieved to be on my way. The noise, the crowds of people running here and there, and concrete as far as the eye could see soon turned into one quiet freeway, with a carpet of green on both sides and an open blue sky above. I could already feel the tension slowly leaving my body.

My first stop was Springfield, to check in with the parole office. Maggie met me at the bus depot and drove me to the parole office in her dad's 1985 Ford Fairlane. Her big brown eyes widened as we entered the parole office—it was obvious this was all new to her. I checked in, and we both took a seat in the rows of plastic chairs, along with my fellow convicted felons. I waited to be called in.

"Robert Carney," yelled a voice from the doorway that led to the offices.

I stood and turned to Maggie, leaned down, and whispered in her ear. "Try not to make eye contact or talk with anyone. I'll be right back."

She nodded her head yes, and I headed toward the doorway and officer. I glanced back at her. She looked like a sheep in a den of wolves. I followed the officer through the doorway and into an office.

They took my mugshot and fingerprints and asked for the address and phone number of where I would be staying. There were two male parole officers questioning me. The younger one spoke first.

"We'll be out to the Helms's house in a week or two to see the home and talk to the family."

"Okay," I replied. "Are we done?"

"Yes, for now," the older one answered.

Their eyes followed me as I exited the office. I could feel them boring into my back. I nodded to Maggie as I entered the waiting room, and off we went. On the way down in the elevator, she looked a bit out of sorts.

"So did anyone bother you in the waiting room when I was in the back?" I asked.

"One guy asked me what I was in for, but I just ignored him," she said.

"Next time just say *homicide* and they'll leave you alone," I said, then started laughing and gave her a hug before the elevator doors opened. I was pretty sure she liked the excitement.

We drove through the trees and mountains. The change of scenery would do me good. I was fighting a losing battle of staying clean and sober in New York City. Probably because I wasn't attending as many Twelve Step meetings as I should have or taking any suggestions. Every time I turned a corner, there would be a memory or trigger, and the obsession to get high or drink would kick in, and I would be off again.

The drug and alcohol runs had been getting worse now. The thoughts and obsessions of having a drink to calm me down and the rush I got from a shot of cocaine were haunting me constantly. I would get a few days or weeks sober, but then I would give in. Once the little man was out of the cage, I would drink and drug for days until I was completely broke and had exhausted all avenues to get more. One more felony and the Department of Corrections would have me for life, with the new three-strike law, but even that didn't scare me. The obsession and compulsion to continue to use drugs and alcohol ran deep, very deep.

We pulled up to Maggie's quaint home, which was over one hundred years old and sat on the side of a mountain surrounded by miles and miles of countryside. This city boy was out of his element, for sure. Their home sat on eighty-six acres on the side of that mountain. An old barn behind their home had been turned into a wooden workshop. Bob Helms, Maggie's dad, had lost the use of his legs due to diabetes, and he now got around on a walker. Bob used his workshop to make wooden clocks, which he sold.

Then there was Gram, Maggie's grandmother, a large gray-haired woman who dressed in knock-around clothes she got from the thrift store she worked at in town. She was one of the sweetest, kindest women I had ever met. Gram was in her early eighties and had married Bob Helms's father when she was in her teens. She had worked in a factory in town most of her life, until it closed down, and had lived in that house on the mountainside since she was married. Gram certainly got a kick out of me when Maggie had invited me up for Christmas that past winter.

Maggie and I had entered the house and were greeted by Billie Jean and their hound dog, Sneakers. Billie Jean was Maggie's younger sister by a couple of years. She welcomed me with open arms and a big smile. It took Sneakers a minute to get up off the couch and come say hello. He was a bit on the heavy side, and it was obvious he hadn't run in a while. I bent down and gave Sneakers a big hug. I put my duffel bag in Maggie's room, and we headed down to the workshop to say hello to Bob. Gram was still at work in the thrift store in town.

Bob smiled as we entered the workshop. He sat at his worktable, with his walker parked next to him. Maggie's father was a big man, and his blue farmer jeans and white T-shirt were covered in small wood chips and sawdust. The walls were covered with wooden clocks of all shapes and sizes, including cuckoo clocks. He swung around in the swivel chair and took my hand in his big paw and squeezed it tightly.

"I'm glad you made it back out here, Robby. We're all glad to have you here, especially Maggie." He smiled, even as his top dentures loosened and began to slip down. He quickly closed his mouth and moved his jaw side to side to adjust his dentures, while I grabbed his big paw with both hands.

"Thank you so much for having me, Bob. You have a wonderful family, and I'm grateful to be here," I replied.

Maggie and I started attending our Twelve Step meetings, and I began to adjust to this new way of life. I got a job at a local moving company through a man named Ray, whom I asked to sponsor me, from my Twelve Step meetings. Like a good sponsor, he didn't tell me there was a job opportunity there. Ray just said we were stopping by to see an old friend of his at his place of business, which happened to be a moving company. I later remembered that I had told Ray that I'd worked for moving companies in New York. Ray left me and the owner alone in conversation for a few minutes, and the next thing you know, I was employed. I was glad and relieved to be able to earn some money so that I could give Bob and Gram something toward the house and food. I was barely down to cigarette money when I arrived a couple of weeks earlier.

Ray would drive up to the Helms's house once a week and take me to a meeting, then lunch. On our second trip out, he asked me a question on the way to the meeting.

"Robby, have you accepted the fact that you are an alcoholic and an addict?"

"Sure, Ray, just ask my parole officer, or my last girlfriend, or the last guy I worked for. They'll tell you."

"Well, let me ask you this. If I invite you to my house for dinner on Friday night and you say yes, have you accepted my invitation?"

"Well, sure."

"No," he said. "When Friday rolls around and you're home from work and cleaned up, picked up some dessert, knock on my door, and sit at my table with my family, and begin to eat the meal with us, then you've accepted my invitation."

"Huh?" I waited for more, but he just left me hanging there. Later on I thought about it. It made sense. I could say yes, I was an alcoholic and addict all day long, but if I wasn't going to meetings, have a sponsor who will take me through the Twelve Steps, join a home group, or find a Higher Power I can pray to for help, then I wasn't accepting anything. I was just making noise and saying yes. I had to partake in my recovery. In those eighteen months of trying to stay clean and sober and failing, I learned many things, none of which was lost.

Those first couple of weeks in Monson were certainly a change. Two things occurred that let me know I had arrived on another planet. Maggie and I had gone into town with a shopping list from Gram. I pushed the shopping cart, following her around. As Maggie was filling a bag with potatoes, a passing elderly woman looked me in the eye and said hello. I stared back at the woman, as if she had been playing with a short deck, and kept walking. A few minutes later a middle-aged man with a kid in the cart caught my eye and said hello. I shrugged and gave him the gangster nod—a slight lift of the chin, straight faced, and no eye contact.

I quickened my pace and caught up to Maggie. "What's up with these people saying hello? They don't even know me. What do they want?"

She just looked over her shoulder at me, shook her head, and laughed. "Stop being paranoid. They see a new face in town and they're just saying hello."

I looked at her, puzzled. "Where I come from, if a total stranger says hello to you, they want something."

"Oh boy." She rolled her eyes and laughed.

On our way through town, heading home from the market, Maggie pulled over to a garage sale. The person's yard had a bicycle, coffee table, some chairs, a television, albums, a radio, some clothes, the usual. Everything had a small white sticker with the price written on it. I found a couple of T-shirts I wanted to buy.

"Maggie, where are the people selling this stuff?" We happened to be the only potential shoppers there.

Maggie pointed to a large glass jar on a table with a few bucks and some change in it.

"I don't know where the people are, but if you see something you want, just put what it costs in that jar on the table. It works on the honor system."

I gazed around the yard, then up at the windows to see if anyone was peeking through the blinds. "That's crazy. In my neighborhood this stuff and the money jar would be gone in five minutes."

Maggie just shook her head and rolled her eyes and sighed. "Well, you better get used to it." She laughed.

A few weeks had passed, and things were going well. Maggie and I were making our meetings, I was getting some good hours in at the moving company, and I was making a dent in a project I'd started, digging their house and surrounding area out from under a few years of brush and overgrown weeds. I had also adopted a baby rabbit I named Bugs from a pet store in town, while getting Sneakers some dog bones. The big hound dog was coming along well. Our hikes up and down the mountain were getting longer, and his breathing was getting better. Sneakers started to trim up, and my head was clearing.

The constant obsession of drinking and using drugs was subsiding. The Twelve Step meetings, talking with my sponsor, the change of scenery, and keeping busy were really paying off. Although, sitting down for breakfast and watching Bob take out his hypodermic needle to take his insulin really bugged me out, but even that was getting easier. I was starting to feel human. My favorite part of the day was watching TV with the Helms family at night in the living room.

Bob in his rocking chair eating his nightly bowl of ice cream. Gram and Billie Jean had their spots on the couch (Gram knitting), and Maggie, Sneakers, and I were lying on the thick rug on the floor. Me using Sneakers's stomach as a pillow while we passed around a bowl of popcorn or some other treat while watching *Wheel of Fortune*, seeing who could figure out the words first. I hadn't been part of a family for a very long time. It felt good.

In my fourth week in Monson, I received a call from the Springfield parole office. They would be making that trip to check out my living arrangements and speak to the Helms family. That night I told Gram they would be coming by the following morning. The whole family got a little wide eyed and shrugged their shoulders and said "okay" in unison. Especially Gram, with her nervous and contagious laugh. I called into work and took the following day off.

The next morning I sat impatiently, waiting as the black sedan climbed the mountain and pulled up in front of the house. Three parole officers emerged from the car, two men and a woman. They wore plain clothes, but their shields and guns were visible from their beltlines.

I turned and looked at Gram and Bob. "Here they come."

Bob sat in his recliner in his sawdust-covered overalls, his walker parked next to him. He looked at me with a serious face, adjusted his upper dentures as they fell loose again, and gave me an assuring nod. "No worries, Robby. We're good."

Gram sat in her corner of the couch with her knitting and winked at me, and the doorbell rang.

"Well, let them in," she said with a smile.

I opened the door and invited them in. "Good morning," I said as they entered the house. I recognized the two male POs from my visit to the Springfield office, but the woman PO was new.

"Where is your room, Mr. Carney?" the older male PO asked.

"Please be quiet. Maggie is still sleeping. She has asthma and had a rough night," I whispered as I led them to the back of the house and her room, which we were sharing. I opened the door, and they peeked their heads in and looked around. Maggie was still sound asleep, her blond head barely sticking out from under the covers. You could hear her wheezing from her labored breathing. I showed the officers the rest of the house, then led them back to the living room. They seemed satisfied with the living arrangements but had some questions for Bob and Gram.

"Mr. Helms," said the female officer, "are there any firearms in the house?"

"No," Bob replied.

"Does anyone else living in the house have any felony convictions?"

"No, ma'am," Bob replied.

Then the older male looked over at Bob and Gram and began his questions.

"Mr. and Ms. Helms, are you and your family aware of Mr. Carney's criminal background?"

Gram looked over at him. "He did mention that he had been in some trouble in the past but was doing his best to stay on the straight and narrow now," she answered with a smile on her face while wringing her hands in her lap.

The older PO looked at Gram, then Bob, and continued. "'Been in some trouble' is putting it mildly. Just so that you and your son are aware, Ms. Helms, Mr. Carney has been getting in trouble since he was fifteen years old, and in and out of institutions since he's was twelve. He's been arrested numerous times. His crimes include car theft, possession of illegal firearms, armed robbery, assault, and the list goes on. We just want to make it clear that you know what you're getting yourself into."

Bob and Gram sat there in silence for a moment, taking it all in. My smile disappeared, then my chin dropped down to my chest, and I closed my eyes for a few seconds. Yes, *that was me they were talking about. Well, me on drugs and alcohol anyway.*

Bob finally looked up, leaned forward in his recliner, and looked from one officer to the other. "Well, we thank you for that information and appreciate the three of you coming out here to inform us." He then continued. "In the time we've got to know Robby, we believe he's going to do just fine, and our home is his home for as long as he likes."

The officers then looked over at Gram.

She looked up from wringing her hands. "That's right, officers. Our home is Robby's home. He's part of our family now." Then she glanced at me, smiled, and winked.

I felt the color return to my face, along with the smile, as my heart swelled.

"Okay," said the older PO as he shrugged. "You're now fully aware of your situation. Here's my card if you have any questions or want to contact me."

As they exited the house, the younger PO looked back at me. "We'll be in touch, Mr. Carney, to let you know when to start reporting to the Springfield office. Here's my card. Call in once a week until we get you set up with a parole officer."

"Will do." I shut the door behind them. I walked back into the living room and thanked both Gram and Bob for opening their home to me.

"No problem, Robby," Bob answered.

Gram, however, just looked at me with puzzled eyes and patted the seat next to her on the couch. "Come and sit next to me."

I plopped down on the couch next to her, and she put her arm around my shoulders, tilted her head sideways, and with a surprised look said, "But you seem like such a nice boy." We just looked at each other for a moment and busted up laughing.

"I am a nice boy, Gram. It's just that once you add any alcohol or drugs to this nice boy, I become that guy they were talking about."

Months had passed, and winter set in. The snow-covered mountains of Massachusetts were beautiful, unlike the city, where the snow turned dirty and into slush the next day. The heavy snow put a damper on my hikes with Sneakers. Though we still got out, we just couldn't hike as far, depending on the depth of the snow. Work had slowed down a bit, which was not unusual for the moving business in the winter. My boss trained and began to use me in the office, answering the phones and giving prices and quotes. I was getting to know the moving business from the inside out.

Things were going well for me in Monson. I did a lot of growing up there. The Helms family and my boss, Jed, put all their trust in me, and as a result, I became trustworthy. I had lived on that mountainside for the better part of six months now, and I had finally gotten a driver's license at thirty-four years old. I bought an old 1976 Plymouth Volare right out of a new friend's backyard for $500. It had been sitting in the yard so long it had sunk three or four inches into the dirt, but it started right up and drove out. I bought the car first, but Gram made me promise I wouldn't drive it until I obtained my driver's license.

My relationship with myself, Bob, Gram, and Billie Jean was great, but not so much with Maggie. We were growing apart in our sobriety. I was beginning to resent her for her selfish behaviors and taking advantage of her family emotionally, physically, and financially. I kept those feelings to myself. Imagine me, a twice-convicted felon, recovering alcoholic and addict, and a thief and liar, judging poor Maggie. I look back now and laugh, but I do wish I was more understanding and less judgmental then. She was doing the best she could, as we all were.

Having lived with the Helms family for six months, I had grown close to them. One morning at breakfast, Bob looked across the table at me.

"Robby, I've been meaning to talk with you," he said seriously. "I've got five acres picked out for you and Maggie to settle on if you want?"

I took a second to swallow my oatmeal, then replied. "Thank you, Bob. Are you and Gram gonna be around tonight after dinner? I really need to talk with you guys."

"Sure, Robby, we'll talk tonight."

Though close to the Helms family, I didn't want to be there under false pretenses.

That morning I drove to Palmer, Massachusetts, and put in five hours at Able Movers, helping pack and move a two-bedroom apartment, then headed back up the mountain to take Sneakers on our daily hike. We were hiking three to five miles a day now, depending on snow and the weather. Sneakers had dropped ten to fifteen pounds and now had some get up and go in him. The hikes helped me to clear my head and try to pray again. I ended the afternoon by pulling and gathering a load of weeds and brush and bringing it down the mountain in a trailer I pulled with Bob's tractor. I still had quite a few loads to go, but the property surrounding the Helms's house was starting to get cleared and look better.

That night Maggie went off to a meeting, Billie Jean went to meet some friends, and I stayed back and helped Gram clear the table and get some alone time with her and Bob. After the plates were put away, I sat at the kitchen table with them.

"You guys have been so kind and helpful, and I don't know how I could ever repay you," I said with a solemn face and sincere voice. "I just want to be as honest as possible with you guys. I don't think Maggie and I are going to work out."

Bob looked over at me with a sad face. "I'm sorry to hear that. I was hoping it might."

Then Gram looked over and chuckled. "I kind of figured that. She's a handful, all right," she added.

I looked at them both sadly. "I'll start looking for a place this weekend."

"Oh no you won't," Gram replied. "There's a big ole room right up in the attic you can have, with a window that looks right down over the mountainside. We'll get it cleaned up this week for you."

Then Bob looked over at me, shaking his head yes. "Oh yeah, there's plenty of room up there, and remember, this house is yours to stay in as long as you like." He put his hand on my shoulder. I hugged them both.

I moved up to the attic and made that my room for the next three months. Maggie was none too happy with the move but would come hang out with me up there a lot. We remained good friends and supported each other's recovery. I was thinking about getting my own place close by that coming spring. Everything was going great. my Twelve Step meetings and working with my sponsor, my job at Able movers, and my relationship with the Helms family, along with the new friends I had made in Massachusetts. If this was what feeling human was, I liked it.

Then the dreaded day came when I received the call from my parole officer in New York. I got home around 3:00 p.m. I heard Gram's voice as soon as I closed the door behind me.

"A Mr. Levy called from the parole office in New York and wanted you to call him as soon as you get home."

"Thanks, Gram." I thought that was odd. I was making my bimonthly check-in calls, and everything seemed fine. Although the Springfield parole office still hadn't accepted me and assigned me a parole officer yet, I was still checking in with them. I reluctantly picked up the phone and dialed the number to the New York parole officer.

"Mr. Levy, Rob Carney here in Monson, Massachusetts. What can I do for you?"

"Hello, Mr. Carney," he answered. "I have some bad news for you. I was just assigned a new supervisor who reviewed all my case files. After seeing yours and realizing Springfield parole hasn't accepted your case yet, he wants you back here within forty-eight hours. You are to report to me in this office by 5:00 p.m. the day after tomorrow."

"Okay, Mr. Levy, see you then."

I hung the phone up and stood there for a few minutes in silence. Sneakers had sat down next to me and was leaning his warm, furry body against my leg. Gram and Billie Jean were sitting at the kitchen table, waiting to hear what Mr. Levy wanted. I bent and petted, then hugged Sneakers. I walked into the kitchen and looked at Gram and Billy Jean.

"I have to go back to New York." I then repeated what Mr. Levy had told me.

They both looked at me in disbelief.

"Can he do that? Is there anything we can do?" Gram asked.

"I don't know," I answered. "But if I'm not back in New York by the day after tomorrow, they'll put a warrant out for me."

It was a long, cold February night in the Helms's house.

The next morning I threw my packed green duffel bag, along with a small suitcase, into the trunk of my '76 Volare. With a broken heart, I turned and headed back into the house to say my goodbyes. They were all gathered in the living room. Both Maggie and Billie Jean were visibly upset and made me promise to call them when I arrived in New York. Bob put his big paw out to shake my hand and pulled me in for a hug.

"You're going to be okay, Robby. You've got a good handle on your sobriety now, and you know you always have a home here when your parole is over."

"I know, Bob," I replied. "I can't thank you enough for opening your home to me."

Then came Gram, who stood there with tears in her eyes while wringing her hands. I hugged her.

She took my face in her hands and looked me straight in the eye. "You stay on the straight and narrow now, and don't forget about us." She held my face tightly.

"I won't, Gram, I promise." I turned to walk out the door, with Sneakers following me. I stopped, bent, and hugged him tight and stroked the top of his head. With tears welling up in my eyes, I told him to be a good boy now, and out the door I went.

It was a gray, cold, and windy February morning as I drove down the mountain toward Interstate 95 South. Tears rolled down my cheeks as I motored away from all the love and trust I'd found in that house. More love than I had ever encountered.

Bob was right. I did have a handle on it now. I managed to put nine months clean and sober together in Monson. I was driving my own car with a valid license, and I had saved a few dollars. The constant screaming in my head for another drink and drug had toned down to a loud whisper. This was the best I had felt about myself in the past twenty years.

Driving south on 95 that cold and gray day, many thoughts went through my head. The closer I sped to New York, the louder the thoughts got. There would be a few more months of fighting my drug and alcohol demons, but this grateful and loved guy driving back from Monson, Massachusetts, would have a fighting chance now.

38

Back in the Hood

I t was a long five-hour drive from Monson, Massachusetts, back to New York. The little man in the cage would not shut up for most of the ride. My resentment with the New York State Parole Office grew the closer I got to the city. The concrete, heavy traffic, tall buildings, and no-nonsense faces of my fellow New Yorkers greeted me. I drove directly to Brooklyn and checked in with my PO, then I was supposed to go straight to my aunt Anna's apartment in the Bronx. She said I could stay with her until I could get on my feet. She lived in the neighborhood I had left almost seventeen years ago, the schoolyard days. As I drove to her house, the little man in the cage started whispering to me again.

"One last hurrah," the little man said, while rattling his cage. "We tried to do the right thing, and look at what they did," he whispered. "We have all this money and the car now. Just one night of drinking and a half a gram of coke, and we'll go to Aunt Anna's in the morning. Who will know? It will be our secret. You can always go back to meetings the next day." The little man would not shut up, and I let him out.

Two days later I showed up at my aunt's house, none too well to wear after drinking and doing coke. I made up some story about getting here late and staying with a friend for a couple of days. That first day and night at my aunt and uncle's place was really tough. The urge to drink and use again was overwhelming. I had let the little man out, and he did not want to get back in his cage. I picked up the phone and called the hotline for Twelve Step meetings in my area. They informed me there was a meeting about to start in twenty minutes just a couple of blocks from my aunt's apartment.

I parked across the street from the church. I could see the sign for the Twelve Step meeting hanging from a side door of the church. I sat in the car for a few minutes, being pulled in two directions as I watched people enter the meeting. The taste of alcohol and the rush from the cocaine was still fresh in my mind. I quickly said the Our Father prayer to myself and pushed the car door open. I dreaded having to start all over again. First Brooklyn, then Massachusetts, and now the Bronx, and I had to start counting my clean and sober time again from day one.

I pulled the heavy wooden door of the church open and climbed the dozen steps to the meeting room. To my surprise, I spotted a few familiar faces here and there. People that I drank, drugged, and spent the better part of my teenage years with. I was welcomed with open arms. I had arrived. I was back home where it all started seventeen years earlier.

I stayed with Aunt Anna and Uncle John for a couple of months until I saved enough money to get my own place. I stayed clean and sober and attended meetings regularly. My aunt Anna had taken care of me for a few years when I was an infant and my mother worked. She loved me like I was her own, and her door was always open to me. Knowing I had been clean and sober for nine months in Massachusetts, she agreed to let me stay with her and get on my feet once again.

I did not tell her I relapsed when I got back. The same rules applied when I stayed with them this time. I left with them at 7:00 a.m. in the morning when they went to work. Then I would return at 6:00 p.m. when they returned from work.

A friend at the Twelve Step meetings told me about a moving company in Harlem that was always looking for good movers. I drove down every morning at 6:00 a.m. to shape up. I was a good worker, so I got picked to work most days and began to save some money. If I didn't get on a truck that morning, I would go and make a couple of Twelve Step meetings.

Within two months I had saved enough money to get a one-bedroom apartment on Mosholu Parkway in my old neighborhood and not far from my meetings. I moved in with a mattress, small television, a coffee maker, and a clock radio. I clearly remember my first night there in my own place. I slept like a baby on that mattress on the shiny wooden floors. The sun coming through the fourth-floor windows woke me up the next morning, as there were no blinds yet. I made a pot of coffee, put some soft rock on the clock radio, sipped my coffee, lit up a smoke, and looked out the window over the courtyard and Mosholu Parkway. I was thirty-four years old, and this was the first time I had keys to my own apartment, with my name on the lease. I spotted my car parked across the street from the building and thought, *Maybe I could do this adult thing legitimately.*

I furnished my new apartment with furniture people were getting rid of on moving jobs. There was a purple velvet couch, red leather recliner, fake palm tree, big red Indian rug, but it was home. I retrieved my rabbit Bugs from my sister's apartment in Brooklyn, where I had dropped him off when I first got back to New York. He was pure white with one ear straight up and the other hanging down most of the time. I'd kept him in a plastic laundry basket next to my bed in the attic at Grams's, then had bought him a rabbit cage as he grew. Bugs was a great distraction for me with my constant mental battle with alcohol and drugs. Bugs and I settled into our new apartment.

It felt great to finally have my own place and car. I was attending my meetings with guys and girls I had grown up with, and making new friends. My job at the moving company was going well. I had earned a spot on the trucks and was going out regularly. I was learning from some of the best movers I had ever worked with. I could now pack, pad, load, and drive. I was in touch with my family in Brooklyn and on good terms with my mother and sisters. I had only one small problem remaining. That little man in the cage would not shut up when I was alone. He would escape from his cage one more time in those last few months and almost kill me.

We had a short moving job that day, and I had gotten off work early. I had some free time, and a thought entered my head. *I have a lot of free time today, and I could miss just one meeting tonight. Just a six pack of beer and a half a gram of coke.* Then the little man chimed in. "No one will know. It'll be our secret. Besides, we've been working real hard and deserve a little break," he said, while staring at me through the bars of his cage. "I promise I'll get right back in," he pleaded. I could almost taste the beer, and the thought of the cocaine rush made my stomach flip and the hair on my neck stand up. I exited the Major Deegan at Fordham Road and went straight to the coke spot, then to a bodega for some beer.

After two and a half months sober in my new apartment, I let the little man out of his cage, and I could not get him back in. I locked myself in the apartment for three days, only leaving to get more coke and booze. I hadn't slept or eaten the entire time. At one point Bugs tried to pull the syringe out of my hand by biting at it while I sat in the bathroom, shooting up coke, or perhaps I was hallucinating. At the end of the third day, I began to shiver uncontrollably. I called an old friend, whom I had recently run into who wasn't sober, to come and help me. I also called a girl in the building I had made friends with at the meetings and who was sober. I refused to go to the hospital, so they both sat with me and held me. I was ice cold and shaking like a leaf. The girl made me eat a sandwich and drink some hot tea. They stayed with me for a couple of hours until I stopped shaking. The next morning I checked myself into the hospital for some damage I had done to my arm from the coke. That was April 4, 1992, the first day of my long-term sobriety.

Part Five: My Second Life

A Day At a Time Publishing

39

Day One

I spent that day and the next couple of days in the hospital on an IV drip of antibiotics. On my second day in the hospital, I was visited by a friend I had made at my recovery meetings. His name was Danny, and he was an older gentleman I had come to know. Danny brought me a coffee, bagel, the daily newspaper, cigarettes, and had my TV turned on. I knew Danny was just getting by financially, because he was living on disability in a furnished room, but I'd seen and learned that a recovering drunk or addict will give you the shirt off their back. I was released from the hospital and picked Danny up to go to a meeting.

He looked over at me as we were driving. "Robby, can you do me a favor?"

"Sure, Dan, what's up?"

"Can you try to stay clean and sober? I really hate hospitals. I've been in and out of them my whole life."

"I'm trying, Dan."

"Well, try harder."

I had heard in the meetings that it would be helpful to find someone whom I could talk to about what was going on in my head, because that is where the relapse begins. I searched and found this young man named Johnnie W. He was in his mid-twenties and was tall, thin, and had a buzz cut. He was always laughing and was well liked by everyone. I heard the older girls say he reminded them of James Dean. He was two years clean and sober.

The story was that before he got sober, he was a homeless dope fiend and wino. They called him the McDonald's doorman because he would hold the door open for people going in and out of McDonald's to hustle a few bucks. I only knew him sober, but knowing where he came from, I thought, *How could you not trust the McDonald's doorman?* After that first Twelve Step meeting out of the hospital, I asked Johnnie for some help.

"Hey, Johnnie, I have a question for you."

"Yeah, what's up, Robby?"

"How do you stay clean and sober? I know how to get clean and sober. It's the staying part I'm having trouble with."

"Well, Robby, it was suggested to me to do these five things, which have been working for me for the past two years. One, don't drink or drug a day at a time. Two, make a meeting every day for at least the first ninety days. Three, get a sponsor who will take you through the Twelve Steps. Four, join one of the meetings and take a commitment. And five, pray your ass off, asking God for help."

"Thanks, Johnnie. Can you repeat them so I can write them down? At this point I'm desperate and will try anything."

"Anytime, Robby. Check in and let me know how things are going."

Two weeks had gone by, and I was staying clean and sober and making a meeting every day. I had asked an old friend who I used to drink and party with, but who was now sober, to be my sponsor. I joined a small and new Twelve Step group in the neighborhood and later took the chairperson commitment. I would say the Our Father prayer every morning on my drive down the Major Deegan to work.

I seemed to be doing okay when I was busy at work, or at a meeting, or on the phone with my sponsor, but when I was alone with myself, I was not okay. I would constantly be thinking about drugs and alcohol. The thoughts and memories of the relief and effects of alcohol and the rush from cocaine, along with the pictures of them in my mind, were unbearable. At the end of three weeks, I met with Johnnie for some coffee.

He sat across from me in the booth of the diner, smiled, and shrugged his shoulders. "So how's it going?"

"I'm doing everything you suggested, but when I'm alone with myself, I can't stop thinking about drinking and getting high. I'm even dreaming about it now. It's literally haunting me."

"Have you asked God for help with that?" Johnnie asked matter of factly, while leaning on the table and sipping his coffee.

"You can ask for help with things like that?" I asked, surprised.

"Of course. You can ask God for help with anything."

My relationship with God had not been good for a long time. In fact, my faith had dwindled down to almost nothing, so this was the prayer I came up with.

"God, if you're up there, please help me. Help me battle these thoughts and feelings and get through this day clean and sober." Then I would say the Our Father prayer over and over to myself. I noticed that my relapses would begin with a thought, then the little man in the cage would start spewing lies about how it will be different this time. Then a picture would form in my mind's eye of a drink or drugs, and I would have a physical reaction. My stomach would flip, and the hair on my neck would stand up and I would be off on another drug and drinking run.

I learned to interrupt that process by praying. As soon as the little man in the cage started talking and the pictures appeared in my head, I began to say the Our Father prayer wherever I was. Focusing on the prayer drowned out the man in the cage's voice, and soon the picture in my mind's eye would change, almost like flipping the channel on a TV, and the urge to use and drink would pass. Sometimes this would happen four or five times a day. As time went on, it happened less and less. After five weeks I actually had a day with no mental thoughts or obsessions to drink or drug at all. A few days later, I had three days in a row free of the obsession, then it was gone. The obsession and compulsion had been lifted. My just-in-case-you're-up-there prayer had worked. My mind opened up a little that maybe God was looking out for me and had been all along.

After all, two heroin overdoses, stabbed in knife fights in prison, shot at in the streets, electrocuted, and the many street fights and car and motorcycle accidents, and I sat there alive and in one piece at thirty-five years of age. I thought God had abandoned me, but after a sober look, it appeared he'd been carrying me all along.

With a couple of sober months under my belt, I was driving my Volare up Broadway in the Bronx and spotted Rick, one of my childhood friends, walking along Van Cortlandt Park. I hadn't seen him in many years. I pulled up alongside him and jumped out of the car.

"Yo, what's up brother?" I yelled with a smile and open arms.

He stopped and looked at me like a deer-in-the-headlights expression. It took him a second to recognize me, then the smile appeared and his eyes sparkled. "Hey, man, how are you?"

I could tell he was not in a good way. His face was drawn, and his clothes were hanging on him. Rick was five foot seven and about 140 pounds, 20 pounds lighter than his normal weight. His brown hair was stringy and unkept. The look of disappointment and urgency in his blue eyes told me everything I needed to know.

"You look good. Did you just get out?" he asked.

"No." I laughed. "I've been out for a year and a half now. I was in Massachusetts for a while, but I'm back and have a place on Mosholu Parkway. The car's mine too. It's even registered and insured."

Rick rolled his eyes and smiled.

"No shit, Rick. I'm doing okay now. I went to a Twelve Step meeting over on Bainbridge Avenue, and I ran into a bunch of our friends from the schoolyard. I have a couple of months clean and sober now, and things are going really well." I rattled off half a dozen names.

His eyes lit up as I mentioned each name.

"What are you doing now? Do you need a ride somewhere?"

"No, I'm just staying with my mother up the block, and I need to get up there," he answered.

I could see the urgency in his eyes and knew all too well what he needed was to get straight. I wrote my number and a couple of our sober friends' numbers down, gave the matchbook cover to him, and told him to call us, that we would help him. I hugged him and watched him walk up Broadway. I was glad to have found my friend.

I had inquired in the meetings about my old childhood friend Wally, whom I had run with for many years in my youth. I'd heard he was hanging around 198th Street and Valentine Avenue with his girlfriend and dingo dog, running coke for the Puerto Ricans. Later that week I drove by 198th Street and saw him standing on the corner. The neighborhood had certainly changed. Not only was he the only White guy around, but he stood six foot and was pale white, with freckles, and had a dingo dog next to him. He certainly did not blend in.

I sat across the street parked for a minute watching my old friend. We had grown up together, ran the streets, and watched each other's backs as kids and young men. He had a pint of wine sticking out of his back pocket and his thin six-foot frame sort of leaned forward a bit, like a tall tree leaning toward the sun. A car pulled up in front of the building with two young White guys looking to cop some coke. Wally approached the car, then entered the building to get their coke, with the dingo dog on his heels.

Once he completed that transaction, I slid out of my car and crossed the street. "Yo, brother, what's up?" I said with a big smile as I approached him.

His eyes lit up when he recognized me. "Yo, what's up?" he said as I gave him a hug. "Man you're looking good. Did you just get out?"

"No." I laughed. "I've been out of the joint for a while now." I told him of my travels to Massachusetts and how I now had my own place on Mosholu Parkway, only a few blocks away. As we talked, I watched his eyes scanning the streets and passing cars for potential customers, so I got right to the point. I pulled my sleeves up and turned my bare arms upward.

"Look, brother, no marks. I've been clean and sober for a couple of months now. I've had a few relapses, but I'm back on track now and doing great. I have my own place, my own car, and I'm working full time. I found this new stuff that really works, bro." Then I told him about the Twelve Step meetings and all the people we had grown up with that I had met there. Wally seemed interested, but a car pulled up in front of the building that he had to attend to. So I gave him my number on a matchbook cover and made him promise to call me. He took it and walked toward the double-parked car, with his dingo dog close behind.

He called me a few days later and was interested in this new stuff I was peddling. I met with him, and we spoke at length about his current situation, which was not good, especially his living arrangements. He was renting a room from someone who, like my aunt Anna, made you leave when they went to work in the morning, and you couldn't return until early evening, when they were home. The past winter had been brutal on him and the dog, and his landlord was also an addict and treated him and his dog cruelly. I asked Wally if I could take a bat to him, but he said no, he still needed a place to live. We stepped into Sal's Pizza parlor on 198th Street for a few slices and continued our conversation. The dingo dog followed us in and sat on the floor next to Wally.

"So listen, Wally, let me help you? How much are you drinking? Let me put you into a detox, then you can stay with me awhile until you get on your feet."

"I'm drinking about ten to twelve pints of wine a day, and I'm on methadone. I've been on the methadone program for a few years now."

"Don't worry about the methadone. We can deal with that later. Let's try and get you off the alcohol now. You can tell them you're on the program, and they'll give you your methadone in the detox."

"Okay, let me see if my sister will watch the dog for me. I'll call you in a couple of days."

I was happy he was actually considering it. The seed was planted.

Rick, on the other hand, called a mutual friend whose number I had given him and was getting help. He was staying with our friend and his family and making Twelve Step meetings regularly. It clicked for Rick right away. He went back to work, got his own place in the neighborhood, and was doing well.

Wally called me back a few weeks later, and I got him in a detox for the alcohol. They detoxed him from the alcohol but maintained him on the methadone. He completed the detox and stayed with me for a few weeks. Our deal was he could stay with me and Bugs as long as he needed to get on his feet, as long as he made his meetings and stayed sober. After two weeks I came home one day, and he was drunk and the kitchen was a greasy mess. He had been trying to make bacon and eggs. I'd thought he might be nipping, but there was no question now. I had to ask him to leave, and it broke my heart. I stared out my fourth-floor window over the courtyard and watched Wally stumble out of the building and into the street. I cried for the first time in twenty years. I knew if I let him stay, I might get drunk before he got sober.

Rick called me a week later and said he ran into Wally and he wanted to get sober again. I suggested we get him into a thirty-day rehab, but since Rick had gotten his own place now, he let him stay on his couch. Wally slowly came off the methadone, and within a few months he was completely clean and sober. At three months Wally picked up his ninety-day token at one of our Twelve Step meetings. The following week he stood up with the ninety-day token in his hand.

"I took this ninety-day token last week, but I have to give it back. I smoked a joint a couple of weeks ago and didn't say anything, but I'll be back for it." Then he sat down.

I knew right then that he was going to make it.

One Saturday afternoon Wally, Rick, and I went to a pool hall to shoot some pool. We were all within six months of being clean and sober. As we were playing, we started to goof on one another. After all, know one knows you like your childhood friends. The three of us laughed so hard, we started holding our stomachs and crying. Laughing from deep within our bellies. It had been a very long time since I had laughed that hard. It was a beautiful gift, having my best two childhood friends back in my life twenty years later, all three of us having survived hell.

At my last attempt at trying to stay clean and sober, I began to take suggestions. One of those suggestions helped me tremendously and, I believe, was the turning point in my sobriety. Because of my dark past, the man in the cage had plenty to work with. I could be having a perfect day in sobriety, and he would whisper some awful deed I had done in the past and steal it away. I would feel as if I weren't worthy of a clean and sober life. I called my sponsor and shared these thoughts with him.

"It sounds to me like you're ready to clean house, Robby."

"Sure, Kyle, just tell me what to do next."

"Are you still asking your Higher Power for help on a daily basis, like we talked about?"

"Yes, I say the Our Father prayer every morning on the way to work, and I ask God to look over my family and friends."

"Good," Kyle responded. "Because you're going to need him now more than ever. I want you to take some time this week to sit and write. Write down every one of those things that haunt you and you're ashamed of, for as far back as you can remember, everything. All the bad behaviors. I also want you to write down the positive qualities you see in yourself. As soon as you're finished writing, call me, and we'll go over it together."

"Okay, I'll get right on it." This was the part of my recovery program where some of the harder work began. I guess if you were going to attend a Twelve Step meeting on a regular basis and expected to stay clean and sober, you should probably do the Twelve Steps. What a concept. In all the Twelve Step meetings I had attended, I would read those steps hanging on the banner and cringe at some of them. What Kyle was asking me to do was one of them.

In all fairness, when I asked him to be my sponsor, he did ask me what I was willing to do to stay clean and sober. My answer was, anything. In the two years I had been out of prison and trying to stay clean and sober, I had been doing what's called two stepping. I would practice only the first and twelfth step. I would not drink and drug and would go to meetings, then try to spread the word and help the new guy coming in, but I wasn't ready to look at myself and do some work. It became apparent that the two-step thing was not working out well for me. I did not want to relive the horrors of relapsing again, waking up hungover, strung out, broke, disappointed, and disgusted with myself to the point of even considering suicide. No, I did not want to relapse again.

I went out and bought a spiral notebook and a new pen and set them on my kitchen table. I wanted to do this perfectly, leaving no stone unturned. I went back in my memory, gathering up all my past misdeeds. I wasn't going to start writing until I could remember them all. A week had gone by as my memory search continued.

I pulled into a gas station on Webster Avenue on my way to a meeting to gas up. I opened the hood of my Volare to check the oil, held the hood open with a small metal bar, because it was broken, then went into the office and paid the attendant $10 to gas up. An Indian fellow who worked there checked my oil and was closing the hood of my car. I noticed the small metal bar sticking out of the hood as he was pressing down on it.

"Yo, what are you doing, man? You're gonna bend the hood," I yelled. I could feel the rage climbing up out of my chest.

"Sorry. I was just checking the oil for you," he replied as he backed up.

Now two other Indian men came out of the office. "What's going on here?" one of the approaching men yelled. I opened the driver's door and took a tire iron out from under the seat.

"What's the problem?" I asked loudly, with the tire iron hanging by my side. All three men ran back into the office, locked the door, and called the police. I stood there alone in the middle of the gas station, six months sober, and asked myself, "What's wrong with this picture?" I jumped into my car and skidded out of there.

I needed some help. My sponsor wasn't available, so I called Rita, my friend Skino's Mom, whom I trusted and who had many years of sobriety. I told her what had just happened, and she told me to come by for some coffee.

"You're lucky you didn't get arrested," she said as we sat at her kitchen table, sipping coffee. "Where are you in your program?"

"I'm on my fourth step."

"How much of your fourth step have you done?"

"Well, I haven't written anything down yet. I'm trying to remember everything before I start writing, so I can get it all down."

"Well, it's no wonder you're feeling like crap and are about to explode. You're walking around with all that crap floating around in your head with nowhere to go. The idea is to get it out, so pick up your pen and start writing and don't stop until you're finished."

I thanked Rita and went home and opened my spiral notebook, with pen in hand.

Looking out my kitchen window as night began to fall, I stared down at the blank white page in front of me. I closed my eyes, said the Our Father prayer, and asked him to please give me the courage to be as honest as possible and get it all down. My furthest memory back was me stealing change out of my father's pants while my parents slept, during one of his rare visits. I was probably three years old. I'd taken a few coins and sneaked out of the apartment and went up the hill to the corner candy store on 176th Street. I'd plopped the change on the counter and ate chocolate jelly bars and rings until the coins were gone, then I'd moved on to the next thing.

For the next three days, I got home from work, went to a meeting, then sat down at my kitchen table and continued writing for at least two hours. It poured out of me. I wrote down everything—the lying, the cheating, the stealing, embarrassing sexual experiences, all of it. Many feelings arose: anger, embarrassment, shame. I cried; I prayed; I wrote. On the third night around eight thirty, I was finished. I called Kyle, and we met at a diner in Yonkers. We sat in a booth and over some pie and coffee, and I began reading to him out of my spiral notebook.

Kyle listened, and when I finished, he asked for the spiral book and read the ten pages back to me, asking me to elaborate on a couple of things. Then he shared some of his deepest, darkest secrets with me. I relaxed and didn't feel so different and alone.

He asked me to tear the written pages out of the notebook. We went out to the parking lot. I held the pages out while he put a match to them. I held them in my hand until the flame grew too big, then I dropped the bright burning pages and watched them as they floated down and the colorful flames danced on the blacktop. The white pages turned to black ash, and a strong wind came along and took them away.

Kyle smiled and looked up at me. "Okay, Robby, now your house is clean," and he gave me a hug.

Driving home that night, I did feel some weight off my shoulders and a feeling of accomplishment. I'd known that I would have to "clean house" one day if I wanted to stay sober, and I'd dreaded it, but it really wasn't that bad. If there were ever an initiation to earn my seat in the Twelve Step meetings, I felt I had just earned mine.

I had heard of people in recovery going through that process and having an immediate transformation. The weight of the world was now lifted off their shoulders, and the sky had opened up. That was not my experience, although the stress of doing it was over, and I did feel some relief.

My payoff began to reveal itself a few days later. I was having one of those really good days in sobriety. It was the weekend, and I had just come from a meeting and was having lunch with some of my sober friends. We were having some laughs over lunch and making plans to have a poker game that night. Then it happened. A memory popped up of when I was strung out on cocaine and had pawned a good friend's jewelry to get more. The little man in the cage began to rattle his cage door and started talking crap.

"Who does that, pawns a friend's jewelry to get more drugs? Do you really deserve this clean and sober life?"

The laughter and smile disappeared from my face for a moment. I thought about that memory and remembered I had shared that incident with God and Kyle. At that moment it had lost its power over me. It was like getting shot with blanks—it had no effect on me anymore. The smile returned to my face, and I joined the laughter again. Now I understood. I had taken much of the man in the cage's ammunition away from him by sharing those secrets. The negative noise in my head had dropped a few decibels. I had much more work to do on myself, but this was a great start.

A few weeks had passed since I'd completed my fourth and fifth steps, and I was feeling pretty good about myself. It was around 5:00 p.m. on a cold November night, and dusk was falling over the city. I stood waiting on the corner of 204th Street and Bainbridge Avenue in the Bronx for a friend to pick me up. He was taking me to his Twelve Step home group meeting to share my story. I had eight months clean and sober. A cold wind blew along the avenue as a light snow drifted down. The street was oddly empty and quiet for this time of day. I stood on one corner in front of a cab service next to a subway station. There was a restaurant across the street on the corner, a busy candy store next to a subway entrance on the third corner, and a bank that was closed stood on the fourth corner.

I watched this young Irish construction worker carrying four bags of groceries across the street, coming from the supermarket just up the block. He was wearing dirty construction boots, worn jeans, and a dusty brown Carhart jacket. He carried two full brown shopping bags, hanging from each hand. The rest of the street was empty and eerily quiet. Snow fell heavier now, as the young man passed me and crossed the street going east. When he reached the middle of the street, bills floated from his jacket pocket onto the freshly fallen snow. A long line of $20 bills trailed behind him. I instinctively looked up and around. There was not one person in sight, just an occasional car driving by.

I stepped off the curb, took a few steps, and began picking up the bills. When I had gotten them all, maybe twenty or more, I looked up at the young man carrying the groceries and called out to him before I could give myself time to think.

"Hey, mister," I yelled loudly.

The guy looked back over his shoulder as he continued walking. "This money just fell out of your pocket as you were crossing the street," I shouted as I held the handful of bills up. He turned and just stood there staring at me. I walked to him and handed him a handful of twenties. "They fell out of your pocket as you were crossing the street."

With a thick Irish brogue, he thanked me. "Jesus Christ, thank you, man. You've no idea the hole I'd be in if I'd gone home to my family without that. I just cashed my paycheck. God bless you, sir." He put his bags down and stuffed the money into his pants pocket.

"You're welcome. You have a good night," I replied as he picked his groceries up and walked off. I turned to cross the street, when I saw the old man standing in front of the closed bank, looking in my direction. I had scanned the corners seconds ago, before I'd handed the money over, and there was no one in sight.

Where did he come from? I wondered.

He stood there staring at me. He wore an old gray baggy suit, a gray fedora, and a black scarf around his neck. He held an overcoat over his left arm. He nodded to me with a slight smile, then just turned and walked off.

My friend's car had just turned the corner to pick me up. I hopped into the car and said, "You're not gonna believe this. You see that old man walking down the block?" I pointed out the back window of the car, but the street was empty. He was already gone.

"Where?"

"Never mind." Chills ran up my arms, and the hair on my neck stood up. I just laughed and thought, *I guess God has his eye on me now, or maybe he always has.*

40

Freedom

I was just a few weeks away from my one year clean and sober anniversary. I had gotten off work early that sunny spring day. My coworkers and I had packed and moved a two-bedroom apartment that morning and were back at the warehouse in Harlem by 11:00 a.m. I was home by noon. I had been putting in a lot of hours at work and was grateful for the break. As soon as I walked into my apartment, I let Bugs out of his cage. Then I changed into some comfortable tennis shorts and a T-shirt, put some smooth jazz on the radio, grabbed a book, and plopped down onto my purple velvet couch. Bugs hopped up onto the couch and nestled between the back of the couch and my side. Twenty minutes into my book, I began to doze off, when the intercom buzzed.

I slowly wandered to the intercom. "Who is it?"

"Parole Officer Harris, just stopping by to do a house check."

"Sure, come on up. I'll buzz you in, Mr. Harris. I'm in apartment 4D on the fourth floor." Instinctively, I scanned the apartment, but there were no drugs, booze, drug-dealing paraphernalia, weapons, or stolen goods to hide. I took a nice, deep breath, let it out, and relaxed. He knocked on the apartment door, and I let him in. Mr. Harris was around my age, maybe in his mid-thirties. He was about five eight and in decent shape, but still huffing from climbing the four flights. He held a file folder in his hand with my name on it.

"Come on in, Mr. Harris. Let me show you around." I brought him from room to room in the one-bedroom apartment. He followed me and made a notation in his file folder.

"You have a nice little setup here, Mr. Carney," he said as he took in the purple velvet couch, white leather recliner, large Indian rug, and fake palm tree in the living room.

"Thanks. I got all this stuff on moving jobs in Manhattan. Either it doesn't fit in the new place, or they just want to get rid of it. Have a seat, Mr. Harris. Would you like a coffee or water?"

"No thank you. What are you reading there?" He pointed to the book on the couch.

"I got off work early today and was gonna catch up on some reading and napping before my meeting tonight. The book is *The Road Less Traveled*. It's eye opening. I read it once before, when I was locked up."

"I know. I've read it also," he replied. "You seem to be doing well, Mr. Carney. No arrests or violations for over two years now. How are you doing with drugs and alcohol?"

"I'm actually doing good. I'll be coming up on my one-year clean and sober anniversary in a couple of weeks. I had a few stumbles along the way, but I seem to be on the straight and narrow now." I smiled inwardly, thinking of Gram.

He opened his file folder and made another notation. He paused and read my file for a moment, then looked up at me, the spotless apartment, and the book on the couch, and just shook his head, in what I thought was disbelief. Then he looked behind me in shock.

Bugs had come hopping out of the bedroom. He had been hiding under my bed.

"You have a rabbit?"

"Yes, I've had him for about a year now. I brought him back with me from Massachusetts."

"I just got one for my five-year-old two weeks ago."

"Cool. They're great pets, except for eating through the phone wires," I said, laughing. "I have two books on rabbits. Let me give you one. They're helpful." We talked about rabbits for a few minutes, then he rose to leave.

"See you next month, Mr. Carney." He shook my hand and left the apartment.

On my next monthly visit to the parole department on 161st Street in the Bronx, Mr. Harris informed me that this would be my last parole visit.

I looked at him, puzzled. "What does that mean? I just have to call in now?"

"No," Mr. Harris replied. "You're done with parole. I'm cutting you loose."

I didn't know what to say. I couldn't remember a time when I hadn't been on probation, in prison, or on parole in the last twenty years. "You mean I'm finished? No more reporting, calling in, or getting visits from you guys? I can even leave the state without permission now?"

"Yes, Mr. Carney. It's over. You've completed your parole."

I just stood there staring at him.

"Well," I said with a straight face, "can I just call to say hello once in a while?"

There was silence for a couple of seconds, then we both broke out into a loud laugh. I shook his hand and walked out onto 161st Street. It was a cool spring evening, and the sun was beginning to set. I looked up and down the block. I was off parole. I could go anywhere I wanted, anytime I wanted. I was free for the first time in twenty years. Free of being supervised by New York State Probation, Prison, and Parole departments, free of worrying about my next fix, free of what I'd done in a drunken blackout the night before. It was getting clearer that by asking God for help, making meetings, and incorporating these Twelve Steps into my life, things were getting better. Who knew?

41

Lady Di

While having sandwiches at my friend Chris's summer rental down in Rockaway Beach in Queens, she walked in. Her name was Diane, and I had seen her before at a couple of our sober gatherings in the Bronx. She stood five feet, with long, curly brownish-red hair and blue eyes. She caught my eye immediately as she entered the house. I was attracted to her, but it was something I'd heard her say that took me over the edge.

"So how is the flower shop doing?" Dee, Chris's wife, asked Diane.

"I had to walk away from it," Diane responded. "My mother opened the flower shop next to her bar to keep me out of the bar." She laughed, her blue eyes sparkling. "After being sober for a while, I realized how much control she had over me with the flower shop, and I couldn't handle it."

"So what did you do?" Dee asked.

"I got a job in a supermarket as a checkout girl, but went back to the flower shop in the evenings to help my mother fill orders until she could get it under control. I recently got a much better job in a doctor's office, and I'm doing well on my own now in my little studio apartment. I was even living above the bar at one point." She looked around the room and caught me eyeing her, and smiled.

I eavesdropped on the whole conversation and was impressed by her. Now there was a girl after my own heart. Not afraid to go for it and walk away from all that security so she could have her independence. I didn't know she had arrived with her friend Richie, but as she was leaving, I made my move on her. I caught her in the front yard.

"Hi, how are you? I'm Robby." I extended my hand to shake hers.

"Hi, I'm Diane." She shook my hand.

"I couldn't help overhearing about your flower shop. It takes a lot to head out on your own. I admire that. Do you have time to head over to 116th Street for a hot chocolate?" The sun was beginning to set, and it was getting chilly.

"No thank you. I actually came here with a friend, and we were leaving now, but thank you," she said politely, and walked off.

I turned to my friend Mickey and nodded. "That one is marrying material." My eyes followed her out into the street and into the car.

I had seen her at meetings in the Bronx before, but never in the light I saw her on that day. If I was going to live this clean and sober life, I wanted a partner who was beautiful, smart, with a good spirit, and not afraid to take chances. I saw her a week later at a meeting in the Bronx and stumbled through asking her if she wanted to grab a slice of pizza after the meeting. She declined for the second time, saying something about having to go home and feed her cat.

On my third attempt, I ran into her as she descended the stairs, leaving the Gun Hill Twelve Step meeting in the Bronx. I stood at the bottom of the stairs in my dirty green shorts, green Liffey Movers T-shirt, and work boots, after a long hard and hot day at work.

"What are we gonna do here?" I asked, with my arms wide open, staring up at her.

"Do about what?"

I thought I caught the slightest glimpse of a stifled smile. "About going out on a date."

"I'm not looking to get in any relationships," she quipped. "I got out of a very bad one almost a year ago, and I'm doing just fine right now by myself."

"I'm not asking for a relationship, just a date. C'mon, the San Genaro feast is going on downtown in Little Italy. We'll have a nice night out, and there'll be plenty of people around."

She rolled her eyes and gave me the once-over. "How long have you been around?"

"Around eighteen months." I knew full well she was asking how long I had been clean and sober. I had been around meetings trying to get clean and sober for eighteen months, but only four months actually clean and sober, so it wasn't a complete lie.

"Okay." She nodded. "I'll go to the feast with you," as if she just agreed to get her tooth pulled.

I picked her up that Friday night, and we have been together ever since. I think she was very impressed when I spent about $20 trying to win her a doll shooting baskets. I finally sank one and won her a stuffed fish, which I believe she still has.

I had such a rough way to go up until I finally got clean and sober. I believed I must be paying a debt for some terrible deed I did in a past life. Then Diane came along, and

I thought, *I must have done one really good thing to deserve her.*

Diane and I have come to find that we have much in common. We've both been abandoned and had to endure things a child should not have to endure. We've both felt less than and have addictive personalities and have tried to fill the hole in our soul with unhealthy things, even sober. We both come from such crazy families that we kid each other. We may not know what to do to sustain a healthy relationship, but we certainly know what not to do. We've learned as long as we keep God and our Twelve Step program up front, we can then be there for ourselves and each other.

After dating for about six or seven months, we moved in together. Or rather, I moved in with her. We both had to work through our trust issues. I had a wad of money with a rubber band around it, and I asked her where I could stash it. She showed me a loose panel in the wall, and I hid it there. A couple of months went by, and she inquired about it.

"So what's up with that stash of money in the wall?"

"Oh, that's my get-the-fuck-out money. Your name is on the lease here, so if we get in an argument and you tell me to get the fuck out, I have enough for a month's rent, security, and a mattress."

"Oh," she exclaimed, "I can understand that," and we both laughed.

We had been together close to a year when I purchased a van and began doing some moving on the weekends on my own. I made some business cards, put an ad in the local neighborhood paper, and in the cold of winter, Wally helped me hang up flyers in supermarkets, on telephone poles, and in some well-to-do neighborhoods. I got a beeper, and I was in business.

I took a job going up to Lake George that winter. It was a large van, an extended Ford Econoline. I packed it tight, using every inch of space, to take it all. The father up north I drove, the colder it got, and the van began to lose power. I sputtered into a town a few miles from Lake George and had the van serviced. They changed the thermostat and gave me some proper fluids for that weather. When I arrived at the unload in Lake George, it was nightfall, windy, and below freezing. I found the key under the mat and unloaded the van with my dolly. On my way home, I stopped to gas up, and called Diane.

"Hey, babe, I'm on my way home now. I had some problems with the van."

"Are you okay? You should have been home by now. Have you eaten?"

"I'm fine. I grabbed some snacks at the gas stop. It's the van I'm worried about. I can feel it losing power again. The cold is messing with it. I'm afraid to turn it off, because it may not start again. Anyway, I'll be home as soon as I can. Love ya."

"Love you too. Be careful."

It was midnight when I pulled into the toll on the Tappan Zee bridge. I had a strong feeling the van would die on me when I stopped to pay the toll, and it did. The toll booth attendant told me to leave the van there, that they would come and tow it. He gave me a card where I could pick it up in the morning. It was freezing cold and snowing. A big truck hauling live chickens in cages pulled into the toll booth next to me. I could hear them cackling under the gray tarps.

"Can you give me a ride down the Deegan to McLean Avenue?" I yelled up to the older gray-haired Latino driver.

"Sure, poppy, get in," he said in broken English.

He did not understand much English, but he knew I broke down and I needed to get to the Mclean Avenue exit. It was a quiet half-hour ride down the Deegan as the snow fell. He pulled off at McLean Avenue so I could jump out. I offered the gentleman $20, but he just smiled, shook his head no, and waved me off.

I began my descent down the hill and into the Woodlawn neighborhood, making fresh tracks in the half-foot of snow. There was no traffic, and it was eerily silent as the snow fell steadily and glistened off the bright streetlights. I pulled my wool hat down over my ears, buried my cold hands in my coat pockets, and with my head down to avoid the wind, I walked the last ten blocks home. I had been going for twenty hours straight, and I was cold, hungry, and tired. I turned the corner onto Van Cortlandt Park East, trekking through the fresh snow, almost home.

Two blocks away I could see the three-story brick house that we lived on the top floor of. There was a light on in the front room. I saw a figure move in the light as I got closer. I knew she had been looking through the window, waiting for me. That light was my beacon home. It meant her warm embrace, a hot meal, and a bath. There were no other lights lit for me. I had found my way home.

42

Who's This Guy?

I walked into the basement studio after a long day's work, and Diane came out of the kitchen to greet me. She stopped short after getting a good look at me.

"Where did that blood on your shirt come from? And your face is red as a beet."

"I had a fight with one of the drivers at work. It's no big deal. I work with a rough crew at the moving company down in Harlem. Sometimes if two guys have a problem, they just punch it out behind a trailer in the lot."

"Well, get washed up. I'll get dinner ready, and you can tell me what happened."

"There's not much to tell really. There's this new guy. A Turkish guy named Ahmed. He started driving for Liffy a couple of months ago. He's quiet, a hard worker, and is married with a little daughter. I'm really surprised we got into it."

"How did the fight start?"

"Ahmed and I bumped heads twice since he started working with us. Once when I had talked him into letting me take that TV off the truck we were working on. It had been left on the truck by accident from a long-distance job. The customer ended up putting a claim in for the TV, and Ahmed gave me up to the boss when questioned. I had to return the TV and pay a $100 fine. The second time was when he was taking his time driving the truck back after a long day, so he could drag the day on and get more hours. I told him to speed it up. We were all tired and hungry and wanted to get home. He drove the truck back fast all right, but he was not happy with me. So we did not get off on the right foot."

"How did the fight start today?" Diane asked as I helped her clear the table.

"About a dozen of us went over to the bodega on Third Avenue to cash our paychecks. Most of the guys bought a beer and sat outside the bodega on a small wall in front of the store. I was one of the last to cash my check, and I walked out with my iced tea. As I walked through the crowd of green Liffey mover shirts, a bottle cap bounced off my chest. I looked in the direction it came from, and Ahmed had a freshly opened beer and a smirk on his face. I asked him if he threw it, and he said yes, and did I have a problem with it? So we went at it right there on Third Avenue on the sidewalk."

"Isn't that right around the corner from the moving company?"

"It is," I answered. "As soon as we started throwing punches, a pretty big crowd formed. The inner circle all had green Liffey shirts on, but beyond that a lot of people had gathered. I got lucky and caught him with a couple of good shots, and he went down on one knee. I backed up a couple of steps to see if he was finished, but he got up and charged me, swinging wildly. After a few more swings, the guys jumped between us and broke it up. Ahmed quickly walked down Third Avenue, turning and cursing me as he walked. I could see he was bleeding from his nose and lip."

"Well, I'm glad you're okay."

I went to work the next day, just like any other day. I stood outside the truck yard on 121st and waited for Linda to assign us to our trucks. I looked up and saw Ahmed walk by me and into the yard. His face was busted up. His left eye was blackened and swollen, and his bottom lip was fat and had been split, and his nose did not look right.

I stared at him as he walked by, and realized he'd had to go home to his wife and daughter like that last night. I started to feel bad, really bad, for having caused that. It was an unfamiliar feeling. It was a weird and different feeling for me, for sure. After all, he did start the fight with that stupid bottlecap and trash talk, but that didn't seem to matter at this point. I caused that damage, and I felt terrible.

I called my sponsor that night and told him what had taken place at work. He said it would be a good opportunity to work my Twelve Step program. I sat down and wrote out the whole scenario, from taking the TV off the truck to throwing punches on Third Avenue, trying only to focus on my side of the street. What had I done wrong? The truth was, I had talked Ahmed into giving me the TV. I told him the TV wouldn't be missed and he'd get in more trouble for forgetting it on the truck. When he told the boss I was in possession of it, I was sure his job was on the line. So the truth was, my selfishness and dishonesty caused the whole problem. As for telling Ahmed to drive the truck back faster, I myself had taken the long way back a few times to build up my hours. I had some work to do.

The following morning I went into work a few minutes early. I bouoght an extra donut and coffee. I parked my car on 121st Street and Third Avenue, where Ahmed turned the corner on foot every morning. When he turned the corner, I scooted out of my car and approached him.

"Good morning, Ahmed. Do you have a minute?"

He looked a little startled, but then looked me over and saw the donut bag in my hand and seemed to relax a little. "What's up, Robby?"

"Ahmed, first of all, I want to apologize for taking that TV off the truck. I had no business doing that, and I don't blame you for telling the boss what happened. I understand you have a family to feed. Also, going back in the truck that day, I was out of line to tell you to speed it up, especially in front of the guys. Now I know how the guys feel when I stretch a job out. Most of all, I'm really sorry you had to go home and face your family like that. I feel absolutely horrible."

Ahmed just stared at the ground, looking over at me once in a while as we strolled along 121st Street toward the lot, then he spoke. "Yeah, going home to my wife and daughter looking like this killed me. My baby girl cried when she saw me."

It felt as if a knife pierced my heart at the thought of his daughter crying.

"Anyway, I shouldn't have tossed the bottle cap at you, but I appreciate that you stepped up, and I do accept your apology."

By now we had reached the truck lot, and all the men were standing around, waiting to be assigned to a truck and sent out. The men began to chatter and look toward us as we walked into the lot together. I stopped and turned to Ahmed.

"The coffee and donuts are on me this morning." I handed him the bag. "Once again, I apologize, and if there's anything

I can do to make it right, let me know," I said within earshot of some of the boys, then shook his hand.

"We're good," Ahmed said as we shook hands at the entrance to the lot.

We never became great friends, but we were able to work together with little or no tension after that. I also benefited greatly from that second interaction. The horrible feeling I had for causing the problem was all but gone and was replaced with a really good feeling for having done the right thing, which again, was unfamiliar territory for me.

43

You da Man!

Have you ever had five people tell you that you were capable of accomplishing something, but you were still skeptical? Then this sixth person comes along and tells you the exact same thing, and you believe him absolutely? Chris, whom I had met in early sobriety, was my sixth person. Chris had been in law enforcement for a short while before his addictions caught up with him. He had been sober a couple of years now and was married, with a young son. He had black hair, blue eyes, and was about five foot nine. He had a friendly and outgoing way about him. He made you feel unafraid and good about yourself. I heard that when he was hustling during his using days, he could sell you a dirty T-shirt. He was one of a kind.

When I first met him, we were all talking after one of our recovery meetings. I overheard him say he was taking a group of elderly people from a nursing home to Yonkers raceway, then to a Jewish deli afterward.

"Hey, Chris, do you need some help with the old people at the track?"

"Sure, Robby, that would be great. The nursing home supplies a small bus and driver. After we get them settled in their seats at the track, you can run and place bets for them. Meet me in the parking lot of Yonkers raceway at 11:00 a.m. on Friday, then we'll take them to lunch after the races."

"Great, see you Friday," I answered.

About a dozen elderly people exited the bus, some in wheelchairs and some in walkers. Chris joked with them all, making them laugh and enjoy themselves. We got them seated and I ran and placed bets for them.

Over lunch at the Jewish deli, I told Chris how I had just gotten off parole and was finally free to travel now. He told me he was visiting a sober friend in San Diego in a couple of weeks. Would I like to join him? I spoke to Diane about it, and we agreed I should go. I had not left New York since rehab in Massachusetts and Canada when I was a teen. We flew to San Diego and stayed with his friend Floyd, who I had met once before in New York. Floyd lived in Ocean Beach, an old hippy town. It was a new world to me.

Floyd had to work, so Chris and I took a boat on a day trip to Ensenada, Mexico. When we walked off the boat, we were surrounded by a group of Mexican women with little children selling Chiclets gum and other candies. We gave them a couple of dollars and waded through the crowd. There were Mexicans in stands everywhere selling everything—jewelry, bags, hats, toys. A gentleman even offered to take my picture sitting on a donkey that was painted with white stripes to look like a zebra. I declined but laughed.

Chris and I separated to go shopping for our girls. We were to meet back at a specific corner in a half hour. I had found a handmade Mexican bracelet for Diane and returned to the corner.

There was Chris in the middle of twenty to thirty Mexican women and their small children, some carrying their infants on their back or side. They were all yelling and shoving Chiclets gum and candy at him. Chris stood towering above them in the middle of the crowd with a handful of bills, mostly singles and fives, giving money away. They were practically on top of him. I made my way through the crowd and pulled him out.

"Are you okay?" I asked, laughing as we walked away.

"Oh yeah," he said, and smiled as he handed out a few more bills to the street beggars.

I learned much from Chris. He was a giver. We made our meetings in San Diego and made some new sober friends. Seeing the beauty of San Diego and the country of Mexico in just a couple of days was overwhelming. This sober life was becoming very attractive. We returned home after a week, and I told Diane of our adventures and promised to one day show her San Diego.

Back in New York, I asked Chris to come and check out a van I was thinking of buying for my Reliable Man with Van business. My current van had been giving me problems. We pulled up to the guy's house in Yonkers, and the big, extended gray van was parked in the driveway. He was asking $1,800 for it. The seller, a young heavyset guy with long black hair and a beard, used the van to deliver rugs. He had carpeted the entire inside, making it perfect to move furniture in.

On the ride there, Chris told me to take $300 of the $1800 and put it in a different pocket.

"Why?" I asked.

"Because you're only gonna pay $1,500 for it." I put the $300 in my back pocket, got out of the car, shook the seller's hand, and inspected the van. It looked and sounded great. Then Chris got out of his black Cadillac and walked over. I introduced him as my business partner. He began walking around the van and kicking the tires.

"These tires are shot. They're gonna have to be replaced. Could you open the hood and start it again?" he asked the seller.

"Sure," the seller replied. "It runs well for me, and I've kept it serviced."

Chris peered into the engine as it was running.

"The starter doesn't sound good, and that carburetor will have to be changed soon. That flywheel is on its last leg and will have to be replaced too. It's gonna cost you a few bucks to get this up to par, Robby. I wouldn't pay more than $1,200 for it," Chris said matter of factly, then walked over and slid back into his Caddy.

The seller stood there speechless. "It's a good van and worth at least $1,800," he said, in a low voice, not seeming so sure of himself now.

"Well, my business partner knows engines, and we still have some others to look at. I'll tell you what. I'll give you $1,500 cash for it right now," as I pulled out the wad of folded bills. I nodded toward the Caddy. "If he asks, just say I paid you $1,200 for it."

He looked at me and the cash, then over at Chris in the car, then at the van. "Okay." He then went in to get the title. We swapped cash for the van, title, and bill of sale. I drove the van home, following Chris back. When we arrived at my house, I looked at Chris and shook my head.

"I didn't know you knew about vans and engines and tires?"

"I don't. I made all that shit up."

I just shook my head and laughed.

Chris was a smart businessman, but he also had a heart of gold. We were driving along one day in his shiny black Cadillac. As we were exiting the Cross Bronx Expressway, we stopped at a light. A homeless guy approached the car with a squeegee, offering to clean his windshield. Chris told him no thank you but gave him a buck anyway, as did I. At the next light, the same thing happened. This time Chris gave the guy a buck, and I didn't.

We were driving along quietly, when Chris looked at me. "So why did you give the first guy a buck, but not the second?"

"Well, the first guy looked like he would use the money for food or shelter. The second guy looked like he would use it to get high or drunk."

"Oh, okay." Chris shrugged, then continued to drive along quietly. After a few moments, I turned toward him.

"Hey, Chris, I have a question for you. How come you give anyone who asks a buck, or more?"

"Oh, that's easy." Chris smiled. "God comes in all different disguises."

Needless to say, he was right, and I followed suit. Chris helped me with many things.

I had been with Diane a couple of years now and wanted to ask her for her hand in marriage, but I knew nothing of such things. In the life I had lived for twenty years prior to meeting her in sobriety, there was no room for that, and I had no idea how to go about it. I went to Chris, who had been married for ten years, and asked how that worked. We had a man-to-man, and he answered some important questions for me.

When I'd first met Chris, he wasn't working but had just gotten an offer to run a parking lot in Hell's Kitchen in downtown Manhattan. The last guy to run it was a wino and couldn't make the $500 a week rent. I watched Chris turn that parking lot into a gold mine. He got contracts with companies in the area and ran it 24-7, with hired help. A year later he opened a deli in Rockaway, in Queens, where he moved to from the Bronx with his wife and son. His wife ran the deli, and the parking lot became successful. Chris was not afraid of hard work and going for the brass ring. I admired him for that, and I was learning much from him during our friendship, including how to be a friend.

I really didn't have a great track record at keeping friends. Mostly because of putting drugs and alcohol ahead of any relationships I had, and I also noticed this weird thing I did when I did make a close friend, which I expressed to Chris one day. We were having breakfast in a diner in the Bronx after a morning meeting.

"Hey, Chris, we're becoming good friends, and I just want to warn you of this dumb thing I notice I do, because I value our friendship."

"What's that, Robby?"

"I do this thing where the minute I see we're not the best of friends anymore, because everything ebbs and flows, I sabotage the friendship. I find some reason to tell you you're not a good friend and to fuck off." Chris looked over at me with a sad, but serious face.

"Well, don't do that to me, Robby. I want us to be good friends for a long time. You know, sometimes God puts people in our lives for us to learn a lesson. When the lesson is learned, he plucks that person out of our life. It doesn't mean we should kick that person in the ass on the way out. We have to thank them for the lesson learned, then be congenial to them when we see them."

"What is congenial?" I asked.

"Say you see that person at a restaurant or meeting after you're not as close anymore. Say hello, ask how their family is doing, and give them a hug, then move on but keep the door open and wish them well."

Thanks to Chris, I have many friends today, some close and some only congenial, but I don't throw them away anymore.

Chris is one of a handful of friends I have made, through my recovery groups, who have helped me change my life for the better. From Chris I received confidence and learned not to worry and take everything so serious. I would stay close friends with Chris over the years.

44

San Diego

In September 1995 Joey T. came along for the ride with me to buy an engagement ring for Diane. Joey was a short, thin Italian kid from the neighborhood. I used to frequent his uncle's pizza shop on 198th Street when I was a teenager. Now we were both in our thirties and doing our best to stay clean and sober.

Joe would crack me up. "So why are we driving all the way down to Canal Street for a ring, Robby?" he asked as we drove down the West Side Highway.

"I'll get the best deal on a diamond ring from the Hasidics on Canal Street. I want to get Diane a nice engagement ring."

"Are you crazy?' Joey said with his hands raised in the air. "You don't give her a real diamond. You give her a nice zirconia."

"A zirconia? Are you kidding? What if she has it checked out?"

"If she really loves you, she won't get it checked out. Believe me, Robby. I've been engaged three times. I know about these things." He said this with his most serious face as we drove along the Hudson River.

I started laughing so hard, it was all I could do to hold on to the steering wheel.

After much bargaining with the Hasidics, I found her the best diamond ring I could, then drove to City Island to her parents' bar to ask for their blessings. Helen and Jimmy were thrilled and gave me their blessings. I was supposed to wait two weeks and propose to Diane on her birthday, but I couldn't wait. That very night I got her to agree to drive down to Rockaway Beach. I proposed to her on the beach, only yards away from where I had fallen in love with her two years earlier. Then we walked down the block to Chris's house to break the news to Chris and Dee.

Less than four months later, we had a beautiful wedding. Both our families and all our friends in our recovery groups attended. It was a proud day for my mother. My younger sister, whom I'd become close with, was part of the wedding party. Keeping my promise to Diane, we honeymooned in San Diego for a week. We had dinner at the Hotel Del in Coronado one night. As we were leaving, we looked up and saw a full moon with a bright ring around it. We believed it was a sign to start a new life there, and we did.

We went back to New York from our honeymoon and sold everything we had, then moved back to San Diego three weeks later. It was Diane; my rabbit, Bugs; Diane's black cat, Cody; and a greyhound/shepherd mix, Griselda, who'd been sick when we'd rescued her from Diane's mother's bar. We had about $10,000, and we mailed ourselves ten boxes of our personal belongings. Our families were in shock but wished us well. Chris reassured me that he would be in my corner no matter what. He actually asked if he could pay our first six months' rent, just to take the edge off. He knew how much I worried about money. I declined but thanked him and told him I knew he would have my back if we got in trouble.

Once there we began to make our Twelve Step meetings and make some new friends. It was a tough transition at first, but we also had each other and God to help us get through the lonely times without our family and friends. Although, it really was paradise, having just come from the Bronx. I bought a fourteen-foot box truck with half our savings and started hauling. Which meant I had a truck and would take stuff to the dump for you, or move your furniture from point A to point B. I ordered business cards, put an ad in the local free newspaper, *The Reader*, and I was in business.

Diane found a job as a medical biller for a doctor's office. My hauling business was slow to start, and money was tight for a while. We bought a used Honda Civic that almost drained us because it kept breaking down. After our first few months there, we began to run out of money. At one point we were down to our last $500. We tried not to panic. Our first job was to remain clean and sober, and that was going well. We were making our meetings and getting involved.

We'd rented a small cottage in Ocean Beach, in San Diego, about fifty yards from the ocean. Every morning I would walk up to the corner with my cup of coffee and cigarette, sit on a stone bench atop a cliff overlooking the ocean, and say my prayers. I asked God to look out for us and our families and help us build a new life here.

My dream when we'd moved to San Diego was to start my own moving company. Being sober for a few years gave me some confidence. I was also trusting in myself and God more. If we were going to start a moving company, we needed a good amount of money for a regular moving truck, equipment, insurance, permits, and fees. I knew it wouldn't be easy. Diane and I sat down and came up with a plan, which I call the Golden Goose theory.

The Golden Goose being the moving company. On the road to the Golden Goose, we would come upon many golden eggs. We would have to bypass and not purchase any of the golden eggs along the way if we wanted to have enough money to buy the goose itself. A golden egg could be described as a trip home for a wedding or visit, or a newer car, or a bigger bungalow. I did buy a Suzuki 700 motorcycle for $500 from someone who was moving. We would pack a lunch, get on the bike, and zoom all over San Diego. It was inexpensive and fun.

We learned to tighten our belts for the next couple of years. No trips back to New York, minimal eating out, shopping at thrift stores for clothes and house accessories. If we went to the movies, we went to the matinee for $3 apiece and snuck in our own candy. We saved what we could. The money was building up, but another obstacle appeared ... me. The man in the cage began talking to me regularly when I was alone, and I wasn't sharing it with anyone. As the man in the cage's voice got louder, my dreams of starting my own moving company faded.

"They'll never give you a moving license—you're a two-time convicted felon. You've been a criminal since you were a teenager, at least nine or ten arrests. They don't give guys like you a license to move people's personal property."

I knew who was talking, but I was starting to believe him.

45

Homer

God would place another sixth man in my life that would tell me I could do it, and I believed him. His name was Homer. I met him at a men's Twelve Step meeting I had joined in San Diego. He was in his mid-seventies and had been sober for many years. He stood about five foot ten. I was sure he was once six feet tall, but age had leaned him over slightly. He was a kind and gentle man with a bit of a scruffy voice, due to age. Homer was a staple in that men's Twelve Step recovery group.

I had accidentally blocked his car in with my motorcycle at an outdoor meeting we attended in the park with our wives, on a Saturday morning. We got into a conversation, and the four of us decided to have lunch together that day. That would be the beginning of a friendship that would last a dozen years, until Homer's passing.

Homer was a successful business broker and had an office on El Cajon Boulevard. We would meet once a week for lunch at the Chicken Pie Shop. He had asked me about my hauling business a couple of times, but I would always try to change the subject. I was just a guy with a truck trying to make a buck. I had no hauling license or anything. It was all cash.

"So tell me more about that business of yours?" Homer asked me again over lunch.

"Well, to be honest, Homer, it's not really a licensed business. I advertise in *The Reader* as a hauler. I use my truck to take people's junk to the dump or do small moving jobs for them for cash."

"Why don't you get a business license so you can advertise correctly and get some real business?"

"I don't know if they'd give me a business license with my record."

"Well, why don't you try and get the business license. If you run into any problems, I'll try and help you with it."

"Okay, Homer, I'll try."

As it turned out, Homer was right, and I was able to get the business license for hauling. I had my box truck lettered with *Reliable Man Hauling Service*, with my contact numbers on it. My phone and pager blew up. I was out either hauling people's junk to the dump or doing small moving jobs every day. If I needed an extra hand, I would go down to the beach and grab a homeless guy living down there. I would pick the cleanest and most sober one. The guys soon yelled and waved at me when I drove by the beach in my truck.

The money began to roll in, but I was getting beat up. No job too big or small was a part of all my advertising. If you wanted a cement wall knocked down and taken away, I got a sledgehammer and did it. Clean a garage out or knock it down and haul it away, done. Want a big pile of dirt taken away? I have a shovel and a truck. I'm your guy. Cleaning out the college beach rentals was easy. I dragged the stuff down the stairs, tossed it in the truck, and off to the dump. But if it was a move, I had to wrap everything in pads and have help carrying it.

At the end of a hard day, I parked the truck on a hill in front of our house. If the truck was dirty from a hauling job, I would hose it out and leave the roll-up door open so it would dry, then throw my dollies and pads on it if I had a moving job the next day. After the truck was done, I threw my dirty boots and T-shirt over my fence and walked up the hill to the cliffs. There were rock steps that led down to an alcove and the ocean. It was my own private beach. I jumped in and let the ocean cool me off and wash away all my dirt and sweat and let the salt water heal any bruises or scratches I had gotten that day.

In our second year in San Diego, Homer and I were having lunch on Thursday at the Chicken Pie Shop, when he inquired about the business again.

"So how's Reliable Man Hauling doing?"

"Good. The money is starting to come in. I'm getting a little beat up with the hauling, but it's all good."

"What do you really want to do with yourself?" Homer asked as we ate our lunch.

"Well, Homer, my dream was to start a moving company when we got here eighteen months ago. Moving furniture is something I've done for a while, and I'm good at it. The reality is, they would never give me a moving license with my criminal record."

"How do you know for sure? Why don't you go for it and see what happens. You didn't think they'd give you a business license for hauling, but you got it. And remember, if you hit a wall, call me, and I'll see what I can do."

Homer and his wife, Ruth, and Diane and I had become very good friends over the past year. The four of us would have lunch after our Twelve Step meeting in the park on Saturdays.

Homer once asked me, "Hey, Robby, you know God wants you to have a good life, right? He wants you to be happy, happy in love, prosperous, and live to your full potential."

I looked at Homer with squinted eyes. "Are you sure?"

"Yes, I'm positive." He laughed. "You know what I like about you, Robby?"

"What's that Homer?"

"You're unscarred," he answered.

"What do you mean, unscarred?"

"Well Robby, I know your whole story, everything you've been through. But if I didn't, I would never know because you're unscarred."

Like me, Homer was an entrepreneur. Born in Hollywood, California, he was raised in a single-parent family and had a brother and sister, and their family was poor. He said he wasn't from the wrong side of the tracks but the middle of the tracks. Apparently his house had actually been in the middle of two sets of train tracks. When he was a youngster, he and his brother had a car and would do tour guides for the tourists all over Hollywood. He said they would drive by a big house, and someone would be in the yard, and they would say, "Don't stare, but that is Marilyn Monroe" or "Jerry Lewis," and the people would gasp and nearly faint. From the back he didn't know who they were, but neither did the tourists.

In his earlier years as a broker in San Diego, Homer had sold a liquor store to a respected elder in the Chaldean community in San Diego. Chaldeans are Christian refugees who have fled Iraq in the face of religious persecution. There was a large population in San Diego, and they owned most of the package (liquor) stores.

The elder was not happy with the purchase of the store and did not want to pay Homer his commission.

Homer said he had given the incident some thought and decided to let it go. He told the elder that he was sorry he was not happy with the sale, that he would not pursue his fee, and that he would do what he could to help him sell it if he wanted. From that day forward, he became the sole broker for the Chaldean community in San Diego. They loved and honored Homer. The community threw him an eightieth birthday party, to which we were invited.

I went ahead and applied for the moving certificate in San Diego with a push from Homer. I received the written application form, which required a good-running moving truck that they would inspect, general liability insurance, and workers comp. I started by contacting the head of the Public Utilities Commission (PUC) in San Francisco and was later directed to deal with the head of the PUC in San Diego, who would also give me a two-hour written test once the application was completed.

A few weeks had gone by, and I was right on top of it. I got my box truck up to par and ready for a DOT inspection. I paid for all the insurances, cargo, general liability, and workers comp. Then I came across this question on the last page of the application: "Have you ever been convicted of a felony crime of moral turpitude?" Were they kidding? Why would they wait until the end of the application to ask me that? I worried and panicked, not sure how that would affect me. I could also picture the little man in the cage laughing and rubbing his two gnarly hands together. "Oh, I'm going to have fun with this." I immediately called the head of the PUC in San Diego to feel them out.

"Hi, this is Robert Carney. I'm applying for a moving certificate, and I'm inquiring about one of the questions on the application."

"Sure, what is it?" he asked.

"The question about the felony crime of moral turpitude. I ..."

"Have you ever been convicted of a felony?" he asked before I could finish my sentence.

"Yes, but ..."

"Then mark yes in that box."

"Okay, thank you." I hung up the phone and sat there stunned.

"I told you this would happen," the little caged man whispered in my ear. I began to pray to shut his voice out, then a thought came to me. *What about Mr. Quinn in San Francisco? He was very helpful to me in the beginning, and he is the head of the PUC of California.* So I called him.

"Hi, Mr. Quinn. This is Robert Carney, from San Diego."

"Hi, Mr. Carney. How is your application coming along?"

"It's coming along, Mr. Quinn. I've gotten everything done, and it's almost completed. I did want to ask you about one of the questions though. The one about the felony. I've been in some trouble as a youth."

"I'm going to ask you two questions, Mr. Carney. Have you been arrested in the last ten years?"

"No, Mr. Quinn," I answered. *I had been incarcerated but not arrested.*

"Second, have you ever been arrested for or convicted of any sexual crimes?"

"No, Mr. Quinn."

"Then mark no in that box, Mr. Carney."

"Thank you, Mr. Quinn. Have a great day." With that I completed the application, took and passed the written test, and started my first moving company. When I received the Household Goods moving permit in the mail, I called Homer, and he, Ruth, Diane, and I went out to dinner to celebrate another dream come true. I looked across the table at Homer with admiration and thanks. He had given me the confidence and the push to go for it.

I could describe Homer in many ways—honest, kind, generous, helpful—but the word that sticks out most is *fatherly*. I could not believe our good fortune. We were living in paradise, only yards from the ocean, where we watched the sunset every night. We were involved in our Twelve Step meetings and making new friends. And now God had blessed us with a business so that I could provide for Diane and me. I also believed that God had given me this business to somehow help other recovering alcoholics and addicts.

I began to hire guys who were trying to get clean and sober and back on their feet again. I hired them from Twelve Step meetings and halfway houses. After two months of picking guys up and dropping them off at their halfway houses and sober-living programs, all the while trying to teach them how to be movers, I reached my breaking point. I stopped by to check on a job in La Jolla and heard one of the guys tell the customer they had to wrap it up because he had a 5:30 curfew at his sober halfway house. I soon realized that no, maybe this was not God's plan for my moving company.

I prayed on it, talked to my new sponsor, and came up with another plan. I would form a moving company that consisted of regular, seasoned movers. Then help one or two guys who were getting on their feet and show them the ropes. I realized without a successful moving company, I could help no one or pay my bills. This plan worked out much better for me, the guys I was trying to help, and my customers.

This chapter would not be complete if I did not tell you about Tommy.

It was 6:00 a.m. as I walked up to the stone bench overlooking the cliffs and ocean only yards from our cottage. I had my coffee and cigarette and was getting ready to say my prayers, when I saw a young man with long blond scraggly hair sitting on the bench. It was obvious he had not showered, and his clothes were well worn.

"Good morning," I said as I sat on the other end of the stone bench.

"Morning," he mumbled, not making eye contact but continuing to stare out over the ocean.

"Care for a smoke?" I took out the pack and offered him one.

"Thanks." He took one but would still not make eye contact with me. We sat in silence smoking our cigarettes for the next few minutes. I prayed silently, and Tommy just stared out over the ocean. Tommy was homeless for sure, but he was about five foot ten, in his twenties, and on the thin side but in decent shape.

"I'm Robby." I extended my hand.

"Tommy," he murmured, still not making eye contact, but shaking my hand. His hand was coarse and dark from not washing.

"Tommy, would you be interested in making some money moving furniture?"

"Yes," he answered, making eye contact for a brief moment.

"Okay. Be here tomorrow at 7:00 a.m., but you have to be showered and have your hair combed, because we'll be in customers' homes. Can you do that?"

"Yes," he answered, nodding his head up and down while staring at the ground.

Tommy showed up the next morning. He'd cleaned up the best he could. He probably used the public showers down at the beach. His long blond hair was in a ponytail, and I was sure he was wearing the cleanest shorts and T-shirt he owned. He was passable, for sure. We moved a one-bedroom apartment that morning, and he did a good job. He didn't talk much, but he followed directions and worked hard.

For the next few weeks, Tommy would be sitting on the bench at 6:00 a.m. I would bring an extra cup of coffee and cigarettes. He would finally tell me his story. He was homeless and living under a small bridge in Ocean Beach.

Tommy was from the Midwest and had been in San Diego for almost a year now. He had been a musician back home. He played bass guitar and had been part of an up-and-coming group. They had actually opened up for a famous heavy metal band during the nineties. He had also been engaged to his childhood sweetheart, and they had set a date to be married. According to Tommy, the success of the band had happened quickly, his head and ego had gotten too big too fast, and his constant partying had gotten the best of him. After a few embarrassing incidents, he was asked to leave the band, and his fiancée left him shortly afterward.

Before he could drink himself to death, he took what little money he had left and some expensive guitars and moved to San Diego. He worked for an auto parts store and was doing okay for a while. He had even put the alcohol and drugs down. He then had an awful run of bad luck. His apartment had been burglarized, and they took the money he had stashed and his expensive guitars. He could not make his rent that month and was soon evicted. He then lost his job because of his living conditions. He gave up. Tommy had been homeless for almost a year when I'd met him on the bench that morning.

He began to work steadily for me and asked me to hold some money for him. I spoke to Homer about him, and he suggested we get him in a sober-living home that we were involved in. Tommy agreed, and we got him into Heartland House the following week, when a bed opened up. Tommy was quiet, respectable, and paid his room and board there, but was a loner and stayed to himself.

After a couple of months, he found a more secure job. One that offered him forty or more hours a week on a regular basis. I was happy for him and wished him well. I also reminded him he could always come back to work for me if it didn't work out. About a month later, I was told Tommy had left Heartland House. I did not see or hear from him for about three months. When I was driving through downtown San Diego with Diane one night, I thought I spotted him on a corner panhandling. I pulled the car over and told Diane I would be right back. It was Tommy, all right. He spotted me crossing the street and turned to look in the other direction.

"Tommy." I looked at the back of his blond tangled hair and the long, dirty coat he wore on a warm day. He turned slowly with a paper McDonald's coffee cup with some change in it in his hand. I stuffed a couple of bills in the cup, and he looked up at me with a sad smile.

"Thanks, Robby. I'm sorry," he said with a look of disappointment and stared down at the sidewalk as people hurried by on either side of us.

"Tommy, look at me," I said. "It's okay. I understand," and gave him a hug. I took a step back and looked him in the eyes, "One thing you know, Tommy, is that if you get tired of this life, you can change it. Even if you just want to talk, I'll be on the bench every morning at six o'clock."

"Thank you for everything, Robby." Then he turned, shook his cup, and said, "Spare change for food please."

That would be the last time I ever saw Tommy. I don't know if he had an alcohol or drug problem, but he had been broken for sure, and I understood that.

46

Mikey Bats

We had been in San Diego almost two years when Mikey Bats retired from his doorman job in Manhattan. He called us and asked if we could find a studio apartment for him. We found him a nice place a half a block from the ocean in our little town of Ocean Beach. We made it livable for him. I furnished it with the basics, and Diane put the finishing touches on it—curtains, bedspread, shower curtains. We even filled the fridge for him.

Mikey Bats was a good friend and a helper of God's children, especially the broken ones, like me. I first met Bats on my last attempt at trying to get and stay clean and sober. I walked into a Twelve Step meeting, and he yelled across the room, "Hey, Robby, how's the job search going?"

"I'm still looking, Bats."

"Hey, John," Bats yelled to a guy who'd just walked into the meeting. "Don't you work for a moving company? Hook this guy up, will you. He's a mover." I was working for an Irish outfit down in Harlem the next day.

Mikey Bats had taken a liking to me and was easy to talk to. He looked familiar when I first met him. I was sure he was one of the old dope fiends I'd seen nodding in the neighborhood when I was a kid.

Mikey Bats got sober when he was forty-nine. He had spent thirty-five of those years in and out of institutions as a result of alcohol and drugs, mostly prisons, starting with juvenile lockdowns when he was just a kid. He was down and out and on a soup line in the South Bronx when he was approached by someone who also helps God's children. He brought Mikey up to Graymor, a recovery men's shelter upstate, and the rest is history.

He was blessed by the Franciscan Friars there, and then he began to bless others. He got cleaned up and became a doorman in downtown Manhattan and also learned to be a certified acupuncturist. He would go to detoxes and rehabs and do acupuncture on withdrawing alcoholics and addicts. He later went to school at night and became a certified drug and alcohol counselor.

Mikey Bats was a big man. He stood just over six feet but was leaning slightly over at this stage of his life. He wasn't overweight, but a little plump. One of his outstanding features was that he could touch his big hook nose with his tongue, which would crack the kids up in line with their parents in the supermarket or anywhere else. Mikey was a big kid at heart.

He found out shortly after he got clean and sober that he would eventually need a kidney transplant. He took care of himself holistically from that point on.

In San Diego, he became our third wheel and part of our small family. If we were going out to dinner or buying tickets to a show, we would automatically include him, and Homer and Ruth, if they wanted to join us.

Mikey began working at the Volunteers of America as a certified drug and alcohol counselor. He also used his acupuncture to help alcoholics and addicts trying to recover. I could tell the guys he was working with at the Twelve Step meetings, because they would repeat many of his crazy sayings. "You need a checkup from the neck up" or "Stay away from Lola with the good leg," which referred to a good-looking woman that could be a distraction to a guy in early recovery. There was also "He got the dip in his hip," which meant a guy was slipping back into his old behaviors. If I heard any of those sayings in or outside a Twelve Step meeting, I knew Mikey was working with the person saying them.

Having Mikey Bats close to us in San Diego was good for us. I watched him and realized that the reason he was so helpful to so many was because of what a rough life he had endured. He had run the streets for many years, going from a heroin addict to a full-blown homeless wino, which became the route for many of the old dope fiends back then. Mikey was familiar with street life, and he'd had a couple of good hustles. He was a good booster, which meant he could walk in a supermarket, buy a quart of milk, and walk out with a couple of hundred dollars of expensive meat under his coat. His main hustle, though, was writing prescriptions. If you could get him a prescription pad from a doctor, he could write you a prescription for any drug, even in Latin.

Yes, Mikey Bats knew the streets and the prison system well, but I'd never met one person who helped so many people on their road to recovery from drugs and alcohol. He was also a big fan of Graymor, the holy mountain where he got sober at the men's shelter. He brought me up there to speak in my first year of recovery and suggested I attend the yearly men's retreat, which I did.

Mikey had been in San Diego only a few months when he started a Twelve Step meeting in a storefront down the block from his apartment. Within a year there were three meetings a day in that storefront. I learned much from Mikey Bats. God blesses us ... now we must go bless others.

47

Crash and Burn in San Diego

After nine years in San Diego, I sold my moving company and our house and moved to Reno, Nevada. It appeared that much of my success was a result of running my business the way I'd chased the drugs and alcohol, nonstop. I ran the trucks seven days a week and would take a job call on my cell phone 24-7. There would be a severe price to pay for that.

It was not something I really saw coming. It sneaked up and pounced on me like a thief in the night. My last truck had come in over an hour ago. I sat at my desk in my home office with my head in my hands and began to cry. The business phone rang again and again. I could only stare at it. Diane had just arrived home from work and walked into the office. As soon as she saw me, she knew something was wrong. She stood staring at me, sitting quietly with my face in my hands.

"Are you all right?"

"No."

"What's wrong?" she asked, worried.

"I don't know. I just feel like crying, and I can't take another phone call. I'm done. I can't do it anymore." I wiped my eyes with my sleeve.

"What are we gonna do?"

"We'll sell the business and house and move to Reno. The cost of doing business is so much better there. I won't have to work as hard, and we'll be able to retire at a decent age. I also need a break or I'll end up being the wealthiest guy in the looney bin."

"Okay," she replied. "You haven't steered us wrong yet. I'll give my job notice and start packing."

I was only mentally able to keep one truck and crew up and running while we got our affairs in order. We did well on the house, and I was able to sell the company to one of my employees, who took it on with a partner. In the agreement, I kept one truck and left him two. We packed that truck up and pulled out of San Diego within six weeks of my mental breakdown.

Ruth said she had never seen Homer cry until that day our truck pulled away from that empty house, and Homer and our good friend Wayne waved goodbye. It broke our hearts to leave them. I asked Mikey Bats if he wanted to join us, but he had been in San Diego a few years now and was settled.

I had done some research into the Household Goods moving industry in Nevada, then contacted the Transportation Services Authority to start the process. I spoke with an officer, Tognetti, a number of times, and he sent me an application to fill out, which I did and mailed back. He also set up an appointment for me to meet with him at the TSA office within two weeks after we arrived in Reno.

I showed up at the TSA office on that set date. It was a small one-story building with several private offices and one large room for hearings. At this point, Mr. Tognetti and I had spoken a number of times on the phone and had gotten familiar with each other, but this would be our first face-to-face.

Officer Tognetti was in his late forties, like me. He stood about five foot ten, with short black hair, and was in decent physical shape. He wore casual jeans, shirt, and boots, but I did notice the gun and handcuffs that hung from his belt. He shook my hand and led me into his office.

"Have a seat, Mr. Carney." My application sat on his desk. "It looks like you ran a very successful business in San Diego for the past nine years."

"Yes, sir, I did my best." Then we talked about the moving industry for a few minutes. I learned that the TSA also regulated cabs, private buses, limos, and tow truck companies.

"Well, Mr. Carney, it's a pleasure interviewing someone with your experience in the moving industry. Many of our applicants don't have your experience."

"Thank you, Mr. Tognetti."

"During this initial interview, I'll ask you a series of questions to gather information about you, then we'll set a date for a hearing. At that hearing, there will be four people from the TSA office and a representative from the attorney general's office. All five attendees at the hearing have to agree on granting you a Household Goods Moving Certificate."

"Sounds good. Let's do it."

All was going smoothly until Officer Tognetti got to this section of the questionnaire.

"Have you ever been arrested, Mr. Carney?"

"Yes, I have."

He stopped reading from the questionnaire and looked up across his desk at me.

"You have? Was it a misdemeanor?"

"No, sir, a felony."

"You were arrested for a felony? Were you convicted?"

"Yes, sir, I was convicted of armed robbery."

"You didn't do any time, did you?"

"Yes, sir. I was sentenced to twelve years, of which I did five."

He sat straight up in his chair and adjusted his glasses. "So was that just a onetime thing?"

"No, sir, I actually did another eighteen months soon after that."

"Are you serious? They actually gave you a Household Goods moving license in California with two felony convictions?"

"Yes, but those arrests and convictions were quite a while ago, and they all had to do with drugs and alcohol. I've been clean and sober for the past thirteen years now."

"Well, Mr. Carney, I'm going to have to end the interview for now."

"Why?"

"To be honest, I don't know what to do. I've never been in this situation before. I'm going to have to contact my superiors in Las Vegas and ask them what to do at this point." Then he came from behind his desk and walked me to the front door of the building.

"Is that it?"

"No, I'll call you within a week and let you know where the interview stands."

"Okay, thank you, Mr. Tognetti." The door closed behind me.

I drove home in silence and half in shock, then came the unwanted chatter. I could picture the little man in the cage rubbing his gnarly little hands together.

"Did you think your past wouldn't catch up to you?" he whispered. "You were lucky the first time, but there's no way they'll give you a license here in Nevada. These guys even carry guns and cuffs."

I started praying out loud to myself. By the third Our Father, the little man silently crawled back into the corner of his cage. I parked the car in the driveway of our new rental and entered the house.

"Hey, babe, I'm home."

"How did it go?" she yelled from the kitchen. She was working on her laptop, sending out her résumé to different doctors' offices.

"Not so good. The TSA officer literally stopped the interview when he found out about my criminal background. This move might have been a mistake, but they will be calling me in a few days to let me know where we stand."

"Why don't you give Homer a call and tell him what happened. I'm sure we're going to be okay. God has a plan." She hugged me.

In the meantime, we began making our Twelve Step meetings and making new friends. Of course, our first job was to secure our sobriety. We did the five things Johnnie W. told me to do thirteen years ago. Don't drink or drug a day at a time, make a meeting every day, find a new sponsor, join a new home group, and continue to pray our asses off.

The call finally came at the end of the week.

"Hey, Rob, it's Mr. Tognetti. My superiors in Vegas advised me to complete the interview, and they will set a date for a hearing. I can't promise you anything, but I do suggest that you explain your criminal record in the first few minutes of the hearing."

"Thank you for the opportunity, Mr. Tognetti." I told Diane and called Homer with the good news. The TSA would do

an extensive background check on my finances, criminal
record, make sure I had a good working truck and proper
equipment and the correct insurance, before they would set
a hearing date.

48

The Hearing

It was a few months from the time of the first interview to when the hearing date was set. And a lot of hard work in between. Mrs. Light was handling our finances. She requested years of back bank statements and tax reports, which we produced. She also asked that I put together a "proforma" statement for the upcoming business. I had no idea what that even was, but I found out. I had to figure out how much I would be spending on fuel, payroll, insurance, advertising, and rent, for starters. Also, a projection of what I thought we would be bringing in that first year. I had finally completed it after a week and sent it in. I was proud of myself for the accomplishment, only to get a call back from Mrs. Light.

"Mr. Carney, it appears you forgot to depreciate your trucks in your proforma statement."

After all my hard work, I was annoyed and close to losing my patience.

"You know, Mrs. Light," I responded, "this is not my first time around the block. I built up and ran a successful moving company in San Diego for nine years, which I later sold."

"Well guess what, Mr. Carney. You're in Nevada now, and if you want to operate a moving company here, you'll fix that proforma statement." There was a brief silence on the phone.

"Yes, ma'am, I'll get right on it." I learned how to depreciate the trucks, and she accepted the next one. I satisfied the other TSA officers, and my hearing date was set. I called Homer and told him the good news. He informed me that he would be flying into Reno and accompanying me to the hearing. I thanked him and felt more confident.

Mr. Tognetti called me into his office one last time before the hearing and once again explained the process to me. We had talked many times between the initial interview and the hearing. We got to know each other a little, and I did believe he was rooting for me.

"Okay, Rob," he said. "Your hearing date is set. There will be four people from the TSA office, including the chairwoman and me, present at the hearing. There will also be a representative from the attorney general's office. You will have to hire a court stenographer to take the minutes. I'll give you some names."

"No problem," I answered. "My friend and mentor Homer would like to join me at the hearing. Is that okay?"

"Sure, that's fine. They'll just record his name before the hearing starts. Remember, you have to do a forty-five-minute presentation on why you'll be a positive addition to the moving industry in northern Nevada. Also, remember to take the first few minutes to address your criminal background. We'll all have a copy of your criminal rap sheet right in front of us."

"Okay, I will," I replied.

"Good, because I'm moving at the end of the month and would rather use you than the guys I used last time," he said as he shook my hand.

I departed the TSA office for the last time before my hearing.

Homer flew in from San Diego the day before the hearing and joined us for dinner at our home that night. He wanted to hear the presentation I'd put together. I recited it to him and Diane after dinner.

That was great," he said. "But you only spoke for ten minutes. Isn't it supposed to be a forty-five-minute presentation?"

"I thought what I put together would be longer. I don't know what else to say."

"Listen, Robby, they know about certifying businesses, doing background checks, and checking financial records, but none of them are movers. Talk about your moving history. Starting as a young teen in New York, using those burlap straps to carry furniture up flights of stairs and pushing dollies. All the companies you worked for over the years and how you started with Man and a Van and built yourself up. Also, tell them all the good you, Diane, and your company have done for San Diego."

"Okay, Homer, I'll do my best." I hardly slept that night or the night before. I lay awake trying to formulate my presentation, until I fell asleep. That morning after breakfast, Diane and I went into the bedroom, kneeled down beside the bed, prayed, and asked God to join me at the hearing that morning.

I picked Homer up at the Golden Nugget Casino and drove over to the TSA office for the 9:00 a.m. hearing. We entered the building, and the receptionist led us to the hearing room. We sat at a table with two chairs and a microphone. There were five long tables in a half circle in front of us. All four officers, the representative from the attorney general's office to my far left, and the court stenographer to the far right. The chairwoman sat in the middle, and everyone had a microphone in front of them. The main TSA office in Vegas joined us via satellite.

"Good morning, Mr. Carney."

"Good morning, Madam Chairwoman."

"We're just gonna take a roll call and get started."

"Okay," I replied nervously.

Homer placed his hand on my shoulder and gave a squeeze. After roll call, she introduced me and asked me to begin my presentation.

"Thank you, Madam Chairwoman, and good morning to everyone." I noticed that along with a microphone, everyone also had a four- or five-page printout in front of them. I assumed it was my criminal rap sheet.

"I would like to start off my presentation by addressing my past criminal history. I have to say I had a pretty rough childhood, growing up in the Bronx. My father passed away when I was around nine years old, and he spent most of those years in prison. He was a violent man, and he died that way. My mother is a product of foster care and did not have many parenting tools to work with, but did the best she could, for the most part. All my arrests and convictions you have in front of you are a direct result of drugs and alcohol. I've been clean and sober for the past thirteen years now."

"Do you attend Twelve Step meetings, Mr. Carney?" the chairwoman asked.

"Yes I do, and I've already found some good meetings and started building a sober support group here in Reno. I also attended many Twelve Step meetings in San Diego, and brought meetings and hope into many of the same institutions I frequented when I was drinking and drugging, detoxes, rehabs, lockdown facilities. I was asked to speak at a lockdown youth center in San Diego every few months, just sharing my own journey and letting the kids know what they have to look forward to—jails and prisons. I took some of those kids to outside Twelve Step meetings, after meeting with their parents and having them sign a release form."

The chairwoman nodded her approval.

"You may continue, Mr. Carney." And continue I did. I noticed some of them were glancing through my rap sheet. Especially the gentleman from the attorney general's office. He would read something in the report, then lift his glasses up off his nose and look over at me, in what seemed to me, disbelief. I tried my best to stay focused. I told the hearing members of my history in the moving business.

"I started working on the lower east side of Manhattan for small moving companies as a young teenager, learning how to use burlap hump straps to carry furniture up flights of stairs to pushing dollies. Then I worked for companies affiliated with major Van Lines, where I learned to pack up homes, wrap furniture properly, and line load trucks. I then began to do some side work on my own."

I told them how I married and moved to San Diego nine years ago and started my first legitimate moving company, which I built up to three trucks and operated successfully for the past nine years, then sold. That business had an A+ rating with the BBB and a great reputation.

I also spoke of how we gave back to the community in San Diego. We were part of Operation Homefront, where we would move any deployed soldier's family for cost. Many of my employees in San Diego were men living in recovery homes, or men in recovery just trying to get on their feet. We were also part of the Share program, using our trucks to pick up, then deliver skids of food to a Baptist church, then helping bag it up, and we would deliver some to their homebound clients. I also mentioned some of the other community projects we were involved in.

I spoke of how I would be bringing all my years of moving experience from New York and San Diego to Reno, in hopes of becoming a positive force in the moving industry in northern Nevada. I went on to discuss my business plan. Before I ended, Homer asked to say a few words.

"I would just like to add that I first met Robby and his wife, Diane, and their friend Mike after they had just got back from delivering those homebound meals one Saturday morning. I have known Robby for the nine years he lived in San Diego and can tell you firsthand that he is a good man. Five years ago I asked him to join me on the board of directors of Heartland House, a men's sober-living home I've been associated with for the past thirty years. He was a good board member and a positive influence and will be missed. Reno would be lucky to have him and his wife. Thank you for your time."

I swallowed hard to keep from getting choked up. I ended by thanking the TSA members for their time and for considering me.

It then went to a vote. All present members of the TSA and the attorney general's office had to vote unanimously to grant me the Household Goods Moving Certificate. The chairwoman began. First was Mr. Tognetti, who'd done my background check. "That's a yes from me."

Second was Mrs. Light, who'd done my finances. "A yes from me also."

Next was Mr. Jones, who'd checked my truck, equipment, and working space. "That's a yes. Mr. Carney has met all our requirements." Three down and two to go.

Next was Mr. Sloan from the attorney general's office. He made me the most nervous, with his constant looking at me while reading my rap sheet. I was sure he was going to ask me some questions about my record, like, "Mr. Carney, can you please explain this attempted murder or this gun charge, or what about this drug sale?" but there were no questions. Just a simple, "That would be a yes from me." The last and final vote would come from the chairwoman.

"Mr. Carney," she said, staring straight at me. "You have dug yourself out of some hole. I would go on to say that you are a diamond in the rough. Yes, we would gladly have you join our moving industry in northern Nevada."

"Thank you very much, Madam Chairwoman and the other hearing members."

I then turned to Homer and shook his hand. I have drank alcohol and done many drugs in my day, but none of it could compare to how good I felt during those few moments and afterward. Each TSA member congratulated and welcomed me to Nevada. When Mrs. Light shook my hand, I had a few words for her.

"Mrs. Light, I just want to let you know that I am now a better businessman because of all the work you had me do, especially the proforma statement. I'm now aware of every dime that is going into the business and exactly what my profits should be, so thank you."

"No, thank you," she responded. "In my line of work, everyone I have to assess hates me. You've just made my day," and she gave me a hug.

After hardly sleeping for the past two nights because of the worry and anticipation, I floated out of that hearing room. My first moving job in Reno was ten days later. The day after I received my certification, Mr. Tognetti was my first customer.

49

Reno

We loved Reno. The new friends we made at our Twelve Step meetings were good, solid people. They celebrated recovery. Every month someone would host a party at their home to celebrate the people who had a clean and sober yearly milestone that month. Everyone brought a dish. Sometimes there was live music. Diane and I really grew in our sobriety there.

We skied in the Sierra Nevada mountains. I'd send the trucks out at 7:00 a.m., and Diane and I would be at the slopes by 8:00 a.m. Gliding up the mountains in a ski-lift chair through the tops of snow-covered pine trees, surrounded by untouched glistening snow everywhere. It was truly God's making. We would get eight or nine ski runs in and be back to the office by noon.

We hiked with our Ridgeback pups in the foothills of the mountains surrounding Reno. We'd pack some sandwiches and head out for a two- or three-hour hike. Sometimes we ran into wild horses in the foothills. The dogs did not know what to make of them at first, but we were struck with awe at their beauty. There were times when I'd be driving in the streets of the foothills, doing an estimate, and spot two or three wild horses just walking down the street. Reno was one of a kind.

The clear, crystal blue water of Lake Tahoe was only forty-five minutes away up through the mountains. Once we were settled and the business was running smoothly, I bought a Harley-Davidson that we would spend many hours on, going up to the lake or into California, Diane clinging to my back like glue.

From seeing the sun sink into the ocean off the cliffs overlooking the ocean in San Diego, to skiing the snowy mountains of the Sierra Nevada mountains overlooking Lake Tahoe, to stumbling into wild mustangs in the foothills of Reno, we knew how blessed our lives had become in sobriety. They say a grateful alcoholic or addict will never drink or do drugs again. We had much to be grateful for.

I had finally learned to create some boundaries in my work life with my second moving company. I closed the shop on Sundays, and I would have someone work the office on Saturdays. I had figured out how to get all the trucks to the shop by 4:00 p.m., or before, for the most part. If one truck finished early, I would send it to help finish a bigger job. And I always made sure one truck had a short day. After all, it was all just man hours and time.

I also learned to let the office phones go to voicemail after 5:00 p.m. It turns out, customers actually leave messages so you can call back the next day. I was always so afraid of losing that potential job. These new boundaries helped reduce my stress at work. It was much easier starting my second business. I certainly knew what not to do.

Things were going well in Reno. We found a great, supportive recovery community there. The business was coming along good, and we were enjoying all the beauty of the Sierra Nevada mountains, the foothills, and Lake Tahoe. It was at the end of our second year there, when life began to throw us a few curve balls. I would call the next two years the dark years.

To begin with, death paid us a visit and decided to hang out for a while. My first Rhodesian Ridgeback, Casey, passed away. We had driven to Northern California to get her as a rescue when she was ten weeks old. She had followed me around and stayed by my side for the next eleven years. She went everywhere with me. Diane and I were heartbroken. Then, three of our close family members died within eighteen months. First, my younger sister, Donna, died from a drug-related cause at forty-three, then Diane's mother, Helen, passed from a heart attack. Next was Diane's older brother Billy, from cancer. The trips back and forth to New York were exhausting. We couldn't catch our breath between funerals.

Once we had cleared those hurdles, some of my past began to catch up with me. I had been diagnosed with hepatitis C from my prior drug-use days. It was beginning to affect me, and I had to take some pretty severe medication to fight it. Interferon and another drug were the culprits. I took two pills a day and had to inject myself in the stomach once a week. The side effects were brutal, but the treatment did cure me of Hep C to this day.

One thing is for sure, life is going to happen whether you're sober or not. Sickness, deaths, relationship problems, money problems, all of it. The good news is, if you're sober you have a much better chance of handling whatever may come your way, and you don't have to do it alone.

I've learned that the disease of addiction can take many forms: anger, jealousy, fear, gambling, resentments, spending, financial insecurity, and the list goes on. Over the years I can see myself dealing with my character defects like playing a game of whack a mole—I knock one down and another pops up. Looking back now, it's pretty clear that as long as I've asked God for help and worked my Twelve Step program, everything has worked itself out.

It's also come to light that many of my so-called problems never left that space between my ears. The 10 or 20 percent that did materialize was easily handled by God and my Twelve Step program. There have been times when I've asked God for help and in his own way he has said no. Then a few months later, I see why he said no, and thank him. I don't always know what's good for me.

Of all the problems I've encountered in my sobriety, one solution has helped me tremendously over the years. Working with another alcoholic or addict. It takes my mind off me and any problem I might have, and the rewards are priceless.

50

My Second Moving Company

I t was 6:30 a.m. when I walked out the back door of the building, followed by Rosie and Simba, my two Ridgeback pups, and began my morning check on the moving trucks. All four trucks were parked side by side in the lot behind the building. They were white with green vinyl lettering on them, *Carney's Full Service Movers*, with green shamrocks on either side. Carney's Movers had become a familiar sight on the streets and roads of northern Nevada for the past twelve years. A name I had become proud of.

I unlocked and rolled up the door of each truck and checked the contents to make sure each truck was fully equipped with pads, dollies, and boxes. The men would begin showing up at 7:00 a.m. I began loading the fourth truck with boxes of all sizes for a pack job that day, and we would do the actual move tomorrow. Two sides of my twelve-hundred-square-foot office were lined with skids stacked with cardboard boxes of all sizes. I pulled boxes from each stack and loaded them onto the truck. I climbed up into the back of the truck to secure the boxes.

"Do you need anything else?" yelled a voice into the back of the truck. It was Kevin, one of my drivers—this was the truck he drove.

"No, you're all set. You have a pack job today. I got Terrance and John with you."

Kevin stood six foot, two hundred pounds, with blond hair and blue eyes. He was a quiet guy in his late twenties, and my top driver. There was little damage or drama when Kevin ran the job. I climbed out of the back of the truck and could hear Terrance playing with Simba and Rosie in the office.

Terrance was skinny as a rail and stood about five feet ten. He was one of the best movers I ever had. Those thin guys could be surprisingly strong, and work a straight nine or ten hours, no problem. Terrance was a young Black man in his early twenties.

Three years earlier, I had taken a call on my business line, from what sounded like an elderly Black woman with a southern accent.

"Is this the moving company?"

"Yes, ma'am. How can I help you?"

"Well, my grandson Terrance is heading your way from Alabama, and he needs a job," she said matter of factly.

"Does he have moving experience?"

"Oh yeah, he's a mover all right, and a hard worker too."

"Well, you just send him this way, ma'am, and I will hire him on the spot. The summer is almost here, and we're getting busy. I can always use a good man."

"All right, Mr. Carney, you look out for my Terrance now," and she hung up.

A week later a young, tall, and skinny Black gentleman came into the shop, asking for work. I handed him a job application and told him to fill it out. He was one of many people who would apply for work there. I was making a copy of his license and social security card, when I noticed his first name was Terrance.

I turned to the quiet young man. "Was that your grandmother who called here last week about you applying for work?"

"She might have. We were looking at moving companies online, and she liked the reviews you had, so she might have called you after I left to come here. She's a little pushy."

"Yeah, that was her," I said, laughing. I went into the back room and emerged with a new company green T-shirt. I threw it to him. "I'll see you tomorrow morning at 7:00 a.m. Bring lunch and a jug of water with you."

"Thank you, Mr. Carney. See you in the morning," he said with a smile as he walked away looking at the T-shirt. Terrance would become a great fit for my second moving company.

It was now 7:00 a.m., and the shop was filling up with men. I gave each driver a clipboard with their job on it and went over any details. Rosie and Simba had jumped off the moving blanket that covered the stack of wardrobe boxes and began to mingle with the guys. Two of the men were petting Rosie, while another was playing tug of war with a thick rope with Simba. By 7:30 all four trucks had pulled out of the lot and were heading to their moving and packing jobs that day.

Diane came down the outside steps from our apartment above the shop, on her way to work. She kissed me, Rosie, and Simba and headed to her job at a local doctor's office. The building we'd purchased when we'd first arrived in Reno was two stories. Downstairs was the office, and upstairs were a studio and one-bedroom apartment.

In 2010, after the recession hit, we short sold the home we had bought. I gave my tenants upstairs in the building notice, then Diane and I and the pups moved upstairs. I knocked a wall down and created a huge living room while adjoining the two apartments. We lived above the office for five years and saved our money.

Through it all, we remained clean and sober, and my second moving company had earned a great reputation. We moved many government officials (including the then governor's parents) and many who worked the government office that regulated me. Of course, it was the men who worked for me that made us successful. Although, I have to say, I went through many men to get to those special ten to twelve I employed at that point.

Amber, my office manager, arrived at 8:00 a.m. Amber was heaven sent. I would head out to do estimates, and she would cover the phones and any problems so I could focus on getting the jobs. I had gotten into a rhythm doing the estimates and interacting with the customers. Moving is a stressful business, and I was learning how to make them feel relaxed and comfortable with the process.

I pulled up to my first estimate that morning, a three-bedroom house.

A young mother carrying an infant on her hip answered the door. She led me through the house room by room, then the backyard and garage. I took notes and asked questions. I completed the estimate form, tore off a copy, and handed it to her.

"I estimate the job to take eight hours with three men and one truck. The more prepared and packed up you are, the faster it will go. It's a fairly easy move, and you will only be charged for the time used."

"When we arrive at my new house, will the men put the furniture in each room, where we want it?" she asked.

"Excuse me?" I answered, staring at her blankly. "No, ma'am. We don't bring it in the house. We just set it on the lawn and driveway, and you take it from there." We both stood there staring at each other in silence for a few seconds, until I couldn't contain myself any longer and I burst out laughing.

"Oh my God," she said, now laughing. "I thought you were serious."

"No, I'm just messing with you. The men will bring the furniture into each room you direct them to and place it where you want. When it's all unloaded, they will have you take a look in the truck to make sure it's empty. Then they will walk through the house with you again to make sure everything is exactly where you want it."

"All right, sign us up for August 14. You got the job. We've heard good things about your company."

"Thank you. We'll be here on the fourteenth at 8:00 a.m., and I'll call you the day before to confirm."

And so it went. We would sometimes be booked up for a month or two in advance. It had taken ten to twelve years to build up our reputation and get the right people in place, but we were there. The moving company was running like a well-oiled machine.

The success of the business afforded us some luxuries we'd never dreamed of. We took a cruise to Alaska with some sober friends from New York. On one of the excursions, we flew in a helicopter that landed on a glacier. On the glacier was a dogsled camp, and we went for a ride on a dogsled. We were able to travel to Europe a couple of times. Once to Italy, where we were accompanied by our niece Stephanie, Diane's sister Jackie's daughter, who would visit us every summer since she was seven. Stephie would fly out and stay with us for a few weeks during school break. We would enroll her in all kinds of summer camps: basketball, sailing, modeling. She softened me up and became the closest thing we would ever have to a daughter, keeping us informed of all her life activities during the year. She was sixteen during our first trip to Europe, which was Italy. We flew into Venice, where we were taxied to our hotel in a beautiful wooden boat. We then went on by train to Florence, then Rome. A ten-day trip I will never forget, especially the gondola ride through Venice. I also celebrated and took my twenty-one-year clean and sober coin at an English-speaking meeting in Florence.

Our second trip to Europe, a couple of years later, was to London and Paris. Stephie and Diane's sister Jackie joined us. We had dinner in the Eiffel Tower and attended a show and dinner at Moulin Rouge. In London we stayed at a hotel close to Scotland Yard, saw all the sights, including going on a Jack the Ripper tour. The trips to Europe were life changing.

I've always been an avid boxing fan. My dream of attending live prize fights and meeting some legendary boxers also came true. Of all the things money can buy, my fear of economic insecurity has been lifted. From going hungry as a child to being homeless as an active addict and alcoholic, I knew God had my back now, and I would be okay no matter what. The rewards of a clean and sober life are many. Here is one.

Diane and I would sometimes escape up to south Lake Tahoe for a weekend away to ski or hike. On one of those evenings, we were enjoying a quiet, intimate dinner at a steakhouse, when two loud but happy well-dressed young men were seated a couple of tables away from us. They sat laughing and enjoying themselves during dinner. Diane and I smiled at each other and laughed, sharing in their good evening.

An hour or so had passed, and we were having our dessert and coffee. The two young men had finished their meals, paid their bill, and were leaving the restaurant. As they passed our table, they stopped. One guy stood there smiling as the other approached our table. The young man walked over to me and extended his hand.

"Good evening," he said as I shook his hand. "I just wanted to let you know that I have nine months clean and sober today. You came into the rehab I was in and shared your story. Your story inspired me, and I just wanted to thank you." His voice held the utmost sincerity.

"You're welcome, and congratulations. Keep up the good work," I responded, then they turned to leave the restaurant.

Diane looked over at me with a big, beautiful smile. I had drank a lot of alcohol and taken many drugs, but nothing had made me feel as good or satisfied as I did at that moment. All those cold nights that I'd forced myself off my warm couch to keep my sober commitments paid off in that one encounter. You never know what you're going to say or do that will help someone.

My life in recovery has been like that. As my man Mikey Bats would say, "You've been blessed. Now go bless others."

51

The Gifts of Sobriety

When I'd received my license for my first moving company, I'd thought God had given me this gift to help recovering drunks and addicts, which was all I'd hired. Then after a couple of months of trying to herd kittens, I realized maybe that wasn't God's plan. I'd then formed a moving company of seasoned movers and hired one or two guys in recovery who were trying to get on their feet. Looking back, I must retract that statement. God did give me this gift to help other recovering addicts, alcoholics, and some people just down on their luck.

I look back at the people who gave me a hand up and the ripple effect it has had. Chicken Charlie giving me his business card at my first meeting. Kevin slipping me that five bucks to go have coffee after a meeting with the group. Tommy Time offering to be my first sponsor. Gram and Bob opening their home to me in Massachusetts, which changed my life. And the list goes on.

I sold my second moving company in 2020 and retired to Florida with my beautiful wife, Diane, and our two Ridgeback puppies, Leo and Abbey. The first things we did when we got here were: not drink or drug a day at a time, make a meeting every day, get a sponsor to work the steps again, join a home group and get active, and pray our asses off. Once again, putting that first, everything else has fallen into place.

I look back at how God has worked in my life up to this point. This is a good analogy. Life is in front of me in the form of a huge pile of dirt. The pile is one hundred feet high and fifty feet across. I have to move that pile of dirt one hundred yards down the road. At the time it seemed an impossible task, so I asked God for help. "Please, God, help me move this huge pile of dirt." Suddenly the clouds move, and the sun shines through, and a dirt shovel falls from the sky, clank, clank at my feet.

I look down at the shovel, then up at the sky. "Really, you're kidding, right?" I think I hear a slight chuckle in the distance. Apparently, my God has a sense of humor. I pick the shovel up and fill it with dirt and walk the hundred yards and dump it. I put five grueling hours in the first day, eight hours the second day, and my little pile of dirt starts to grow. About three hours into my third day of walking one hundred yards with full shovels of dirt, a guy comes along driving a backhoe loader and asks if I need a hand. "Yes please," I say. He makes a number of trips back and forth with the loader, and the pile is moved. I thank him and offer him some money, but he refuses and says he is happy to help.

The point being, if I'm not standing there on that third day with shovel in hand, sweating and tired, at that very moment, I miss the guy going by with the backhoe loader. Looking back, God has sent many angels my way driving backhoe loaders. Chris, Mikey Bats, Homer, and many more, but they've all met me with shovel in hand.

Since I'm living the good life today, the little man in the cage doesn't have much to work with, so he has to reach back and try to finish an argument I had with someone years ago, or find something in the future I should be fearful of. I know today they are both fake. The past is gone, and God will take care of the future. The only thing real is this moment. If I find myself in the past or the future in my head, I have some simple exercises I use to bring myself back.

I take three or four deep breaths and let them out slowly, then I look around and take in everything I see—the laptop in front of me, my living room through my office door, the sun coming up outside my window, and the stillness of the trees in my yard. Next, I inhale through my nose and try to pick up any smells—foods, fresh-cut grass, or animals. Then I listen for any noises—birds chirping, traffic in the distance, the air flowing out of the AC vent above me. Then I feel my bare feet on the cold linoleum floor under my desk, my hands resting on the glass alongside my plastic keyboard. I engage all my senses, and it brings me back to this very moment and out of my head, which is not real.

The truth is, I'm clean and sober. I have a roof over my head. I have my health, my beautiful wife, and two pups still asleep in the bedroom, and they love me to the moon and back. I have a few bucks in the bank. I have the love of my friends and family. That is real.

The man in the cage is still there in my chest, but he rarely shows his face these days, maybe a slight rattle of his cage door or a whisper here or there. I believe the reason is because my faith in God has grown over the years and all the work I've put in in my Twelve Step program. After all, I have over thirty-two years of proof that God has had my back the whole time.

Today is July 20, 2024, two and a half years from the day I sat at this desk and began this writing journey. Diane and I have just returned from the beach with our two Ridgeback pups after our two-and-a-half-mile morning walk, and we're ready to start another beautiful day in recovery.

Thank you so much for taking this journey with me. My hope is that you may have found some hope, some answers, and some entertainment in these pages. No matter how far down you may have fallen or what traumas you've been through, you can pick yourself up, dust yourself off, and have a happy and healthy life. I also hope you may have a deeper insight into the struggles an active alcoholic and addict may have and how you can help them and yourself. The Twelve Steps have been a blessing in my life, and maybe they can be a blessing in yours. There are programs out there for everyone if you need it and want to make a change. If you don't have a God in your life, perhaps you can try some just-in-case-you're-up-there praying. Thank you and God Bless,

Robby

Acknowledgements

First, I would like to thank my Higher Power, Jesus Christ, for having my back and carrying me through the darkest of days, and for relieving me of the obsession and compulsion to drink and drug. Secondly, I would like to thank the founders who created a Twelve Step program that gives me clear cut directions on how to have a happy, healthy, and prosperous second life.

I would like to thank my beautiful and loving wife, Diane, for being my sounding board and putting up with my moods after having revisited some of the dark parts of my life. When she asked me, "What part of the book are you on now?" It was always a sign to bring myself back to the present. Diane also bought me the book, *The book You Were Born to Write* by Kelly Notaras. It was very helpful, as was KN Literary Arts and their online writing course. Kelly's YouTube videos have been priceless. KN Literary also introduced me to David Jahr, my book coach. David's guidance and friendship helped me from start to finish in writing my first book *Unscarred*.

Thanks to my sister-in-law, Mary Taylor, for her honest insight in reviewing and pointing out things in the book I should consider. And to Laura Kelley, for helping ground me and remember what is truly important. Thanks to Bob Posch, my Catholic Big Brother, who along with my wife prompted me to write the book. Thank you Bob for investing your time and energy in me during my youth. It clearly paid off.

I would also like to thank my sober support in New York, San Diego, Reno, and Florida whose fellowship, friendship and guidance help keep me trudging the road to happy destiny.

About the Author

Author Robert Carney's greatest accomplishment, besides marrying his soul mate, Diane, is being clean and sober for thirty-two years and counting. He grew up on the streets of New York, which led to dealing drugs, becoming addicted, and serving time in prison. Along the way, he learned a lot about life and himself. Eventually, Robert would build up and sell his moving business, which allowed him to retire in Florida, where he now resides. Active in Twelve Step meetings, Robert volunteers in hospitals, institutions, and organization and is often called to be a guest speaker at various support groups. In his free time, he enjoys playing golf, yoga, writing, and taking long walks on the beach while living one day at a time.

Stay in touch with Robert by signing up at robertcarney-author.com.

www.ingramcontent.com/pod-product-compliance
Lightning Source LLC
Chambersburg PA
CBHW031437160726
47994CB00005B/1763